The Upper Layers of Open Systems Interconnection

The Upper Layers of Open Systems Interconnection

*Proceedings of the Second International Symposium
on Interoperability of ADP Systems,
The Hague, The Netherlands, 25-29 March 1985*

Edited by

Rainer W. G. Herbers

*Head, Telecommunications Division,
GFS-METRA, Munich, F.R.G.*

Conference hosted and sponsored by
SHAPE Technical Centre (NATO)

D. REIDEL PUBLISHING COMPANY

A MEMBER OF THE KLUWER  ACADEMIC PUBLISHERS GROUP

DORDRECHT / BOSTON / LANCASTER / TOKYO

Library of Congress Cataloging in Publication Data

International Symposium on Interoperability of ADP Systems (2nd: 1985: The Hague, the Netherlands)
The upper layers of open systems interconnection.

Includes index.
1. Command and control systems–Europe–Data processing–Congresses. 2. Command and control systems–North America–Data processing–Congresses. 3. North Atlantic Treaty Organization–Armed Forces–Communication systems–Data processing–Congresses. I. Herbers, Rainer W. G. II. SHAPE Technical Centre. III. Title.
UB212.I6   1985   355.6   87–4302
ISBN 978-94-010-8197-9   ISBN 978-94-009-3815-1 (eBook)
DOI 10.1007/978-94-009-3815-1

Published by D. Reidel Publishing Company,
P.O. Box 17, 3300 AA Dordrecht, Holland.

Sold and distributed in the U.S.A. and Canada
by Kluwer Academic Publishers,
101 Philip Drive, Assinippi Park, Norwell, MA 02061, U.S.A.

In all other countries, sold and distributed
by Kluwer Academic Publishers Group,
P.O. Box 322, 3300 AH Dordrecht, Holland.

TABLE OF CONTENTS

Editor's Foreword

Interoperability has been a requirement in NATO ever since the Alliance came into being - an obvious requirement when 16 independent Nations agree to allocate national resources for the achievement of a common goal: to maintain peace.

With the appearance of data processing in the command and control process of the armed forces, the requirement for interoperability expanded into the data processing field. Although problems of procedural and operational interoperability had been constantly resolved to some extent as they arose over the years, the introduction of data processing increased the problems of technical interoperability. The increase was partially due to the natural desire of nations to support their own national industries. But it was definetely also due to the lack of time and resources needed to solve the problems.

During the mid- and late -1970s the International Standards Organisation (ISO) decided to develop a concept ("model") which would allow "systems" to intercommunicate. The famous ISO 7-layer model for Open Systems Interconnection (OSI) was born. The OSI model was adopted by NATO in 1983 as the basis for standardization of data communications in NATO.

The very successful (first) Symposium on Interoperability of ADP Systems, held in November 1982 at the SHAPE Technical Centre (STC), gave an extensive overview of the work carried out on the lower layers of the model and revealed some intriguing ideas about the upper layers. The first Symposium accurately reflected the state-of-the-art at that point in time.

Since 1982, however, there have been many advances, and this Second International Symposium on Interoperanility of ADP Systems was intended to identify the status of research and development on the upper layers. Further progress made on the lower layers was addressed as well as some new aspects not identified in 1982.

Additionally, the Symposium served as a platform for the discussion and free exchange of information between research and development agencies, industry, and military users.

This volume contains the results of the collective endeavour of contributors to the conference. I present it to you in the hope that it will be a useful medium of reference and study in your professional activity.

The symposium was sponsored and organized by the SHAPE Technical
Centre. I would like to thank the management of the Centre who gave
strong support in all aspects and who approved publication of this
book.

Major credit for the success of the symposium must be given to all our
colleagues who submitted papers for presentation and to the session
chairmen who ·were responsible for the selection of topics and speakers:
I. Groenbeak, A.J. Hill, M. Kesselman, Ch. Köhler, S. Oxman, W.H.P.
Schmidt, and J.F. Wilkes.

My special thanks go to Murray Kesselman who is now back with the Rome
Air Development Center (Rome, N.Y.) . Murray was my co-chairman during
the symposium as well as acting chairman during periods of my absence
in the preparation of the conference. Without him I would not have been
able to organize this event.

Finally, I would like to sincerely thank Ms Susan May and Mrs Norma
Glenton of STC who handled all the administrative functions, and Mrs
Edeltraud Falch of GFS-METRA who, with the support of Mrs Ursel Hild
re-typed the proceedings for publication.

Without the outstanding contributions of all the people mentioned and
of the many I could not mention here, the success of the symposium
would not have been possible.

Munich, 1986

Rainer W.G. Herbers
Symposium Chairman

Opening Session

Session Chairman: Rainer W.G. Herbers

NATO POLICY AND TRANSITION STRATEGY FOR
THE MILITARY APPLICATION OF THE ISO/CCITT REFERENCE MODEL AND ITS
ASSOCIATED STANDARDS FOR OPEN SYSTEMS INTERCONNECTION

Klaus Kühn
NATO HQ
International Staff
B-1110 Brussels
Belgium

1. NATO POLICY

1.1. INTRODUCTION

The NATO approach to improving interoperability is described in a NATO
interoperability management plan. This plan indentifies three complementary sets of interoperability standards: operational, procedural,
and technical. Technical common interface standards (TCIS) specify the
functional, electrical and physical characteristics necessary to allow
the exchange of information between different equipment systems. TCIS
are structured in compliance with the OSI Reference Model and comprise
service definitions (which define the service provided by the lower
layer, and used by the upper layer, at the boundary between adjacent
layers of the Reference Model), and protocol specifications (which
define the procedures used within a layer to achieve the required
service features).

1.2. DEVELOPMENT OF TECHNICAL COMMON INTERFACE STANDARDS

The main motive for developing TCIS is to construct a single architecture of TCIS (SATCIS). If TCIS are developed only in response to
specific requirements it is unlikely that widespread interoperability
will be achieved. Therefore, the co-ordinating technical authority in
NATO will ensure that whenever practicable TCIS are taken from a single
architecture of preferred standards. By building up a SATCIS the co-
ordinating technical authority will have a set of preferred standards
to meet newly-stated requirements, with augmentation if necessary. This
will give great flexibility and will avoid the need to develop special
standards in each case.
    To develop the SATCIS, the co-ordinating technical authority will
identify, in consultation with a variety of NATO groups, the general
military features which are not provided by the civil ISO/CCITT
standards (examples are given in 2). The agreed NATO requirement will

3

R. W. G. Herbers (ed), The Upper Layers of Open Systems Interconnection, 3–9.

then be represented to ISO through the national standards insitutes of
the individual nations participating in the meetings of the co-
ordinating technical authority. The latter group provides technical
support to this initiative and looks forward to the potential advantages of more widely recognized standards, and cheaper, commercially-
available equipment meeting the military requirement.

Whenever a specific requirement for TCIS will be identified, the
co-ordinating technical authority will consider whether the requirement
can be met by an existing standard from the SATCIS. If so, the available standard will be used. If not, a decision will be made whether the
requirement is sufficiently general for inclusion in the SATCIS and
necessary augmentation of the respective civil standards.

1.3. DOCUMENTATION OF TECHNICAL COMMON INTERFACE STANDARDS

TCIS will be stated by reference to the civil standards. They will
specify, where appropriate, which optional features of those standards
are adopted for NATO use, and where it has been found necessary to
augment the civil standards to meet the military requirement. Such
augmentation will be kept to a minimum in order not to loose the
advantages of a wide commercial market. The augmented standard will
have a unique NATO interpretation.

The SATCIS will be composed of a family of documents which are as
follows:

- One STANAG describes the NATO Reference Model for OSI. This is by
  reference to the corresponding ISO/CCITT Reference Model. The title
  "NATO Reference Model" is used intentionally in order to give the
  military the flexibility to augment the ISO/CCITT Reference Model
  should ever a need arise. The military community has already
  identified the requirement for a connectionless mode of operation on
  which, indeed, ISO experts have prepared a proposed addendum to the
  ISO/CCITT Reference Model. However, should ISO efforts fail to cover
  this requirement by their Reference Model, it is foreseeable that
  this would become an augmentation of the existing Model for military
  purposes.
- A series of seven STANAGs will give the service definitions for
  Layers 1 to 7 respectively to the Model. Again will this be mainly by
  reference to the corresponding civil standards. However, where
  necessary, separate annexes will deal with individual network
  technologies or application types.
- A further series of seven STANAGs will give the protocol
  specifications for Layers 1 to 7 respectively to the Model, again
  mainly by reference to the corresponding civil standards with
  separate annexes on individual network technologies or application
  types, where necessary.

1.4. APPROACH TO ISO

In general, ISO is respective to military needs. The basic input to
ISO, covering NATO agreed military features, has now been made by 11

nations to their respective national standards bodies (one nation hopes
to do so soon) and has usefully influenced ISO debate.

2. SPECIFIC MILITARY REQUIREMENTS/FEATURES

The following represents an agreed position within NATO where a
technical group has studied the problem of interoperability between
diverse military networks and applications and has concluded that there
would be considerable benefit in using ISO OSI protocols for this purpose rather than developing separate military protocols.
    A number of military requirements have been identified and their
effects on the OSI Reference Model at the layer 3/4 and 4/5 boundaries
considered. There may be effects at other layers but these have not
been fully presented. Although these requirements have arisen from
consideration of military environments, they have parallels in the
civilian community.
    Extensions to the Reference Model to include these requirements is
considered to be preferable to the development of a separate military
model and protocols. The following eight capabilities are not adequately covered in the current OSI standards development.

2.1. MULTI-HOMED AND MOBILE HOST SYSTEMS

There is a need in a military network for a host computer which is not
collocated with a network node to have links to two or more nodes on
one or more networks for increased survivability. For the foreseeable
future, it will be adequate in such cases for only one link to be in
traffic at any time, the others being regarded as "standby" links, only
to be used following a failure of the "normal" link. The changeover to
a standby link involves the clearing and re-establishment of all host's
calls. This appears to a network as similar to the case of a mobile
host which periodically disappears from one network service access
point and re-appears on another. One of the principal problems associated with the mobility of host systems is that of addressing and
routing. Open system management and the Network Layer services may also
be affected by multi-homed and mobile host systems.

2.2. MULTI END-POINT CONNECTIONS

A conventional method of providing source to multiple sink connections
would be to use the facilities of a host-to-host protocol (i.e. within
the Transport Layer of OSI Reference Model). This method of multi-
addressing will have no impact on the present protocols. However, in
many military networks, transmission capacity is at a premium and the
injection of separate copies of the service data for a variety of
destinations would be unacceptable. Hence, there is a need to provide
an efficient facility to handle data in which more than one destination
is associated. In principle the potential exists to optimize communication resources and comminication delays by providing a multi-destina-
tion date service in order to take advantage of inherent "broadcast"

features in underlying networks where these are present e.g. satellite
transmission facilities and local area networks (LAN).

2.3. INTERNETWORKING

There is an urgent military requirement to see the agreement of a
standard for internetworking between vastly different types of networks
including LANs, packet radio networks, demand access satellite networks, message switched networks, and public data networks (both
circuit and packet switched). This should take into account the requirements for robustness and security. This may require interactions
between host systems and sub-networks over routing decisions. It must
be pointed out that administrative differences between types of networks are often as great an impediment to intercommunications as the
technological differences.

2.4. NETWORK/SYSTEM MANAGEMENT FUNCTIONS

Some management functions required for military applications, such as
error diagnosis, network and system status enquiries and security key
and password distribution may need support from both the Transport and
the Network Layer. Equally some management functions may be applicable
processes in their own right, e.g. directory services. Also a notification to applications of degraded quality of service would be a useful
feature so that, for example, users can adjust their communications to
suit the available resources.

2.5. SECURITY

Military systems and many civilian systems such as banking systems
using ISO protocols will need to incorporate protection mechanisms so
as to control access and information exchange. ISO work undertaken in
this area must be restricted to those visible aspects of a communications path important to assisting end-systems in achieving secure
communications. To this end there is a need to signal security level
and to provide for closed user groups.

2.6. ROBUSTNESS AND QUALITY OF SERVICE

Military applicatons will have a wide variety of delay and reliability
requirements. The Reference Model's approach to such quality of service
requirements must be integrated coherently through the entire architecture. While reliable data transmission is important for many applications, reliable management of distributed applications is equally
important. The ability for routing around damaged or partitioned networks is important for a military internetworking system. Also anti-
jamming techniques should be addressed as it may apply to protocol
layer functions. This should include the case where no cryptographic
protection is provided.

2.7. PRECEDENCE AND PRE-EMPTION

The requirement for precedence in future privately operated data
networks may differ from that in present day systems. The very short
transit times encountered in packet-switched networks may well make the
preferential positioning of high-precedence data in queues unnecessary.
Precedence may however affect the criteria for pre-emption, such as
discarding packets during congestion and those for accepting or reject-
ing virtual call requests.

The existing network and transport services satisfactorily show
priority as a parameter. The existing Transport Protocol also shows a
satisfactory encoding of priority. It is required that this be incorporated in any network protocols in such a way that networks may
provide this service as an additional option.

2.8. REAL TIME AND TACTICAL COMMUNICATIONS

Applications such as the transmission of radar, packet voice or
telemetry data are adopting a type of communication on which the
delivery of data in its original order and without loss or duplication
is not guaranteed. The advantage of such a facility is that data would
be delivered as quickly as possible, with no delays for either retransmission or re-ordering. It requires the host to structure the data
within the Protocol Data Units as independent clearly-identifiable
messages, and may constrain the network not to fragment them.

These requirements reflect the need to request various qualities
of service. The existing quality parameters of delay, throughput and
error rate are considered satisfactory as specified in the Transport
and Network Services and Transport Protocol. However an additional
parameter specifying variance of delay is required (for example to
express the requirements for packet voice). The expected maximum
variance required could be expressed in the order of tens of milli-
seconds.

3. NATO TRANSITION STRATEGY

3.1. GENERAL

International standardization carried out by ISO and CCITT in the area
of OSI is unlikely to be completed before the second half of the
Eighties. Based on the close connection between international standardization and the development of technical common interface standards
(TCIS) (see 1 above), the single architecture of NATO agreed standards
will not be available until after the international standards have been
worked out.

Time schedules in connection with the development of national and
NATO command, control and information systems show that technical
solutions for their inter-connection will be required already in the
near future, if not today. These facts lead to the conclusion that a
time lag exists between the emergence and the satisfaction of require-

ments for TCIS. This situation is characterized by three typical time
periods; periods in which TCIS are either unavailable, or partially
available, or fully available. Especially in the first, but in part
also in the second period, there is a danger that, in the absence of
standards, technical solutions will be agreed which might hamper rather
than promote standardization.

However, although international standardization takes a long
time, the technical content of a standard is often stable before its
final agreement. Where political acceptance is also widespread, a
standard could - with some small risk but very considerable advantage -
be introduced into service before completion of all the acceptance
procedures.

The "NATO Transition Strategy" aims to identify and promote
standards at this stage of a near agreement. It is thereby in good
company with an intercept strategy for OSI recommended by the United
Kingdom Department of Trade and Industry and also with a recommendation
by the Joint European Standards Institute where it is stated: "Some of
the standards in current use which predate the internationally adopted
model for OSI do not conform in all cases to thismodel. Nevertheless
they shall be implemented in this first stage, however, in such a way
that a smooth transition to OSI be possible in a subsequent step."

3.2. INTERCEPT RECOMMENDATIONS

The criteria for making intercept recommendations are:

- widespread agreement on the function of, and need
  for, the standard;
- a high degree of technical agreement internationally;
- a credible source;
- an assured future.

Intercepts will be "recommendations" not "standards"; they will be
available as precursors to future standards expected from ISO and
CCITT. NATO will support an intercept recommendation as soon as the
criteria are satisfied and this will be made widely known. However, at
this stage the documentation will probably be imperfect, and will be
necessary to define the use of options and parameters, and generally to
tighten up the specification.

Documents forming the intercept recommendation will usually be
based upon an ISO Draft Proposal or document of equivalent status.
These documents will be issued as draft STANAGs. The confidence level
behind "intercepts" is such that they should all mature into full
standards: they should never be withdrawn or fulfil only temporary
functions.

3.3. INTERIM RECOMMENDATIONS

For some time to come, the coverage provided by full TCIS/international standards and intercepts will be incomplete: there will be gaps. In new systems it will be necessary to decide how the gaps might be filled in a way which is most compatible with future standards. In existing systems, piecemeal conversion from old to new standards may often be required. To reduce the number of solutions where full standards or intercept recommendations are not available, a number of "interim recommendations" will be made. They will be of temporary nature, but nonetheless they will devote some effort to strengthening their specifications and adapting them to fit with true OSI standards.
Criteria for interim recommendations are more difficult to identify, but they must:

- fulfil a need;
- be proven specifications which do not run counter
  to perceived future standards; or
- be aligned with the general direction of NATO
  standardization.

4. CONCLUSIONS

The development of the single architecture of ICIS in co-operation with ISO/CCITT requires a great amount of time due to the necessity to assess all interoperability requirements and the indirect wax to address ISO through national chanels. This means that ICIS for some NATO/national requirements will not be available on time. However, the NATO Transition Strategy provides an approach which allows for the recommendation of technical solutions at any time and which also allows for the continuation of the development of TCIS without being under pressure of time.

ACKNOWLEDGEMENTS

The writer is Secretary of the co-ordinating technical authority in NATO concerned with the Reference Model of Open Systems Interconnection, the development of technical common interface standards and their applications. He is most grateful to all the members of this group who have contributed to the various NATO documents from which the baseline for this paper was derived.

EUROPEAN INITIATIVES ON STANDARDS

David J. Williams
Defence Systems, ICL
R.V.S. Lloyd
Technical Directorate, ICL
International Computers Limited
Lorelace Road, Bracknell
Berkshire RG12 4SN
United Kingdom

ABSTRACT

The role of the European Commission in harmonising practices across
Europe extends to include the use of Information Technology Standards.
This paper describes the way in which the Commission itself, as a user
and as the instigator of the ESPRIT programme, the IT Industry, and the
European Standards Institutions (CEN and CENELEC), are putting this
process into effect. It also covers the role of the European Computer
Manufacturers Association (ECMA) in the development of Standards.

1. THE BACKGROUND

In 1979, the Dublin summit meeting decided to promote the suppression
of trade barriers by increased use of Standards. In response to this,
the European Commissioner for Industrial Affairs (Vicomte E. Davignon)
invited representatives from the European IT industry to meet with him
and senior CEC officials on an occasional basis to seek ways of implementing this decision and of involving them in fundamental cooperative
activities. This became known as "The Round Table". The companies
involved were:

UK	GEC, ICL, Plessey
France	Bull, CGE, Thomson-CSF
FRG	AEG, Nixdorf, Siemens
Italy	Olivetti, STET
NL	Philips

11

R. W. G. Herbers (ed), The Upper Layers of Open Systems Interconnection, 11–19.

2. ESPRIT

The first outcome of the RT was the evolution of the concept of ESPRIT,
in which the accent was on IT research in a pre-competitve environment,
with industry itself taking a lead in defining the content of the programme and in carrying it out. During 1981 and 1982, preparatory
studies were undertaken, out of which grew not only the five main areas
of research now being undertaken, but also the concept of the Information Exchange System. It was recognised that the communication needs of
the participants in ESPRIT could be met by an ambitious programme of
adoption of OSI principles and standards, backed up by a degree of
central organisation to manage their use. (The prime concept was not a
separate and distinct "Network", but rather the perception that OSI
Standards would suffice, it compatibly implemented on the back of the
available infrastructure of public data networks). A pilot project was
put in place, based on provision of linkages between UNIX-based
systems, originally known as EIES, and this has now developed further
into a full infrastructure project under ESPRIT, known as ROSE. The
IES also incorporates a separate Conferencing and Electronic Mail
system, EUROKOM, run under contract by University College, Dublin.
      The current programme of ROSE is a mixture of the application of
stable draft OSI standards, (including the production of portable UNIX
implementations of layer protocol handlers), ad-hoc arrangements to
fill gaps in current OSI (e.g. use of common inter-UNIX protocols), and
experimental developments in less stable OSI areas, especially LANs and
internetworking.

3. STANDARDISATION POLICY

A second outcome of the RT was more specifically directed towards the
development of a policy for IT Standardisation in Europe. The CEC
already had in existence the committee WGS which had a separate sub-
committee WGS-OSC for OSI work. It also had a specific unit, the ITTTF
which was responsible for managing the introduction of ESPRIT and the
CEC's multi-annual plan for standardisation. However, there had been
little visible output in the form of definitive policies, and the
advice of the RT was that such a formal basis was required. The
industriel members of the RT undertook in March 1983 to consider this
issue, and formed an Ad Hoc Group for Standards, which was later
renamed "SPAG" - The Standards Promotion and Application Group. In
October 1983 SPAG was invited by the Commissioner to make a proposal.
This was done in January 1984, and a substantial document submitted,
outlining the essence of such a policy, based firmly on the common
adoption of International Standards, by the CEC and by its member
states; not just their formal adoption as National Standards, but their
application as the basis for procurement by institutions and the user
community at large, backed up by clearly established mechanisms for
verification and certification.

The technical content of the policy was contained in an annexe, which identified the need for a new concept of Functional Standards - groups of standards selected to be used together in specified ways to provide a defined user-perceived function. The list of standards selected was firmly based on the current state of the art of OSI, using stable standards where available from ISO and CCITT, with additional components, where suitable, from ECMA. A further annexe identified a long list of other areas which would be pursued once stability was achieved.

The twelve companies involved in SPAG subsequently endorsed the content of this annexe of the proposal as the basis for their own corporate policies in evolution of support for OSI, aiming thereby to accelerate the development of the sort of mult-vendor marketplace which was the overall objective of the CEC policy. This endorsement was widely publicised at the time.

In parallel with the work of SPAG, a separate initiative ("EHA") was under way with the blessing of the CEC/ITTTF, which involved representatives of a group of European Research Networks under Professor Zander of DFN. This was aimed at establishing a common understanding of the way in which OSI standards would be used in order to ensure interworkability between the separate networks. Their conclusions were published in a series of five COS documents, which were promoted to a limited extent by the WGS before it was itself dissolved. Much of the technical content of this work has been taken over by SPAG.

Within the countries of Europe, national initiatives were being taken to exploit the increasing maturity of OSI, by establishing suitable policies and data communications architectures. For example, in the Federal Republic of Germany, the series of EHKP standards; in France, the Architel technical specifications; and in the UK, the FOCUS committee published an Intercept Strategy, and the ITSU of the Department of Trade and Industry is publishing Technical Guides (TGs).

4. CEN AND CENELEC

The next step in the process of developing a European Policy was taken in May 1984, when the Ministers of Industry from the 10 EEC countries created a committee to invite the Joint European Standards Institution (CEN and CENELEC) to take part in the establishment of harmonised European Standards (ENs) according to the existing rules of CENELEC. Their first action was to launch a Public Enquiry (PQ) on a draft Harmonisation Document (prHD 40 001) in June 1984, which included verbatim the original technical annexe of the SPAG proposal to the CEC. A steering committee (ITSTC) was established, with four representatives each from CEN and CENELEC to which were later added four from CEPT. This HD presented the concept of Functional Groups of Standards, and a list of related base standards, with the requirement that national activi-ties aimed at adopting standards in these areas be at a stand-till pending the issue of harmonised ENs. The general response to this HD from the 17 members of CEN/CENELEC was favourable to the concept, and critical in detail on some areas of the technical content. As a result, the ITSTC produced a definitive version of the draft HD in November 1984, based on approximately 30 of the standards in the original list which reflected the consensus of the members, as expressed in their responses to the first draft.

Meanwhile, ITSTC had decided to extend the scope of the programme to include the means of developing the required Functional Standards, and of establishing policies for acceptable verification and certification procedures based on these standards, and aimed at establishing the legal infrastructure of harmonised procurement policies throughout Europe. The immediate result of this was the creation of two ad hoc expert groups; the first of these, ITAEGS, is advancing the definition of CEN, CENELEC, CEPT and SPAG members; the second. ITAEGC, is reviewing the current status of verification and certification procedures and facilities. The further development and approval of ENs, (possibly going through an "experimental" stage before final ratification). ITSTC also envisages that the source material for the production of ENs as Functional Standards will come from already existing work, where this is suitable, such as that undertaken by the EHA in de COS documents, SPAG in the GUS, ITSU in its TGs, CEPT in its working committees, etc.

5. SPAG DEVELOPMENTS

While the CEN/CENELEC activity was getting under way in 1984, SPAG extended the scope of its work in response to the commitment from its members to the adoption of its policies. Also, because of the historical link between the RT companies and the ESPRIT programme, the CEC/ITTTF asked SPAG to provide technical back-up to the planned call for tenders for the IES projects. The result of this was the formation of a Technical Committee of SPAG, which between June and October 1984 elaborated the concept of Functional Standards into the format of a "Profile" specification, and produced a first set of such profiles, related both to the contents of the original SPAG proposal to the CEC and the actual requirements of ROSE. A representative of the EHA was also invited to contribute to this work, to pass on the benefits of the work undertakenthere.

These profiles were put together into a document known as GUS (Guide to the Use of Standards) which was supplied to the CEC for use in IES in October 1984. A revision of this was completed in January 1985. Further work is under way to extend the scope and refine the detail of these profiles, taking into account both the increasing understanding of OSI work and its stability, and the requirements outlined originally by SPAG in a second annexe to the January 1984 proposal. SPAG is also making plans, as anticipated in that proposal, to set up a public demonstrator project based on the ideas and actual standards used in the GUS; these will feature in subsequent profile material in the GUS, as also will the specific SPAG contributions to the development of ENs by CEN/CENELEC.

6. FUNCTIONAL STANDARDS

The purpose of a Functional Standard is to make a recommendation as to
when and how certain IT standards should be used. Thes recommendations
are of the form:
  "If you want to provide function X then use standard(s) Y, like
this".

  Each function must however be clearly defined, so as to avoid
confusion with any other function, and to allow easy recognition of
instances of the function in the real world.
  Most IT standards are written to define a specific sub-function,
and they rely on an explicitly stated relationship to other standards
in order to provide a complete, working capability. This is particularly true of the layer standards which derive from the OSI Basic
Reference Model, where the Service Definition standards govern the
logical relationship between the Protocol Specification standards of'
adjacent layers.
  In the OSI Context, three distinct classes of function can be
identified:

- those governing the relationship between local and remote
  systems (independently of the telecommunications
  facility being used).
- those governing the relationship between an end system
  and a telecommunications facility.
- those governing the operation of intermediate systems
  which providea relay function between different functions
  of the same class.

  Functional Standards are required which correspond to these three
classes of function. The main content of the document which defines
such a Functional Standard is the description of the provided function,
and the identification of the standards being used.
  However, it is not sufficient merely to identify a working set of
standards needed to provide such a function. The state of stability of
each standard, the interrelationship between standards, and the aspects
of each standard relevant to the function all have to be taken into
account if an unambiguous specification of the function's support is to
be given.

Each Functional Standard is therefore a combination of a simple definition of the function, an illustration of the scenario within which the function is applicable, and a single working set of standards. Each working set includes references to standards, and recommendations for options, parameter values and interpretations to be followed in each standard.

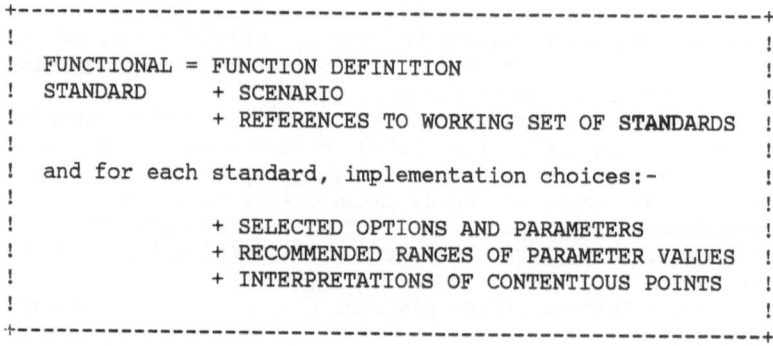

```
+-------------------------------------------------------------+
!                                                             !
!   FUNCTIONAL = FUNCTION DEFINITION                          !
!   STANDARD    + SCENARIO                                    !
!              + REFERENCES TO WORKING SET OF STANDARDS       !
!                                                             !
!   and for each standard, implementation choices:-           !
!                                                             !
!              + SELECTED OPTIONS AND PARAMETERS              !
!              + RECOMMENDED RANGES OF PARAMETER VALUES       !
!              + INTERPRETATIONS OF CONTENTIOUS POINTS        !
!                                                             !
+-------------------------------------------------------------+
```

7. THE ROLE OF ECMA

The European Computer Manufactures Association was started in 1961, and now represents 32 companies with a substantial European interest (they must market, develop, and manufacture in Europe to be full members). Compared with SPAG, it therefore represents a wider cross-section of the European industry, since it includes the larger American-based companies, besides all the important companies from the EEC countries and one or two from EFTA and Japan.

It has always set out to "develop, in cooperation with appropriate national and international organisations, methods and procedures in order to facilitate and standardize the use of data processing systems." It has aimed to do this "in the general interest", including, especially of course, that of the users. Although its name might suggest it, ECMA is not in any ordinary sense a trade association. Its By-laws in fact expressly forbid it to engage in any profit-making or commercial activity whatever. Thus, it refrains from expressing views outside the field of standardization. Adoption of standards by ECMA members is entirely voluntary.

Its practice has always been to submit its standards as drafts to international organizations like ISO or IEC, both directly as a liaison member, and indirectly through the activities of ECMA members in national bodies. Thus a high proportion of international standards in the computer field, and especially in OSI work, originated as ECMA drafts. Participation of US firms in the work of ECMA has enabled a close working relationship to grow up, with the corresponding technical committees of ANSI, starting in the 1960s. As a result, ECMA and ANSI drafts have usually been closely aligned, if not identical, and the eventual standards have reflected both European and American needs.

With the rapid growth of interest in IT standards in Europe as a whole, stimulated by the CEC, ECMA is currently reviewing its aims and working practices, though it is thought most unlikely to depart from its original positon of not engaging in any commercail activity.

8. THE ISO DIMENSION

None of the participants in this European Initiative suggest or expect that the results of the work will be unique to Europe, or that it can stand apart from the work of ISO and CCITT. This actitivty has grown up in recognition of the gap between the formal ratification of layer standards in conformity with IS 7498, the establishment of effective conformity testing and certification procedures related to the needs of users, and the desire of users and suppliers to put the good work of OSI into practical use.

Ways will have to be found to ensure that the outcome of this work is incorporated into a wider scenario involving the other major participants in OSI, particularly the USA and Japan. Contact already exists with the USA in the involvement of European industry with the NBS-sponsored LAN demonstrations last year, and in the planning for those proposed for this year. Contact also exists at the technical level in the work of ECMA. CEN/CENELEC member bodies will need to find a way to promote their European accord into ISO, and CEPT member administrations will likewise have topromote it into CCITT.

ALPHABET SOUP

IT	Information Tecnology
CEC	Commission of the European Communities
ITTTF	IT and Telecommunications Task Force
WGS	Working Group on Standards
EHA	European Harmonization Activity
DFN	Deutsches ForschungsNetz (German Research Network)
COS	Common use of OSI Standards
ESPRIT	European Strategic Pre-competitive Research Programme for IT
IES	Information Exchange System
ROSE	Research Open System for Europe
CEN	European Committee for Standardisation
CENELEC	European Committee for Electronical Standardisation
CEPT	European Conference of PPTs
HD	Harmonization Document
EN	European Norm
ITSTC	IT Steering Committee
ITAEGS	IT Ad-hoc Expert Group on Standards
ITAEGC	IT Ad-hoc Expert Group on Certification
SOGITS	Senior Officials Group for IT Standardisation
RT	Round Table
SPAG	Standards Promotion and Application Group
GUS	Guide to the Use of Standards
ITSU	Information Technology Standards Unit
TG	Technical Guide
ECMA	European Computer Manufacturers Association

DIAGRAMMATIC SUMMARY OF INTERRELATIONSHIPS

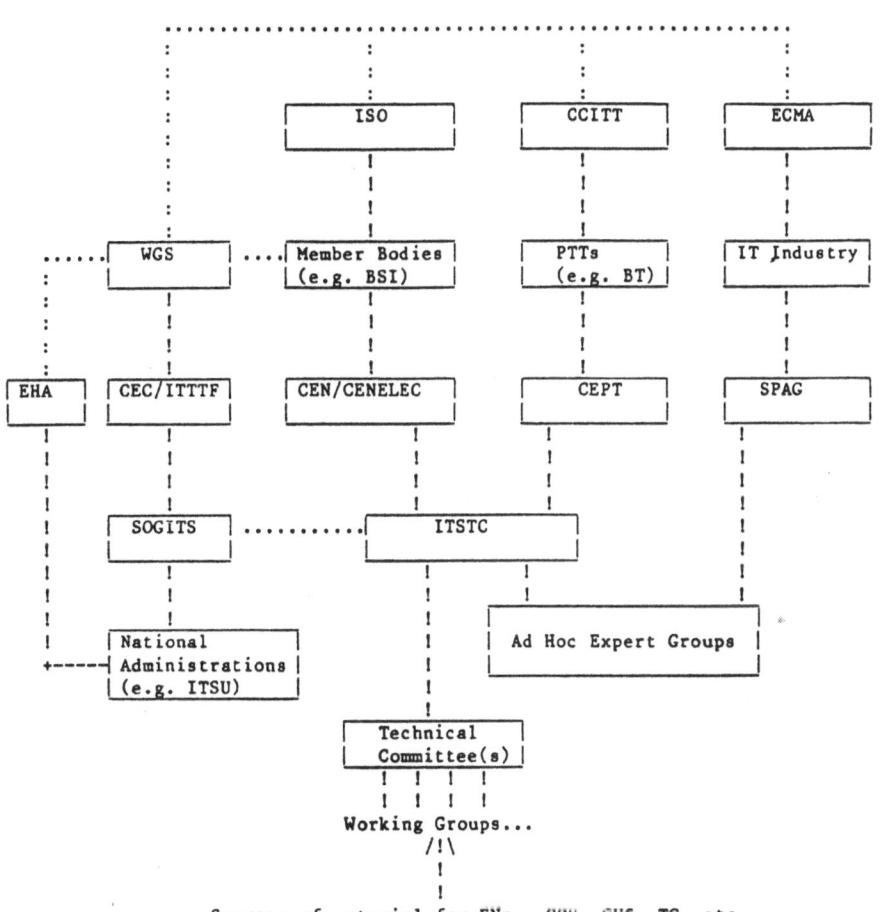

```
              ....................................................
              :               :               :               :
              :               :               :               :
              :            _____        _____        _____
              :           |  ISO   |      | CCITT  |      |  ECMA  |
              :           |_____|      |_____|      |_____|
              :               !               !               !
              :               !               !               !
              :               !               !               !
              :               !               !               !
      _____  :            _____     _____        _____
.....|  WGS  |....        |Member Bodies|  |  PTTs  |      |IT Industry |
  :  |_____|           |(e.g. BSI)   |  |(e.g. BT)|     |_____|
  :      !               |_____|  |_____|            !
  :      !                     !               !                !
  :      !                     !               !                !
  :      !                     !               !                !
 ____  _____        _____      _____        _____
|EHA ||CEC/ITTTF|     |CEN/CENELEC  |    |  CEPT  |      |  SPAG  |
|____||_____|     |_____|    |_____|      |_____|
  !      !                  !                 !               !
  !      !                  !                 !               !
  !      !                  !                 !               !
  !      !                  !                 !               !
  !   _____    ........._____           !               !
  !  | SOGITS|          | ITSTC  |            !               !
  !  |_____|          |_____|            !               !
  !      !                 !  !               !               !
  !      !                 !  !_____    _____
  !   _____          !  | Ad Hoc Expert Groups          |
  | | National  |          !  |                               |
  +-| Administrations |    !  |_____|
    |(e.g. ITSU)|          !
    |_____|       _____
                       | Technical  |
                       | Committee(s)|
                       |_____|
                        ! ! ! !
                        ! ! ! !
                     Working Groups...
                         /!\
                          !
                          !
       Sources of material for ENs - COS, GUS, TG, etc
```

Session 1

Status of the Lower Layers

Session Chairman: Inge Groenbaek

THE ROLE OF THE NETWORK LAYER

Jeremy B. Tucker
Logica Communications and
Electronic Systems Limited
64 Newman Street
London W1A 4SE
United Kingdom

1. INTRODUCTION

The role of the Network Layer is to enable any two open systems
anywhere to exchange data with one another, irrespective of the types
of network the two systems are attached to and of the means of interconnecting those two networks. With this basic communications facility
it achieves half of the dream of OSI: the other half, using that
communications facility in an appropriate way to support distributed
processing, is the task of the Transport and higher layers of OSI.

The raw materials that the Network Layer has at its disposal are
real networks in the field (which, to avoid confusion, are termed
"subnetworks" in OSI), end systems and gateways. In the short term, OSI
can be expected to influence the operation of end systems and gateways
rather more than subnetworks, and so the job of the Network Layer is to
specify how end systems and gateways can cooperate to support communications across arbitrary combinations of subnetworks. In the longer
term, OSI will influence subnetworks themselves; and this is already
happening with public packet-switching networks since CCITT agreed to
modify X25 so as to support the connection-oriented Network Service.
But the main problem today is to cope with the great variety of network
technology and to develop general methods of interconnection.

2. NETWORK SERVICE

A crucial step in this direction is the standardization of OSI Network
Service. The main problem in interconnecting subnetworks in general is
that they offer different facilities to their users: for example X25
networks enable users to resynchronize using Reset, and to send short
urgent messages as Interrupts; by and large, other networks do not
offer these facilities. At a gateway between subnetworks of the two
types it is therefore not possible to map the facilities of one into
the facilities of the other: no such mapping can exist. For each facility available on only one side, there are two possibilities: either

R. W. G. Herbers (ed), The Upper Layers of Open Systems Interconnection, 23–30.

its use is denied over the interconnection or additional protocol is
developed to emulate the facility over the subnetwork that does not
provide it. Either possibility will affect the end systems, which are
therefore involved in the interconnection problem.

The only general approach to interconnection can be to standardize
in essence the set of facilities to be expected in OSI communications
paths. This will then serve as a specification for the solution of any
particular interconnection problem, as well as give a target for future
network design. This standard is the OSI Network Service, DIS 8348. Its
application to interconnection is illustrated in figures 1 and 2.

3. CONNECTION-ORIENTED AND CONNECTIONLESS SERVICE

One thing that threatens to spoil this rosy prospect of global interconnection is that ISO has seen fit to standardize two quite different
Network Services, connection-oriented (CO) and connectionless (CL),
rather than just one. It is not appropriate here to go into why this
has happened in detail but it is largely a legacy of the datagram
versus virtual circuit dispute of the '70s coupled with some miscon-
ceptions of the role of the Network Layer. Nonetheless, the existence
of these two standard services opens the unpleasant possibility of two
incompatible communications environments in OSI, with the supporters of
CO-Network Service unable to communicate (in OSI) with those who adopt
CL-Network Service - a split in OSI. Indeed, since connectionless service is not restricted to the Network Layer, a similar problem could
appear at other layers too, multiplying the potential incompatibi-
lities.

However, the connectionless addendum to the Reference Model
currently lays down the following constraints on the use of CO and CL
services in combination.

1. Where CO Presentation Service is used ...
   (i)   CO Session Service shall be used
   (ii)   CO Transport Service shall be used
   (iii)   CO Network Service shall be available;
              optionally, CL Network Service may be used by
              agreement

2. Where CL Presentation Service is used ...

   (i), (ii), (iii) as above with CO and CL interchanged.

3. A system that does not satisfy (iii) is not a fully open
   system in OSI.

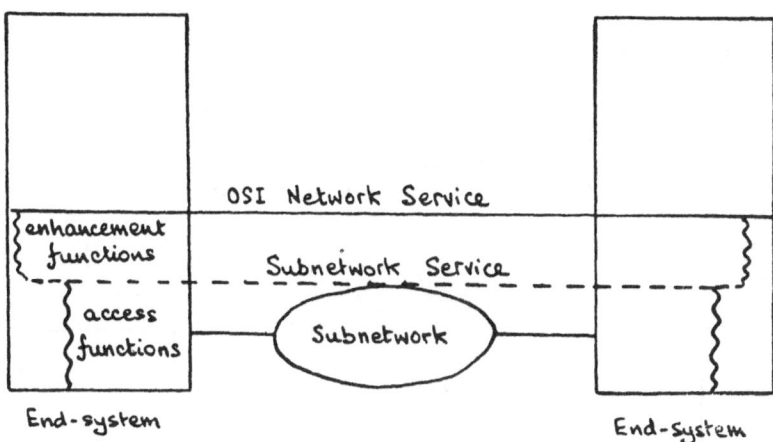

Figure 1.   Subnetwork service enhanced to full
            OSI Network Service

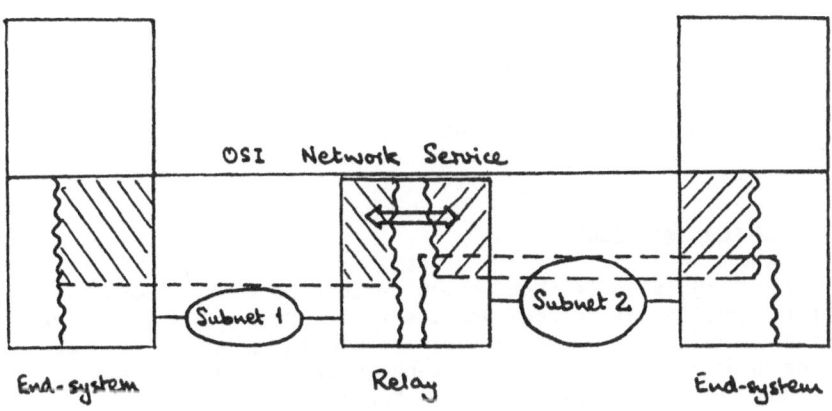

Figure 2.   Use of OSI Network Service for
            interworking

Whatever it may say in the connectionless addendum, however, it is
clear that many organizations will, at least in the short term, provide
CO Transport Service over CL Network Service without the capability of
doing so over CO Network Service, preferring the mild stigma of not
being fully open to developing the extra protocol that would be required for full openness. Interconnection between domains using dissimilar Network Service is possible in practice, but requires the use
of a Transport Relay, which is not permitted by OSI.

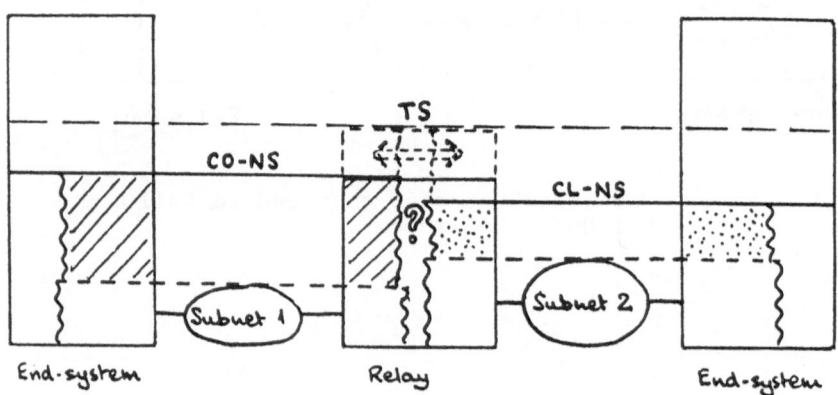

Figure 3.   Incompatibility of CO and CL Network
            Services: Transport relays not permitted in OSI

4. PROTOCOLS FOR INTERCONNECTION

The long-term objective is that communications networks should be
designed to provide OSI Network Service fully. Such "OSI-subnetworks"
will not need additional protocol message exchanges operating over them
within the Network Layer. Until all subnetworks are "OSI-subnetworks",
however, additional mechanisms will be needed.
      ISO has developed a standard, currently DP 8648, which illustrates
the protocol combinations that can arise in providing OSI Network Service over real subnetworks and introduces some infelicitous terminology
to describe them. It does, however, highlight two quite different practical approaches to the development of protocols to support interconnection of networks. These are the use of internet protocols and hop-
by-hop enhancement.

4.1. Internet Protocols

An internet protocol is a protocol that will provide the desired ser-
vi:e over almost anything. That is to say, it expects little an underlying subnetwork other than the ability to transfer a data unit of some
reasonable size across ist. In this way, one single protocol can be
used to provide Network Service facilities overall the subnetworks in a
chain, with the result that this protocol is seen as running end to
end. This is illustrated in Figure 4. Gateways do, however, participate
in its operation: they affect its parameters and will be affected by
it. This generality is very attractive. The price paid may be overkill,
in that internet protocol mechanisms may duplicate facilities inherent
in real subnetworks and thus lead to communications overhead.

4.2. Hop-by-Hop Enhancement

In complete contrast, the objective of hop-by-hop enhancement is to
avoid unnecessary overhead by developing a tailor-made enhancement
protocol specific to a particular type of subnetwork that adds just the
necessary facilities that are not provided by the subnetwork itself.
This is illustrated in Figures 5 and 6. The price paid for this
efficiency may be the development of a fairly large number of Network
Protocols.

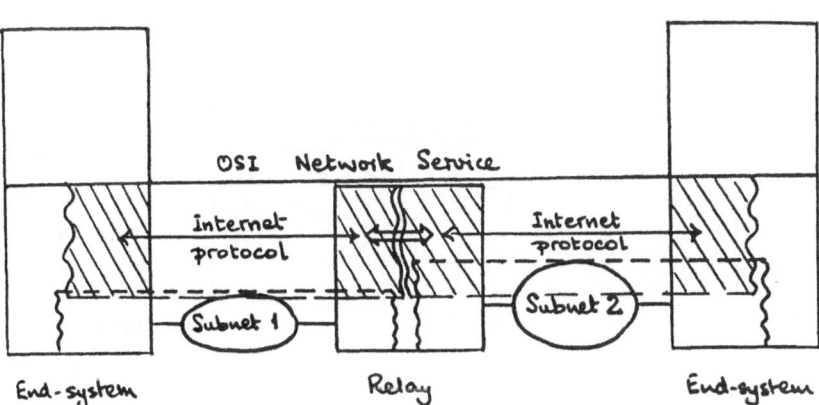

Figure 4. Interworking: internet protocol

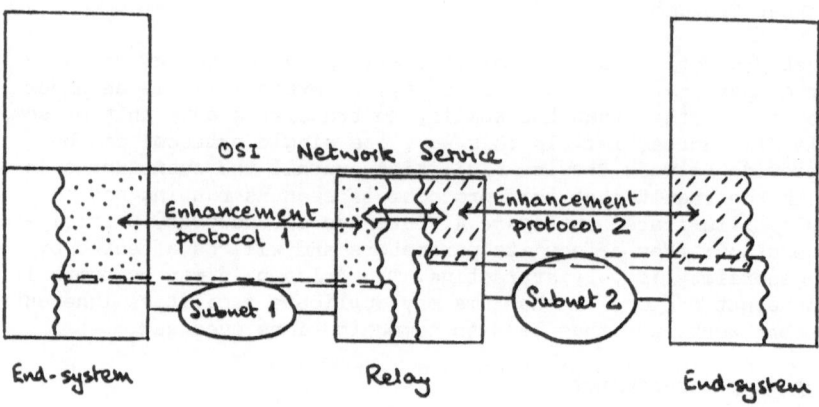

Figure 5. Interworking: hop-by-hop enhancement

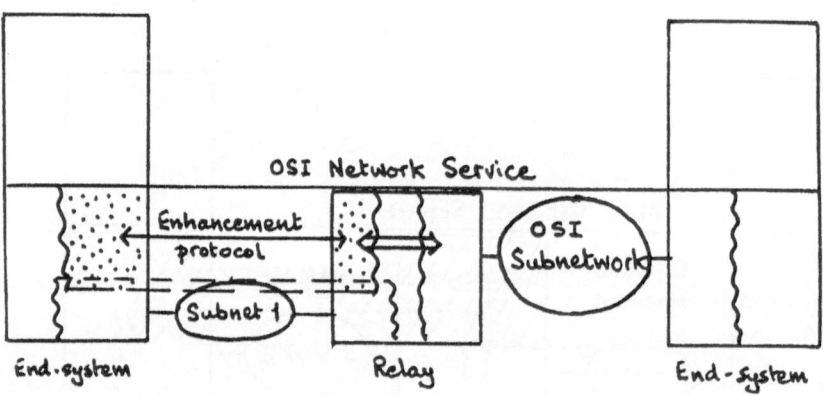

Figure 6.   Interworking : hop-by-hop enhancement

The internet protocol technique was the one adopted in order to provide
CL-Network Service, leading to the CL Internet Protocol Standard DIS
8473, which was based very much on the ARPA IP. To provide CO-Network
Service, on the other hand, the hop-by-hop enhancement technique was

chosen. At first it was expected that this would lead to the development of many different enhancement protocols, but in reality it has proved otherwise: almost all CO convergence protocols are level 3 of X.25 as standardized by ISO in DIS 8208, or (possibly) a slight variant of it. The only types of subnetwork where DIS 8208 may not be always appropriate are:

(i)   general CL subnetworks, where a Network Protocol (NC4) derived from Class 4 Transport Protocol is the only current candidate;

(ii)   LANs operating LLC-1 - here a debate is still going on as to the relative merits of NC4 or a modified version of DIS 8208;

(iii)   X.21 circuit-switched networks, where DIS 8208 is certainly possible but some interest remains in a tailor-made single-connection protocol based on the Network layer part of T.70 with some extensions; however, work on this apparently ceased eighteen months ago.

So to provide CO-Network Service, the general picture may look very like an X.25 Internet, with DIS 8208 enhancement protocols on some hops and 1984 X.25 provided by real subnetworks on others.

5. ADDRESSING

Finally, addressing. Another major problem of interconnecting subnetworks is inadequacy of addressing. Typically, a subnetwork enables a user to supply a destination address which it can use to derive a route. Thus knowledge of address structure, or part of it, is built in to the subnetwork; stated another way, addresses as currently used by subnetworks are constrained in their structure (and length) by the subnetworks themselves.

Just as with the service facilities discussed earlier, OSI needs a global solution to addressing; it therefore needs a global address structure; and since no subnetworks cater for a unified global addressing scheme - even public networks cater only for the public domain, and have different numbering plans for different technologies - existing subnetwork addressing capabilities are all inadequate. Save again 1984 X.25, which, in an attempt to align with the CO-Network Service, is expected to offer an additional address field long enough to meet OSI needs. ("Expected" because final agreement has still not been reached on the length of the field.)

ISO, in collaboration with CCITT, is developing a standard DIS 8348/DAD2 which defines a new address structure rich enough to meet all needs currently envisaged. Largely because this standard is so new - at the time of writing it is out for a 2nd DP ballot - no subnetworks in existence or planned for the immediate future are capable of routing on OSI Network addresses. In consequence, except for 1984 X.25 networks, enhancement protocols, internet or hop-by-hop, will be needed to convey OSI Network Addresses across them; and even in 1984 X25 called DTE address as well as the called OSI Network Address. In the longer term it is expected that subnetworks themselves will more and more be capable of routing upon OSI Network Addresses directly, though a lot of work has to be done on directories before this can come about on a large scale.

X.25, INTERNETWORKING AND MILITARY ENHANCEMENTS

Trevor Benjamin
Royal Signals and Radar Establishment
St. Andrews Road
Great Malvern
Worcs. WR14 3PS
United Kingdom

1. INTRODUCTION

CCITT Recommendation X.25 has become the widely accepted protocol used
for connecting host computer systems to communications networks. X.25
has evolved since its first appearance as a published recommendation in
1976. This paper describes the current status of X.25 and puts it in
the context of complete communications systems.

There is a need in all communications systems to define a complete
set of protocols which can perform together to provide for the needs of
the user. X.25 has a vital role to play in this set, and not just as an
access protocol to wide area networks. The paper will first describe
the organisation of such a set of protocols which has been developed in
the UK MoD for strategic communications systems. This will show the
position and roles that X.25 can be used for. This leads to a comparison of the two latest versions of the protocol, 1980 and 1984, to
highlight its direction of evolution. This is necessary because the
1980 version is already widely implemented and changes will be a major
cause for concern.

The paper continues with the description of some of the associated
recommendations and draft standards that are referred to in this paper
and are of interest in the context of X.25.

Within NATO there has been concern over the use of civilian
protocols in a military environment. This has lead to the overall
strategy of the Tri-Service Group on Communications and Electronic
Equipment, Sub-Group on Data Processing and Distribution, (TSGCEE SG9),
on the adoption of ISO standards and its approach to influencing the
direktion of international standards making efforts. (See Refs. /1/ and
/2/). The paper discusses some perceived extensions to X.25 to satisfy
the military requirement and outlines some agreed solutions. It also
describes the impact of these extensions on the current ISO work at the
Network Layer and the efforts being made to influence this activity.

31

R. W. G. Herbers (ed), The Upper Layers of Open Systems Interconnection, 31–48.

2. PROTOCOL SUITES

International Standards and Recommendations for Communications protocols are beginning to appear at a number of layers corresponding to
those of the ISO Reference Model. Various organisations including NATO
have seen the need to define an intercept strategy that details usable
protocols and those which they predict will achieve future acceptance
and ratification by the standardization bodies. This effort has been
directed at helping implementors chose the right protocols to implement
at the various layers. Within the UK MoD we have perceived the need to
define the useful emerging protocol standards and also the way in which
standards at different layers can be combined to produce complete work-
able suites of protocols suitable for a variety of communication scena-
rios. (It should be stated that at this time the emphasis has been on
defining protocol suites suitable for strategic, fixed communications.)

Figure 1 shows, in diagrammatic form, a current draft RSRE proposal for these protocol suites. This proposal is being put forward for
adoption by UK MoD. The diagram shows protocols which we believe to be
implementable now (with the possible exception of the ISDN standards).
This paper will first briefly describe layers 4 to 7, as these layers
are the main topic of this symposium, and will then describe the
choices made at layers 1 to 3 together with the rationale for the
choices. This will form the background to the further discussions of
X.25.

APPLICATION LAYER	TELESERVICES (VTP, FTAM, JTMP, MHS ETC.)			
PRESENTATION LAYER	PRESENTATION SERVICE - SC16 N1828 (WKNG PAPER) PRESENTATION PROTOCOL - SC16 N1829 (WKNG PAPER) (NULL - INITIALLY)			
SESSION LAYER	SESSION SERVICE - IS 8325 SESSION PROTOCOL - IS 8326			
TRANSPORT LAYER	TRANSPORT SERVICE - IS 8072 TRANSPORT PROTOCOL - IS 8073			
NETWORK LAYER	NETWORK SERVICE - DIS 8348 ADDRESSING - DP 8348/DAD2			
	X 25 (1984) DIS 8208	X 25 (1984)	X 25 (1984) DIS 8208	I.451 (1984)
DATALINK LAYER	HDLC	X 25 (1984)	DIS 8802	I.441 (1984)
PHYSICAL LAYER	X 21 (1984)	X 25 (1984)	DIS 8802	I.441 (1984)
SUB-NETWORK	CIRCUIT SWITCHED NETWORK	PACKET SWITCHED NETWORK	LOCAL AREA NETWORK	ISDN

Figure 1 - Data Communication Systems Standards Protocol Suites

2.1 LAYERS 4-7

At the Transport Layer, the connection oriented Transport Service (ISO IS8072) shall be provided. All implementations shall provide both class 0 AND the explicit flow control option of class 2 of ISO IS8073, the Connection Oriented Transport Protocol, over the Connection Oriented Network Service. The implementation of classes 3 and 4 is optional for those applications that require the additional services that they offer.

At the Session Layer, the Connection Oriented Session Service, as defined in ISO IS8325, shall be provided. Implementations shall initially just provide the Basic Class Protocol of ISO IS8326.

At the Presentation Layer, ISO have yet to agree standards, thus this will initially be a null layer. ISO standards for the Presentation Layer will be adopted as soon as they become available.

Various Application Layer standards will be adopted when they mature within ISO, for example, the File Transfer, Access and Management (FTAM) specification (currently ISO DP8571), the Virtual Terminal Protocol (VTP) specification, the Job Transfer and Manipulation Protocol specification and the ISO Management Model and standards.

Currently for interactive remote system access applications the CCITT Triple-X (1984) recommendations operating over the Session Layer will be used. However, it is recognized that vendor specific VTPs may have to be used for specialised applications until the ISO standards are fully defined.

For electronic mail applications the CCITT X.400 (1984) series of recommendations for Message Handling Services (MHS) will be used. It should be noted that these recommendations include protocols at both the Presentation and Application layers and it is expected that they will be adopted as standards by ISO.

2.2 LAYERS 1-3

The objective here has been to provide the Connection Oriented Network Service (ISO DIS8348) over four different types of networking technology and combinations of the same, so that the protocols specified for the higher layers can be independent of the underlying technologies.

For packet switched networks CCITT X.25 (1984) has been recommended. At present there are few implementations of 1984 X.25 available, but it is believed that all new implementations will be built to this standard and that manufacturers will seek to upgrade existing implementations. Part of the purpose of this intercept strategy is to declare a commitment to this set of protocols to encourage manufacturers to build products that conform to these standards.

For Local Area Networks the recommendation is to use ISO DIS8802 with the Logical Link Control 2 which provides a connection oriented link service. We are then recommending that ISO DIS8208 be implemented by systems using the LAN. ISO DIS8208 is the definition of X.25 Packet Level for Data Terminal Equipment (DTE), allowing DTE to DTE operation (see section 4.2).

For circuit switched connections or point-to-point links providing a CCITT X.21 service then the symmetrical version of HDLC LAP-B will be used for the Data Link layer with the X.25 Packet Level protocol as defined by ISO DIS8208.

From this description it can be seen that all the network technologies defined have been enhanced to provide the same network service. The only remaining differences being in the qualitiy of that service. The internetworking technique will thus be connection oriented. We propose that routing at gateways be initially static, but with alternate routes. This could be upgraded later, as the connectivity of networks becomes richer, to a dynamic situation in which gateways exchange routing information about the state of the internet. Such mechanisms should be defined within the Network Management functions, but there are no ISO standards in this area at present. The use of gateways with static routing would also provide a testbed in which the real requirements for dynamic routing could be ascertained.

Addressing within this proposed standards architecture would be provided by the Draft Addendum to ISO DIS8348 covering Network Layer Addressing. This allows a very flexible hierarchical structure of addressing to be employed. However, it does require that address registration authorities are established to manage addresses and their allocation within addressing domains. It is necesaary that NATO form a policy on its relationship to ISO in this area, as well as its relationship to individual MoDs.

2.3 ROLES AND TYPES OF X.25

It can be seen from the above that the use of X.25 has evolved beyond its original network access role. Within CCITT it is still defined as a DTE to DCE protocol, although more emphasis is being placed on its end to end nature in providing the connection oriented network service across single networks. This provides a common basis over each of a concatenated set of networks for the connection oriented approach to internetworking.

In addition to its traditional wide area role we have proposed the use of X.25 over Local area networks and point to point circuits as an end system to end system protocol (ie. DTE to DTE). In the LAN case it may be argued that using such a protocol will significantly degrade the performance achievable. This may be the case, although this has not been demonstrated in practice with realistic patterns of traffic flow, but the advantages of using a common network layer protocol are also great. A significant portion of the cost of communcations systems is not in their operation, but in the control, maintenance, availability and testing of the protocols. This cost is dramatically increased if special military enhancements are required. It is therefore highly desirable to limit the number of different protocols that are required in military systems, although some trade off against performance may be necessary.

3. X.25 1980 AND 1984

Subsequent to the enhancement of X.25 at the 1984 plenary of CCITT the
state of the recommendation may give rise to some concern amongst implementors and purchasers of X.25 systems. The questions that arise
will be mainly about the differences between 1980 and 1984, and the
possibility of interoperability between the two versions. This section
provides a flavour of the changes that have been made and attempts to
answer these questions.

3.1 PHYSICAL AND LINK LEVEL CHANGES

At the physical level, the X.21 bis interface is no longer recommended
just for an interim period. It is now available to an Administration as
a permanent alternative to full X.21.

At the Link level, HDLC LAPB remains as the main protocol, and one
that will be provided in all networks. The main changes at this level
are the inclusion of two subscription-time options.

The first option brings X.25 into line with X.75 in allowing
"multiple physical circuit operation" (known as Multilink operation).
This option allows the use of more than one physical circuit, each
operating LAPB independently, between a single DTE-DCE pair. This
provides a graceful degradation of the performance of X.25 in the
presence of circuit failures. This option is based on the ISO Multilink
Control Procedures.

The second subscription-time option allows the use of LAPB
modulo 128 sequence numbering, rather than the basic LAPB modulo 8.
This option is available for links with high transmission rates and
long delays such as is the case with satellite circuits.

3.2 PACKET LEVEL CHANGES

The main procedures and formats on the X.25 packet level protocol
remain unchanged, although some extensions have been defined. For
example, the optional maximum data packet sizes have been increased to
allow 2048 and 4096 octets of data. The interrupt user data field has
been increased to allow between 1 and 32 octets of data instead of the
1980 limitation of just one octet. This extension has been carried out
to allow X.25 to support the OSI Network Service Expedited Data
feature. Also the facility field length in Call Request, Incoming Call,
Call Accepted and Call Connected packets has increased its maximum
length from 63 to 109 octets.

The Datagram option of X.25 (1980) has been removed entirely from
the recommendation. CCITT Study Group VII, concerned with Data Communications Networks, does now have a new study Question, for the 1985-1988
session, which relates to Connectionless services in public networks.
The Group will be seeking input on the user requirement for such a service and the nature of that service.

3.3 NEW OPTIONAL USER FACILITIES

Other changes that have been made to X.25 relate to the additions and
modifications of the optional user facilities. In all CCITT have added
9 new facilities and extended the Closed User Group features. The
facilities describe services which a user may subscribe to if the
network offers them. The description do not specify how networks
provide these extra facilities. It is believed that some of these facilities will be useful in enabling certain military features to be incorporated into X.25.

One of the most fundamental new facilities is that of "On-line
Registration". This is important because it defines two new packet
types and it extends the use of logical channel 0. This logical channel
was previously used only for the Restart packet to initialize the X.25
Packet Level and the Diagnostic packet in error conditions. The purpose
of the facility is to allow a DTE to request modification or registration of other facilities or to obtain the current states of facilities
from the DCE. The DTE does this by issuing the new Registration Request
packet specifying the facilities he is interested in and receiving the
new Registration Confirmation packet in reply from the DCE.

Another of the new facilities is the Hunt Group. This allows incoming calls addressed to the Hunt Group address to be distributed
across a set of DTE/DCE interfaces, each of which may have its own
separate DTE address. In addition to this, there is the Call Redirec-
tion facility. This allows incoming calls to be diverted from the
destination DTE to another nominated DTE, when the destination is out
of order, busy or at the prior request of the original destination DTE.
Associated with these are two further notification facilities which may
be used to inform the final destination what has happened.

The other new facilities provide the ability to select and indicate the transit delay on a per virtual call basis, allow the handling
of charging information and permit user identification to the network
for each new virtual call.

3.4 X.25 AND THE OSI NETWORK SERVICE

The other major change from X.25 (1980) is contained in the Annex G to
X.25 (1984). This Annex defines CCITT specified DTE facilities to
support the OSI Network Service. New facility codings are specified to
permit both calling and called address extension to add up to a further
32 digits to the X.25 addresses. There are also facility codings to
allow quality of service negotiation to cover minimum throughput class
indication, end to end transit delay and the use of Network Service
expedited data.

3.5 INTEROPERABILITY

The Interoperability problem between 1980 and 1984 versions of X.25
must be considered at various points of X.25 applicability. X.25 is no
longer aimed at being an access protocol, and has elements that relate
to DTE to DTE (end to end) as well as DTE to DCE (local). The extens-

sions to X.25 as described above must be viewed in this light if their
impact on interoperability is to be assessed.

The Physical and Link layer changes to X.25 are of purely local
significance and will only affect the DTE/DCE operation. Within the
Packet level enhancements the new facilities are of local significance
only, with the exception on Transit delay selection and indication. It
should be noted that the On-line registration facility is only invoked
at the request of the DTE and hence the new packet type will never be
sent to a DTE without it first having requested the action. The other
enhancements noted have end to end, or DTE to DTE significance.

3.5.1 DTE to DCE

The changes to X.25 are all enhancements which leave the 1980 version
as a subset of 1984. It should therefore be possible for a 1980 DTE to
interoperate with a 1984 DCE, because it will never be capable of initiating interactions that the 1984 DCE will not understand. The DCE
will need to know it is handling a 1980 DTE. (see section 3.5.2).

The alternative of a 1984 DTE interoperating with a 1980 DCE is
more complex. It would require the DTE to be configured and controlled
to only use the 1980 equivalent subset of its mechanisms. The ease with
which this is possible is, of course, implementation dependent, but
should not pose too great a difficulty if 1984 versions have been developed from existing 1980 implementations.

3.5.2 DTE to DTE

The question to be resolved here is whether it is possible or desirable
for a 1980 DTE to interoperate with a 1984 DTE. It is assumed that the
underlying network can support both styles of working and carry the relevant extensions from local DCE to remote DCE. Obviously some of the
features that the 1984 DTE could generate, such as a 32 octet interrupt
packet, can not be accepted by the 1980 DTE. Thus there is a problem if
the 1984 DTE transmits such a protocol element and it is passed across
the network and the remote DCE forwards it to the 1980 DTE. This problem exists, and is not dependent upon which style of DTE originated
the virtual circuit.

Similarly a 1984 DTE issuing a call request packet seeking to
negotiate a maximum window size of 4096 should be completely refused by
a 1980 implementation if it is forwarded to it by its local DCE. Indeed
the call should be cleared as an error, rather than negotiating down to
the default and letting the call proceed. 1980 DTEs may regard some of
the possible 1984 extensions as protocol violations of sufficient
magnitude not just to affect that particular virtual circuit but to
warrant restarting the whole link, thus losing all the virtual circuits
the DTE was operating.

At present there does not appear to be a mechanism for signalling
from DTE to DTE what style of X.25 is being operated, let alone the
ability to negotiate down to the 1980 version. Thus it is not possible
for DTE implementations to adapt themselves to operate the restricted
1980 X.25.

Given the above problems, and if 1980 to 1984 operation is
necessary, it would be incumbent upon the DCE implementation, knowing
what version of DTE it was handling locally, to police the interactions
of each virtual circuit and only allow the 1980 subset of features to
be used on virtual circuits between differing DTEs. It would then have
to clear or reset the circuit if either DTE violated this limitation.

This only serves to highlight another problem. An end-system is
presumably using X.25 as one protocol in a suite which provides a
complete application. Given that this suite consists of the ISO layers,
then interaction between 1980 and 1984 may be further limited, if not
impossible. In order to provide the Network Service a 1980 X.25 service
must be enhanced using the X.25 Convergence Protocol, e.g. to extend
the addressing capability. No enhancement is necessary for 1984 X.25.
Thus one end-system or DTE would be operating an extra protocol, the
X.25 Convergence Protocol, which the other end-system would not normally be using. At the very least the 1984 DTE would have to recognise the
Protocol Identifier in the call user data field and select the use of
the Convergence protocol. This implies that the 1984 DTE would have to
implement this extra protocol, which under normal circumstances it
would not require.

An alternative approach to allow interoperation of the two styles
of X.25, if a network will support both, is to only allow 1980 DTEs to
communicate with other 1980 implementations and similarly with 1984
DTEs. This would need to be controlled by the network management, perhaps by using closed user groups. The two logically separate communities as supported by two distinct subnetworks.

4. RELATED STANDARDS

X.25 must be viewed in the context of an overall set of standards that
can be used to make up a communications system. In Section 2 this idea
was elaborated upon showing some of the other standards that can be
used. This section will briefly discuss some of these standards and
their purpose and relationship to X.25.

4.1 NETWORK SERVICE DEFINITIONS

Within ISO the Network Service definition is DIS 8348. It aims to describe, in an abstract way, the service offered by the Network Layer.
This is the service offered by real networks, with enhancement protocols as necessary, and also by concatenations of real networks into an
internet. This DIS only describes the Connection Oriented Service; the
Connectionless Service being defined in an addendum.

CCITT have defined a parallel architecture to that of ISO, with a
Reference Model and a set of Service definitions. These are designed to
cater for CCITT applications. The ISO and CCITT Reference Models are
equivalent. X.213 is CCITT's Network Service Definition. It is recognised that it is desirable that both Network Service definitions should
be in alignment with each other. However, there may be circumstances
where X.213 may define services which are a subset of those provided by
ISO, where it is seen that public networks should not implement all the

facilities which may be offered in private networks (e.g. see section 5.3). X.25 is seen by the PTTs as satisfying the service definitions as described in X.213, rather than DIS 8348. Alignment is thus highly desirable at least to the extent where X.25 can carry all the information that is required to support the OSI Network Service.

4.2 DIS 8208

This ISO document is entitled "Data Communication - X.25 packet level protocol for data terminal equipment". The document fills the need for a definition of X.25 from the DTE point of view, as opposed to the CCITT recommendation X.25 which is defined from the DCE point of view. The DIS covers only the Packet Level procedures and formats, and is compatible with CCITT X.25 Level 3. It also extends the X.25 definition by means of additional procedures to enable the interoperation of two DTEs directly without a packet switched network between them. This allows DTE to DTE operation over private wires, circuit switched connections or Local Area Networks with the appropriate Link Layer protocol. It provides a description of the interface for the Virutal Call and Permanent Virtual Call services. The procedures and formats described in the DIS are designed to be compatible with X.25 (1984) but by restricting the use of 1984 features they can be used for X.25 (1980).

4.3 X.2

This recommendation describes the user services and facilities that are available in public data networks. As part of this it lists all the facilities that can be provided by X.25 packet switched data networks and describes them as "essential", "additional" or "for further study". As the names suggest essential facilities must be provided by networks and the provision of additional services is optional.

The use of this recommendation establishes a minimum level of compatability between PTT provided networks. It is strongly recommended that NATO adopt a similar technique for its X.25 networks, in order to allow a common minimum level of service and to ease inteoperability.

4.4 X.32

X.32 gives recommendations on the interface between X.25 packet mode DTEs and DCEs where the access link is established through a Public Switched Telephone Network or a Circuit Switched Data Network. The recommendation is designed to cover the problems associated with dial-in and dial-out access to packet networks. As such it covers the problems of DTE and DCE identification, including mutual authentication,

and the need for a default profile for facilities and parameter values
for the DTE. 5 methods of DTE identification are provided for:-

    i)   by means of the underlying switched network access
          circuit identification (local loop)

    ii)   by means of a link level XID procedure

    iii)   by means of the X.25 On-line registration facility

    iv)   by means of the network user identification facility
          on a per call basis at set up time

    v)   by means of the calling address field within the call
          request packet.

As is seen, some of these methods allow identification on a per call
basis and some are established before any call is set up. There is also
a variety of levels at which the identification takes place, from the
physical to the packet level.

Recommendation X.32 is not complete and the actual procedural
aspects of the methods are still for further study. However, it is
believed that this recommendation will provide the basis for the military requirement for mobile hosts (see section 5.2.2).

4.5 X.75

CCITT Recommendation X.75 provides for the interworking of public-
packet switched networks over international circuits. It defines the
characteristics and operation of a signalling system operating between
packet switching exchanges. The signalling is performed between
Signalling Terminal Equipments, associated with each exchange and
having equal status. The information exchanged consists of call and
network control together with user data.

X.75 is able to connect two similar X.25 networks together, effectively, to produce one larger network. The connection is made by bi-
lateral agreement and each separate network must arrange for routing of
traffic to from the other network. This form of interworking is on an
lower level than OSI internetworking, the resultant network formed of
two X.75 linked networks being viewed as a single OSI sub-network. X.75
is therefore not a subject for OSI standardisation as it is basically
regarded as a protocol used internally to a network. Similarly X.75
"gateways" do not operate on OSI internetwork information such as OSI
addressing and some quality of service parameters.

5. MILITARY X.25

Since the late 1970s the UK has held the view that the X.25 protocol
was useful for access to military networks, but that in order to fulfil
the military requirement it needed some enhancement. As a result the UK

produced a document as input to TSGCEE SG9 which detailed possible
extensions to X.25 together with the technical details necessary for
their implementation. These enhancements were originally defined for
the 1980 version of the protocol.

The extensions proposed by the UK were defined with three basic
criteria in mind. First, that the military version of X.25 should form
a proper superset of X.25. Second, that they should be compatible with
future CCITT anmendments to the Recommendation and that they should be
acceptable to CCITT for inclusion into the Recommendation. Third, that
they should be achievable using existing products, i.e. without major
alternations to existing software, and preferably accessable as user
features. It was also recognised that all networks offering X.25 services would not necessarily offer the extended features so that their
implementation should be optional.

5.1 REVIEW OF PROPOSED ENHANCEMENTS

The following extensions were considered appropriate for inclusion as
extensions of X.25:

- multi-homing
- mobile hosts
- security
- priority and pre-emption
- multi-addressing
- real-time or low grade virtual circuits.

5.1.1 Multi-homing

It is a requirement in many military systems that communications
mechanisms and especially communication access facilities be, at least,
duplicated for survivability reasons. This leads to the need to have an
end-system connected to a network at two or more different locations,
or in the extreme to two or more different networks. This must have an
impact at the Network layer, and hence the network access protocol, if
routing within the network or internetwork ist to make use of such
redundancy in cases of damage or failure. Such multi-homed end-systems
should not have multiple names at the higher layers as the layers above
the Network layer are not responsible for any routing decisions. The
questions that remain involve how to handle naming of DTEs within X.25
and how to use the multiple links, eq. in cases of no damage, should
load sharing be allowed across the different paths?

5.1.2 Mobile hosts

Many military communications installations need to be mobile, or at
least moveable. The extent of the mobility will depend on the application, and may be within the scope of a single network but also may be
from one network to another. Even within a single network hosts will
require to change their point of attachment to the network, where this
is dependent on geography. In the case of X.25 networks this will

affect the X.25 address, which will be carried from one access point to another by the host. There may also be times when the host will not be available on the network while it is in transit. Therefore it is neces- sary to have mechanisms within X.25 to allow the host to identify it- self, and hence its characteristics, to the network to permit the network to carry out internal routing and management.

5.1.3 Security

This extension is not proposed to provide mechsnisms that will imple- ment secure communications. The requirement is to be able to indicate security levels for connections both to the network and across the net- work to the remote host. This indication will only be useful if the networking system and the hosts participating in the connection have the appropriate security features. In order to signal such information to the network, and to any elements of a wider internet, such as gate- ways, it is necessary to include the indication in network layer proto- cols. Hence the requirement to include security indication into X.25.

5.1.4 Priority and Pre-emption

This extension can be categorised in a similar way to the security extension, in that an indication of a connection's priority level is required both to the network and across the network. The requirement is not to define mechanisms to implement a priority and pre-emption scheme, but to extend X.25 to be able to signal this information.

5.1.5 Multi-addressing

Military data is often destined to more than one recipient, and commu- nications resources are in short supply. Therefore the possibility exists that scarce resources can be saved by only sending the data once, but with many different addresses attached. The data is then only duplicated when necessary, due to differences in routing and location, to distribute it to the recipients. If communications resources, such as link band width, are to be saved by this mechanism, then the mulit- addressing must be done within the network layer. This is because it is only within this layer that the necessary information on network and internet routing is available, and it is only in this layer that infor- mation can be signalled to the particular network implementations that may be able to take advantage of inherent multi-addressing capabili- ties.

5.1.6 Real time or low grade virtual circuits

It is perceived that some military applications have a requirement for a connection oriented type of communication, but where timeliness of delivery of the data is vital as opposed to its guaranteed delivery in sequence. (Examples of this are radar data and packet voice applica- tions.) Many of the mechanisms of X.25 Level 2 and the virtual circuit service of Level 3 are aimed at the qualities of flow controlled,

ordered and guaranteed delivery. Therefore in order to provide such a
low grade virtual circuit it seems that the X.25 interface will have to
be extended to allow the existing mechanisms to be by-passed.

5.2 AGREED SOLUTIONS

In recognition of the importance of these issues, with regard to the
timeliness of influencing CCITT and ISO an Ad Hoc meeting was held by
NATO TSGCEE SG9. This allowed nations to send X.25 Experts to discuss
the mechanisms proposed by the UK, and to agree a set of extensions
that each nation was willing to support as a submission to CCITT. The
meeting was also an opportunity to examine any other features or services that may be military requirements. This meeting was held on 17th
and 18th January 1985 in London. All the above features and the extensions were discussed and some solutions were agreed.
    The first point to note is that the proposals take account of the
1984 version of X.25 and all extensions are oriented towards that
definition.

5.2.1 Multi-homing

X.25 (1984) has defined the Hunt Group as an optional user facility.
(see section 3.3) It was generally agreed that this facility could be
used to provide a multi-homing service, but that its detailed description in the X.25 Specification would have to be studied further to see
if it fulfilled the actual military requirement. It was also proposed,
though without detailed consideration, that there was a need for three
subscription-time options for the user to select the way in which virtual circuits are assigned to physical access lines by the network.
These are:-

   i)   decided by the network possibly based on internal
          routing considerations,

   ii)   decided by the network based on fair distribution of
          virtual circuits over all access lines comprising the
          hunt group,

   iii)   to allow the user to specify a priority order of access
          lines in the hunt group, possibly in a dynamic way (this
          could use the On-line registration facility).

5.2.2 Mobile hosts

It was agreed that there should be a standard DTE to DCE affiliation
mechanism as part of X.25, so that a DTE could signal its arrival at a
particular network access point. This would require the use of a defined logical channel number and may involve mutual authentication
procedures for both DTE and DCE. Some tactical networks, such as
Ptarmigan, already provide subscriber identification by local loop
methods, at the circuit level. Identification information is then

passed from the Circuit switch to the Packet Switch system. These
networks do not require extensions to X.25.

Subsequent to the meeting it has been found that th X.32 recommendation tackles this identification problem for X.25. It allows local
loop identification, as well as proposing other standard mechanisms,
including the use of the On-line Registration facility for this purpose. It would seem that these proposals are satisfactory for military
purposes.

5.2.3 Security

It was agreed that a security parameter was required during call set
up, but not for individual data packets. The security parameter would
contain the security level requested for the call an would' be signalled
unchanged to the remote DTE in the call indication packet. The need for
the DTE to be able supply route selection information at call set up
was undecided. The proposed need for route changes during a call, and
the associated mechanisms, was rejected.

Given that a DTE can signal security level information there is a
need for a new subscription-time option. This would allow users to
state the maximum and minimum security levels that they will use or can
accept. If the DTE does not request a security level the network will
insert a default value to be signalled to the remote DTE. The default
will be the calling DTEs maximum security level.

The extension to X.25 will be the definition of a new facility
code in the DTE to DTE category, to carry this security level parameter. There is also the need to define three new diagnostic codes to
be used by the network when clearing calls for security related
reasons:-

   i)   Network cannot support requested level,

   ii)   Remote DTE cannot support requested level, (cleared by
          network)

   iii)   Level requested is outside requesting subscriber's
          range.

5.2.4 Priority and Pre-emption

It was agreed that the priority requested for a virtual circuit should
be a parameter which is signalled from DTE to DTE. It was also agreed
that the parameter should be encoded using a facility code with a 16
bit parameter field. This was to allow for the encoding of three types
of priority information:

   - priority to gain a connection,
   - priority to keep a connecton,
   - priority of data on the connection.

This will be encoded as 4 bits per priority type. It was also
agreed that the encoding should be such as to allow the top two bits
only to be used to identify four levels of priority, as there was no
requirement for 16 levels. However, it was felt that it was reasonable
to allow for the possibility of expansion. A desire was identified for
a new subscription-time option to allow a DTE to have an agreed priority level for a given period time, as well as allowing the dynamic
selection of priority for outgoing calls.

The need for three new clearing causes was identified:-

i)   cleared due to priority call locally,

ii)   cleared due to priority call remotely,

iii)   unauthorised priority level requested.

If clearing due to priority occurred at an intermediate relay point,
then the already existing "network congestion" cause could be used.

5.2.5 Mulit-addressing

The nations represented at the meeting had so far only identified
requirements for multi-addressing at the Application Layer, for example
in message systems. These systems were usually able to make communication resource savings as well, but only due to the fact that they had
been designed and built with knowledge of the network topology and its
internal routing. The meeting was led to conclude that the requirement
for multi-adddressing at the network layer and especially the type of
service needed was not sufficiently well defined. For example, is an
acknowledged or unacknowledged service required and should there be a
minimum throughput for all participants in a multi-address call, below
which a participant is dropped out so that the others are not held up?
Therefore no extensions to X.25 were agreed at the meeting.

5.2.6 Real time or low grade virtual circuits

The meeting agreed that there is a need to re-assess the user requirement for this service in the light of the qualities of service offered
by modern communicatons networks, especially in terms of throughput and
delay. The characteristics of the service need to be defined such as
whether out-of-sequence data is valuable even if it is late being delivered. Therefore no extensions to X.25 were identified at the meeting.

5.2.7 CATEGORY MARKINGS

The Norwegian NDDN has identified the need for groups of virtual calls
to be gathered together into a category. Pre-emption can only take
place with respect to other calls within the same category. This is
useful for separating, for example, exercise traffic from true operational traffic. The NDDN allows DTEs to indicate up to 16 different
categories. The meeting discussed this as a possible extension to X.25

but saw no immediate requirement for the facility. It was agreed that
the NDDN should continue the use of this feature as special to that
network. Care must be taken in defining the facility codes used, to
ensure that they are within the DTE to DTE set and do not overlap with
other defined standard codes.

5.3 NATO TEST CASE

The results of this meeting make an interesting test case for the
policy of NATO TSGCEE on its approach to adopting ISO standards. In
particular NATO's ability to influence ISO standardization to more
closely reflect the military need. This arises because of recent
changes to the ISO Network Service definition (DIS 8348) with respect
to its Priority and Security parameters. The current DIS 8348 has both
of these parameters as information local to the end-system initiating
the connection, i.e. they are neither signalled to the network nor
across the network to the remote end-system.

   This problem had been identified by the UK, which took action to
get this changed by being the only nation to vote negatively to the DIS
8348 becoming an IS. It is now necessary that the UK be supported at
the meeting of TC97/SC6 in Ottawa taking place at this time, or run the
risk of being overruled by ISO and the DIS 8348 being ratified without
the changes. The nations at the Ad Hoc TSGCEE SG9 meeting agreed to the
necessity of Security and Priority parameters being signalled values,
and also agreed to take this position back to their national standards
bodies to urge support for the UK at the ISO meeting. The results of
the ISO meeting will be known in due course, and it is hoped that the
contents of DIS 8348 will be revised in accordance with military
requirements.

   In close association with this is the necessity of obtaining CCITT
recognition of these extensions, and especially the use of facility
codes. The military do not require that CCITT provide the enhanced
services but that CCITT should recognise the new facilities and carry
them transparently from DTE to DTE. This may give rise to a new standard being defined jointly by ISO and CCITT in which the DTE to DTE
transparent facility codes are listed and controlled to allow PTT networks to police their use, and also to prevent overlapping and inter-
fering usage by end-systems.

6. SUMMARY

This paper has highlighted the need to define complete suites of
protocols for military communications systems. It has shown that X.25
is an important constituent of such protocol sets in various contexts.
As such, it is necessary to understand the evolution of X.25 and the
role it is intended to fulfil. Thus the differences between the 1980
and 1984 versions of the protocol have been described. The possibility
of interoperation between the two versions has also been explored.

   X.25 is not a protocol in isolation, and the paper describes some
related standards and recommendations that are of interest to the military. This has led on to a discussion of possible extensions to X.25 to

allow it to satisfy the military requirement. The main extensions
support the signalling of Security and Priority information both to the
network and across the network to the remote DTE. It is believed that
multi-homing and mobile hosts will be adequately supported by X.25,
together with the recommendations of X.32. The areas of multi-addressing and low grade virtual circuits are subjects that require further
study, both at the requirements level and subsequent to this in terms
of mechanisms to support them.

A test case for NATO's policy of influencing the development of
civilian standards has been described. It is hoped that the results of
NATO's action in this area will soon be known and will be favourable to
the military need.

7. REFERENCES

/1/ Development of Common Interface Standards, TSGCEE SG9, AC/302
(SG/9) D/18, 22nd Feb 1983.

/2/ Approach to ISO (Supported by specialist UK Paper on Data
Distribution Study), TSGCEE SG9, AC/302 (SG/9), D/19,
17 Feb 1983.

/3/ CCITT Recommendation X.25, Interface between data terminal
equipment (DTE) and data circuit terminating equipment (DCE)
for terminals operating in the packet-mode and connected to
public data networks by dedicated circuit. 1980 and 1984.

/4/ ISO DIS 8208, Data Communication - X.25 packet level protocol
for data terminal equipment.

/5/ ISO DIS 8348, Information processing systems - Data communications - Network Service Definition.

/6/ CCITT Recommendations X.32, Interface between data terminal
equipment (DTE) and data circuit terminating equipment (DCE)
for terminals operating in the packet-mode and accessing a
packet switched public data network through a public switched
telephone network or a circuit switched public data network.

/7/ CCITT Recommendation X.75, Terminal and transit call control
procedures and data transfer system on international circuits
between packet switched data networks.

/8/ CCITT recommendation X.2, International user services and
facilities in public data networks.

U.S. MILITARY REQUIREMENTS FOR TRANSPORT
PROTOCOL OPERATING IN AN NATO ENVIRONMENT

John Heafner
Chief, Systems and Network
Architecture Division
National Bureau of Standards
Gaithersburg
Maryland 20899
U.S.A.

Lieutenant Commander Edward Brady
U.S. Defense Communications Agency
U.S.A.

ABSTRACT

We describe U.S. military needs for transport protocol operating in
NATO computer networks. Transport protocol requirements are delineated
with respect to interoperability, performance, reliabiliy, functionality, and availability. We conclude that the ISO class 4 transport,
suitably extended, satisfies these requirements. Survivability and
security aspects of transport are not addressed.

1. ANTICIPATED OPERATING ENVIRONMENTS

The NATO use of computer networks and their attendant protocols can be
examined from the standpoints of normal and emergency use. The most
significant properties of the protocols are likely to differ depending
upon conditions of use. Under normal use the most prominent characteristics of interest are interoperability and cost/performance: that is,
it is desirable to be able to communicate between any two end systems
in a concatenated network in an economical manner. Emergency situations
demand reliability and survivability: that is, it is necessary to provide the robustness to communicate between end systems in a concatenated network in the presence of temporary error conditions and permanent outages of intermediate systems. Thus, different levels of service are acceptable for normal and emergency data transfers, and to
attain these service levels different features of the protocols reach
prominence.
    We examine the transport protocol in terms of its anticipated use
in NATO network architectures and topologies. We reason that one must
select a transport protocol design that accomodates the general case

49

R. W. G. Herbers (ed), The Upper Layers of Open Systems Interconnection, 49–58.

taking into account interoperability, performance, reliability, functionality, and availability.[+] We find that one need not forego efficiency to achieve the necessary levels of interoperability, reliability
and other attributes.

2. INTEROPERABILITY, PERFORMANCE, AND RELIABILITY

2.1. WHY MANY CLASSES EXIST

Why do we have a choice? Five classes of transport have been defined
internatonally /1/. Indeed, it is misleading to label them classes. In
practice they are five different protocols. The dozen or so protocol
mechanisms are either present or absent or differ algorithmetically
with each class. They do not interoperate. They do not provide the same
economics, nor the same levels of reliability. They resulted from the
consensus process aimed at satisfying the perceived needs of diverse
communities of interest. Our feeling is that this is a perfectly
acceptable result of the international negotiation process to arrive at
protocol specifications. Protocol implementations, on the other hand,
are more directly related to the marketplace -- we would not expect
widespread commercial offerings of all five classes.

2.2. WHAT ABOUT CONFORMANCE

The ISO and CCITT are issuing all five classes of transport. The U.S.
National Bureau of Standards (NBS) plans to issue classes 4 and 2. All
three bodies promulgate different conformance clauses. We believe that
conformance statements are policy-motivated and bear little relationship to the practical considerations of operating computer networks.
Our opinion is that the other, more realistic, considerations will take
precedence over conformance statements in product offerings. That is,
it will be important to implement a given class correctly and efficiently for an application, but whether or not it carries conformance
approval is not nearly as meaningful as that it functionally satisfies
the user's requirements.

In selecting a transport class we are concerned with interoperability, performance, and reliability. Let us study these attributes
individually and then as a whole.

[+] Survivability is more closely related to network topology, security,
and internetworking routing than to transport protocol design, and thus
is not considered in this paper.

2.3. INTEROPERABILITY

In the absence of the need to satisfy other constraints, this one is easy. To chieve complete interoperability, each end system must run the same class of transport. This is a given. There is no other way within OSI. Any class will do as long as each end system supports that class. Observe that this does not preclude the implementation and use of multiple classes with the concomitant ability to negotiate classes at connection establishment. There simply must be one class in common among all end systems.

2.4. PERFORMANCE

Performance is related to cost. There are two aspects: the cost of acquisition/maintenance to which we return later, and the cost of achieving certain qualities of service such as throughput and delay. For efficiency, you want the simplist class state machine possible: ideally, class 0. Depending upon tariffing, multiplexing over a network connection can save on costs, so class 2 is a possibility in the appropriate environment. There are other considerations for cost effectiveness as well. Studies show /2/ that to maintain maximum throughput, satellite nodes need at least an 18 bit sequence space. This is satisfied by class 4 with the larger sequence space and window size. Hence, class selection based upon efficiency of operation depends upon rate structure and· the technology employed.

2.5. RELIABILITY

Achieving reliability depends upon the environment in which you are operating. If the subnetwork is totally reliable then, as with interoperability, any class suffices. If, however, the subnetwork is not totally reliable then only class 4 can ensure reliability.[+] If you are operating in either an unreliable subnetwork, a local area network cluster, or a general internetwork environment, then only the robustness of class 4 guarantees reliability.

[+] Class 3 was designed to operate in a relatively error-free setting consisting of a reliable, virtual circuit, single subnetwork. Some of the reliability mechanisms, such as recovery from reset, disconnect, and reject, have been added. These appendages were an afterthought rather than being designed into the protocol. As exception conditions, these resynchronization procedures require separate processing for each kind of error. As a result, the state machine description of class 3 is more complicated than that of class 4. Class 3 should not be a serious consideration from the standpoint of reliability or any other criterion.

Class 4 is the only class that provides the mechanisms for detection and correction of damaged, duplicated, and lost data, and recovery from network-signalled errors. Hence, choosing a transport class in view of reliability depends upon the reliability offered by the network environment and the reliability needed by the user. If there is no difference between the two, then class 0, 1 or 2 can be used. If there is a difference, then class 4 is indicated. More specifically, classes (and 2 may be used with a network providing an acceptable residual error rate and an acceptable rate of signalled errors. Classes 1 and 3 may be used where there are acceptable residual error rates but an unacceptable number of signalled errors, since these classes adjust for signalled error conditions. Class 4, on the other hand, is used where the user otherwise experiences an unacceptable residual error rate on the network.

2.6. SATISFYING MULTIPLE CRITERIA

These criteria, taken singly, do not seem to offer much of a problem. Satisfying interoperability and reliability together requires class 4 because there are faulty subnetworks and there are concatenated subnetworks. Then what can be said about performance? On the single LAN or single PDN running class 4 with the nonuse of checksumming negotiated at connection establishment, we get essentially the same efficiency as with class 2. Memory is relatively inexpensive, so the difference in code space and state table space between class 2 and class 4 should not concern us. So, it is difficult to construct an argument based upon efficiency for the use of class 2 when interoperability/reliability must be foregone as a consequence of gaining theoretically perhaps one or two percent in processing time.

2.7. PROTOCOL CLASS REQUIREMENT

The use of class 4 is necessary, since it is the only class satisfying U.S. requirements for interoperability, performance, and reliability, concurrently. This is based upon the assumption that internetwork communications will be the norm rather than the exception. Internetworking presupposes the use of a general purpose internetwork protocol (IP) operating over local and wide area (both public and private) subnetworks. (Presently, ISO has defined but one IP/3/) Therefore, class 4 transport assumes a minimum of services from concatenated subnetworks, viz., the ability to send data, the ability to receive data, and the bounding of the maximum lifetime of data in concatenated subnetworks. Consequently, class 4 transport contains the necessary error detection and correction mechanisms, as an integral part of its design, to compensate for varying levels of subnetwork service integrity, in order to provide reliable end-to-end data transfer. These mechanisms detect and correct for misorder, loss, duplication, damage, and provide recovery from network-signalled errors as well. Since these mechanisms are fundamental properties of class 4 transport they have been designed to induce relatively low overhead with minimal processing needed.

3. COMMERCIAL VS MILITARY REQUIREMENTS

In most instances and for the bulk of data transferred, military acti-
\ ities are not dissimilar from those of commercial organizations.
Routine transfers in a benign environment are suitable for many unclassified electronic mail, personnel, payroll and logistics purposes. One
\ ight conclude that services provided by commercial providers are
sufficient for military needs. A reliable subnetwork based upon CCITT
Recommendation X.25 may suffice for commercial use and even for military use for unclassified peace-time communications.

We submit that such commercial service is not adequate for many
critical military requirements. Commercial requirements may be thought
of as a subset of military requirements where the military needs additional features to deal with circumstandes not expected by the normal
user. (A subsequent section of this paper discusses the United States
Department of Defense experience in developing protocols suited for
high-stress military applications.)

NATO also recognizes that operations in the environment expected
by its forces are not always the same as for commercial users. Accor-
dingly, Working Group 1 of TSGCEE Sub-Group 9 is working to identify
unique NATO requirements and relate them to the ISO OSI concept. Thus
f ar eight such requirements have been proposed. They are:

    Multi-homed and mobile host systems
    Multi-end point connections
    Internetworking
    Network/system management functions
    Security
    Robustness and quality of service
    Precedence and preemption
    Real-time and tactical communications

These are similar to requirements defined in the United States
DoD. Although the scope of this paper does not allow detailed evaluation of each of these requirements, a brief look at a few issues is
pertinent.

In considering Mobile Host Systems one may picture, for example, a
command post which must relocate quickly but then remain stationary for
some time, or one may consider a host which is in continous motion
(e.g., a ship). The common requirement in these instances is to provide
for connection through various points in a network or catenet. The role
of the transport protocol should be to manage a connection which may be
briefly interrupted while still insuring integrity of vital data. Class
4 of the ISO transport protocol provides basic features on which to
define a solution to this problem.

Internetworking calls for utilization of different types of networks such as local area networks, packet radio networks, demand access
satellite networks, message switched networks, and public data networks. Fortunately, recent work in ISO has yielded an internetwork
protocol to help achieve this goal. it is exactly this need which led

to the concept of a reliable end-to-end protocol such as Transport
Class 4. It is essential in inter-netting for the host to provide the
reliability desired without depending upon the subnetwork.

Solidity and Quality of Service are important transport issues.
Quality of Service is established during the opening of a transport
connection. This idea of solidity leads to problems such as operating
over damaged subnetworks (rerouting), jamming, and reliable data
transmission. It is clear that a robust transport protocol is fundamental to solving these problems. First, one might set aside the worst
case of operation over an inherently unreliable subnetwork and instead
think of service provided by a "reliable" network such as one based
upon X.25. Does the concatenation of virtual circuits give end-to-end
integrity of data? No, although the X.25 protocol does have some end-
to-end features, it is not a reliable end-to-end protocol. Data is
vulnerable to damage at the termination of each hop and further the
user may not be willing to accept the residual error rate which is
allowed by the carrier`s X.25 implementation. The level of residual
errors is especially important in military communications where absolutely reliable transmission of critical messages is required.

We have not addressed the issue of Security because this paper is
unclassified. We do, however, recommend that all security requirements
be studied carefully to determine which may be satisfied by transport
layer mechanisms.

4. FUNCTIONALITY

4.1. ISO PROTOCOL MECHANISMS

Class 4 provides many features and services not offered by the lower
classes. This is evident from studying Table 6 of reference /1/. In
particular, mechanisms not supported by any of the other classes include: the use of multiple network connections per transport connection, inactivity control procedures to cope with unsignalled termination of a network connection, retransmission after a specified time
if protocol data units are not positively acknowledged, and resequenc-
ing of protocol data units. The features and services of class 4 are
required by the U.S. military.

4.2. EXTENDED PROTOCOL MECHANISMS

The ISO class 4 transport must be improved in two respects. Firstly,
mandatory provision of the (ISO optional) 31 bit sequence space and 16
bit window size are required, if use of satellites is required. It has
been shown that the ISO mandatory 7 bit sequence space and 4 bit window
size are inadequate for reasonable throughput, given inherent satellite
technology delays. The ISO optional 31/16 sequence space/window size
does fulfill satellite requirements. Use of local area networks gives
rise to a second need for the larger sequence space. In LAN and LAN
clusters computation time, not bandwidth, is at a premium. The use of

the larger sequence space obviates the need for modulo arithmetic and
hence reduces computation time in LAN nodes.

A second mechanism of transport that is required for U.S. military
purposes is the graceful close mechanism defined in the NBS class 4
specification. This function provides for transport connection termination without loss of data in either direction. This function is not
offered by the ISO class 4 transport, although it is provided in the
ISO session protocol. The ISO specification for class 4 reserves the
protocol data unit code used by NBS for this function so as to avoid
any future interoperability problems with implementations according to
the NBS specification.

5. FORM OF PROTOCOL SPECIFICATION

It is universally accepted that prose descriptions of protocols are
ambiguous and incomplete. The consequence of this fact, borne out in
practice many times, is that different implementations of the same
prose specification fail to interoperate. This is because many of the
design details are ambiguously stated and thus remain as arbitrary
implementation choices.

Thus, it is required that the definitive document of the NATO
transport protocol be expressed in formal description technique notation.

Specifically recommended is ESTELLE /5/ which has recently been
used to prepare the specification for ISO classes 0-4 as well as for
other ISO protocols. Many person-years of supporting software exists in
the public domain that accept the machine-readable version of the specification and provide such assistance as path analysis to determine
the syntactic correctness of the specification, automatic reference
code generation, and automatic test sequence generation that can be
applied to test correctness of an implementation.

6. EXPERIENCE WITH A ROBUST TRANSPORT PROTOCOL

The U.S. Department of Defense has used its DoD Standard Transmission
Control Protocool (TCP /6/) for over 10 years with scores of other
organizations in the U.S. and Europe. This protocol has evolved through
operational use by modifications to solve operational problems of the
nature of the performance, reliablility, and functionality previously
discussed. It is the functional equivalent of the ISO class 4 transport
using the larger sequence space and window size, and extended with the
graceful close function. This experience therefore instills a very high
degree of confidence in the use of class 4 for NATO computer networking. More about our experiences follows.

Fundamental to the development of US Department of Defense computer communications networks has been the concept of internetting; that
is, the concatenation of various diverse subnetworks which might be
available to achieve both economy of resources and redundancy. Since
the early days of basic research by the Defense Advanced Research

Project Agency (DARPA) this notion of a concatenated network, or catenet, operating environment has survived the test of time through many
refinements and has led to the operation of a large and effective
system today.

One problem with concatenating several subnetworks to create a
communications path is that, in general, the worst features of each
network can be expected to influence the character of the total path.
For example, a satellite link will be contribute long delays. A packet
radio network will introduce RF propagation noise and possible path
interruption. A datagram network may lose or misorder packets or may
even accomplish subnetwork flow control by discarding packets. Concatenated, these subnetworks would result in a lossy path with long delays
and the likelihood of missing and misordered packets.

It was recognized that an end-to-end protocol must be used at the
transport layer if the user is to be assured of receiving all data with
an acceptable level of reliability. The TCP is such a robust protocol
for end-to-end reliability. It was designed to operate above any type
or quality of network while assuring the user of reliable data transfer.

In the ARPANET a connectionless or datagram service was chosen and
to provide service over the catenet an internet protocol (IP) was designed. The ARPANET segments messages into packets for transmission
across Internetwork Message Processors (IMPs) and then reorders and
reassembles them at the destination IMP. Inter-IMP acknowledgements are
used as the packet moves through the network. Also, a Ready For Next
Message (RFNM) is sent from the destination IMP to the source IMP. the
RFNM provides an acknowledgment of message delivery.

One may argue that with network service providing packet assembly
and IMP-IMP acknowledgment it would not be necessary to provide such a
robust transport protocol. However, DoD experience has borne out the
intuitive notion that a true reliable end-to-end protocol is needed
when operating over a catenet with potentially unreliable elements. In
fulfilling military requirements this is especially true. After all,
military networks may be stressed by natural disasters, high traffic
loads, or even damage from war or sabotage. The military comminicator
who relies upon dependable network links in a benign environment may be
trying to reconstitute his resources using a variety of surviving network elements with different levels of reliability. Certainly, when
integrating tactical assets into the catenet the military planner can
expect connections to be made via battlefield and fleet digital radio
links (TADILs) and other switched and dedicated (point-to-point) radio
and land line resources.

The TCP was developed with this in mind.

The TCP employs a three-way handshake to open a reliable connection which avoids even the problem of delayed control synchronization
packets during the opening of the connection. Data integrity is assured
by the use of an end-to-end checksum. The TCP is persistent in insuring
proper delivery of correct data in the proper order. In the event of a
network disconnect recovery is possible, and by providing end-to-end
flow control the host's resources can be protected without depending
upon network flow control. By specifying a sufficiently large window

size the TCP allows operation over paths with long delays (e.g., satellites) without the risk of duplicate packets.

At the end of a connection, a graceful close feature insures that no data is lost in transit. Graceful close during connection termination does not abruptly terminate the connection. Rather, the initiator of the request stops sending data but continues to receive and the connection remains open until all data is accounted for.

In operation TCP has proved to be very successful. There have been instances of subnetwork software bugs being revealed because of the thoroughness of the TCP operating above the subnetwork. Since the host-IMP connections are formed below TCP they cannot introduce undetected errors or failures in the end-to-end TCP-TCP path. In actual operation, TCP has recovered from IMP failures and other subnetwork problems and has operated as designed. An option in TCP allows the user to command a connection to remain open without time-out. Thus, a connection can be reestablished after rerouting or repair of a subnetwork. The TCP connections have been maintained open over the catenet with reliable data transfer not just for seconds or minutes but for many hours or even days. In short, DoD's research and operational experience with TCP has convinced network planners of the need for end-to-end reliability at the transport layer. In the context of ISO transport protocol classes, only class 4 approximates these features designed to insure reliability.

7. AVAILABILITY OF IMPLEMENTATIONS

The NBS organizes workshops for implementors of OSI protocols. The purpose of these workshops is to bring together future users and potential providers of OSI protocols so that they may study the standards specifications and agree upon implementation details. Thirteen computer manufacturers and semiconductor manufacturers from the U.S. and Europe demonstrated their implementations of transport class 4 at the National Computer Conference in July, 1984. Some of these companies offered the transport class 4 implementation as a product at that time. Subsequently, we have brought the implementation decisions in line with the complete ISO class 4 as revised in Copenhagen in June, 1984. Other events are planned for 1985 to show the complete and revised standard implemenation. Companies participating in the workshops now number over 50 and include carrier organizations.

A result of these activities is the widespread implementation of the ISO class 4 transport. Chip sets are already commercially available for a price considerably less than one would reasonably expect to pay for the software development of any other transport class. Chip sets, of course, offer operational economies as well.

8. CONCLUSIONS

In its participation in NATO computer networking, the U.S. military is
concerned with interoperability, cost performance, reliability, protocol internal mechanisms, service features, the rigor of the specification, and readily available implementations by many vendors. Class 4
appears to be the only viable choice. Therefore, we recommend the
following. Class 4 should be mandatory, with the extension described.
Any other classes should be permitted to operate but none of them
should be required.

9. REFERENCES

/1/ Information Processing Systems - Open Systems Interconnection
    Transport Protocol Specification, ISO/TC97/SC6 N 3240,
    DIS 8073 Revised.

/2/ The Effects of Satellite Technology on the ISO Model of Open
    Systems Interconnection, Report No. ICST/HLNP-81-18, NBS

                              and

    The Impact of Satellite Transmission on High Level Computer
    Network Protocols, ICST/HLNP-81-17, NBS.

/3/ Information Processing Systems -- Data Communications --
    Protocol for Providing the Connectionless-Mode Network
    Service, DIS 8473, International Organization for Standardi
    zation, Geneva, Switzerland, 1984

/4/ Study for the Interconnection of Open Systems Structuration of
    the "Approach to ISO" Document, Working Document, NATO, TSGCEE
    Subgroup 9, Working Group 1, 14 November 1983.

/5/ A Formal Description Technique Based on an Extended State
    Transition Model, October 1984.

/6/ Transmission Control Protocol, Mil.-Std.-M1778,
    August 12, 1983.

Portable ISONET

Michael AGNEW
LDR SYSTEMS Ltd
Balmoral House
Ash Vale, Aldershot
Hants GU12 5BB
United Kingdom

ABSTRACT

This paper describes the experience gained during the development of
the networking product, ISONET. A first implementation, in Spring 1983,
relied very heaviliy on the host micro-computer s operating system. In
order that the product could be further developed to run on a variety
of computers, it was made portable. The ISONET product and aspects of
its design and implementation are described.

1. INTRODUCTION

There is a widespread user requirement for products to support distributed processing and computerised general office functions. Any product
in order that it can fulfil this requirement needs to satisfy two criteria: it must have a long-term future and it must be available on a
wide range of computer types.
        The ISONET product satisfies both these critera. Firstly, it is
based on the Open Systems Interconnection (OSI) protocols which are
internationally agreed protocols. Secondly, it has been designed to be
portable enabling it to be implemented rapidly on a wide variety of
computers.

2. THE PRODUCT

ISONET is a networking product based on the OSI standards. It is implemented as a layered product in software, with each layer supporting
recommendations from internationally accepted bodies such as ISO,
CCITT, IEEE and ECMA. Only the lower five layers of the OSI Model are
currently implemented.
        At the lowest layer, the Physical layer, ISONET supports a variety
of transmission media from Ethernet to the services provided by the
PTTs. The interfaces to these media are defined by the IEEE and CCITT

R. W. G. Herbers (ed), The Upper Layers of Open Systems Interconnection, 59–66.

in the IEEE Standard 802.3 CSMA/CD Access Method and the CCITT Recommendations V.24 and X.21/bis. IEEE 802.3 enables computers to link
together over the Ethernet Local Area Network (LAN). Of the CCITT
recommendations, the former enables computers to connect locally with
one another or via telephone links and modems; the latter enalbes
computers to access public or private data networks.

At the next level, the Data Link layer, ISONET supports two common
link protocols: LLC and HDLC LAPB. The fist, LLC, is defined in the
IEEE Standard 802.2 Logical Link Control and is used in conjunction
with LANS. Both LLC-1 and LLC-2 are supported. The second, HDLC LAPB,
is defined by both CCITT and ISO and is used with point to point networks and private and public data networks.

Layers 1 and 2 within ISONET are not always separated from one
another. There are, now available, micro-chips which support functions
of both these layers. Generally, these chips or chip-sets provide most
of the functions up to the middle of the Data Link layer, i.e. framing,
CRC checking, collision detection and some retransmission due to error
detection. Standards, too, cross layer boundaries: the IEEE recommendation 802.3 is not wholly contained within the Physical layer since it
also defines Medium Access Control a component of the Data Link layer.
The Network layer in ISONET is divided into two sub-layers: an Upper-
network layer and a Sub-network layer. The highest of these the Upper-
network layer uses X.25 (1980) Network Convergence Protocol. The Subnetwork layer supports access to data networks using the CCITT Recommendation X.25.

At the next level, the Transport layer in ISONET implements the
error detection and recovery class (Class 4) of the ISO Transport specifications DIS 8072 and DIS 8073. Only the connection oriented protocol is supported. The use of Class 4 over a reliable Network service is
an interim choice; Class 3 will be substituted in due course.

The highest level in ISONET is currently the Session layer. This
layer is an implementation of the ECMA-75 Session Protocol Standard-
Subset A. ISONET presents a procedural interface to the top of this
layer called the Session Interface.

The choice of protocols at all the Layers has been greatly influenced by the UK Department of Trade and Industry's "Intercept
Strategy". These are recommendations which are designed to allow the
development of products for Open Systgems Interconnection.

The ISONET product includes two end-user facilities which utilise
the Session Interface: a File Transfer Facility and a Remote Printer
Facility. The former comprises a pair of programs: a File Transfer
Utility (FTU) and a File Transfer Server (FTS). FTU and FTS enable
users to share a common printer for print spooling purposes.

ISONET currently operates under the operating system CP/M-86,
CCP/M-86, MS-DOS, CTOS and VMS. Support for Unix is underway.

3. THE DESIGN AND IMPLEMENTATION

The design and implementation of ISONET has followed three major development phases from an early operating system dependent release to the
current portable version.

The first release in Spring 1983 known as ISONET-SE, was developed
for a specific environment: an Ethernet-like local area network of
microcomputers running the MP/M-86 operating system. A number of factors and considerations influenced the design of this initial release:

- data should not be copied unless absolutely necessary;

- the number of tasks should be kept to a minimum in order that
  context switching is not a great overhead;

- a layer of the OSI model can be modelled very closely by a
  task running under an operating system;

- communications software requires timer facilities and rapid
  responses especially at the lower layers;

- the implementation environment is purely local, therefore,
  running Transport Class 4 over a connectionless Link service
  is sufficient as detailed in ECMA TR/14.

These factors and considerations led to the design depicted in
Figure 1. ISONET-SE comprises the Session, Transport and Link layers;
the Network layer is implemented as a null layer. Each layer is implemented as a single task running under MP/M-86 (the null Network layer
is merged into the Transport layer for efficiency reasons). Additionally, a Timer Task is provided to generate timeouts for the Transport
Task. All software in ISONET-SE is written in MS-PASCAL; special extensions provided by the compiler are fairly extensively used.

The tasks in ISONET-SE are in priority order: the highest priority
task is the Link Task, the lowest is the Session task. The structure of
each task is very similar: each has its own input queue from which it
reads event messages for subsequent processing. Requests to lower
layers cause an event message to be placed on the lower layer task
queue. Likewise, an indication for a higher layer causes an event
message to be placed on the higher layer task queue.

User programs link together with the Session Interface to have
access to procedures to enable inter-process and inter-node communication. These procedures generally queue event messages on the Session
Task input queue or read their own input queues (there are two queues
per session, one for normal flow and one for expedited flow).

Data is passed between the tasks in ISONET buffers which belong to
a shared memory pool. Data copying is prevented through a system of
appending headers to the front of the buffers when they are passed
downwards and similarly stripping headers off when they are passed up-
wards.

ISONET
INITIAL SOFTWARE STRUCTURE

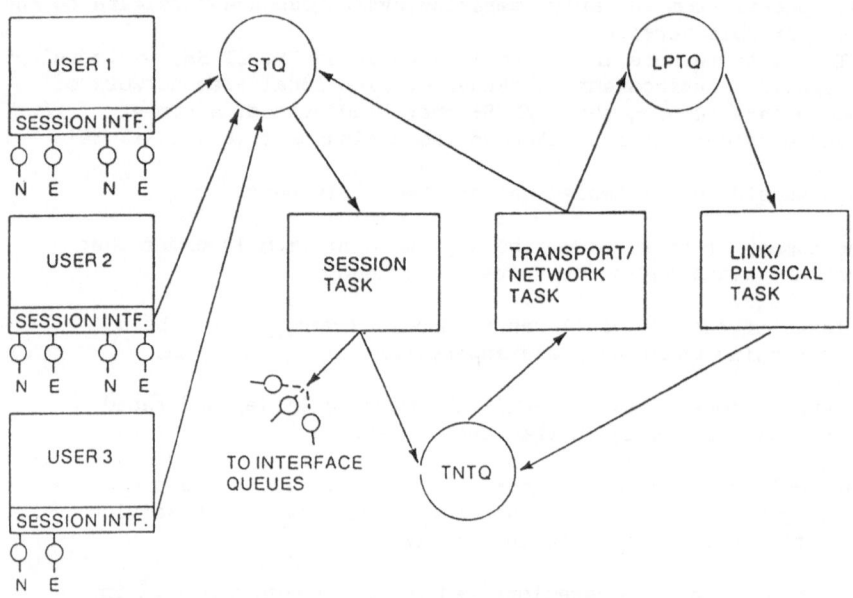

Figure 1 The ISONET-SE Software Structure

ISONET-SE has one major drawback, a result of its very specific implementation: it cannot readily be moved to different environments. It was
for this reason that work began on two parallel ISONET developments
sharing the same portable design: ISONET-SA and ISONET-SXE. ISONET-SA
is functionally similar to ISONET-SE; ISONET-SXE incorporates extra
functions primarily Network layer and LLC-2 software. (Since both developments share the same design, the term ISONET is used whenever it is
not necessary to distinguish between the two developments.)

A number of design and implementation decisions were taken to
achieve true portability. These decisions were based on the premise
that operating system dependency and non-standard programming languages
are the greatest barriers to portability.

The first decision taken was to standardise on PASCAL as the programming language and constrain its use very closely to the ISO-PASCAL
definition. This was based on the knowledge that most computers support
compilers for the PASCAL language and that most of these are supersets
of the ISO definition.

A second decision taken was to have a centralised place for the
development and management of ISONET. This was chosen to be the in-
house VAX minicomputer in preference to a cheaper microcomputer due to
its more extensive programmer development aids and peripheral support.
An example of this is the macroprocessor which is used very extensively
in ISONET to overcome the difference between PASCAL compilers. Current-

ly all source files are maintained in ISO-PASCAL and MS-PASCAL with macro-definitions differentiating between the two. ISONET, therefore, exists in a single master form from which specific implementations are produced.

The major decision taken was to incorporate an executive into ISONET to remove the operating system dependency existing in ISONET-SE. Whilst portability was the main factor in this decision, it was felt that this would lead to a number of improvements. Firstly, efficiency of execution due to the reduction in context switching and secondly, a reduction in total memory occupancy due to the smaller number of tasks. The ISONET executive provides the following functions:

- a priority driven scheduler mechanism;

- queue management routines;

- buffer management routines;

- timer management routines;

- interprocess communications support routines.

The scheduler runs an ISONET "task" when it becomes the highest priority "task" containing a message in its input queue. A "task" runs to completion, that is, it reads its input queue, processes the message and exits before another "task" can be scheduled.

Queues are the means by which ISONET tasks communicate with one another. The Queue Management routines supported by the executive are detailed below:

- MAKEQ   to create an ISONET queue;

- OPENQ   to open an ISONET queue;

- ENQUEUE   to place a message on an ISONET queue;

- DEQUEUE   to read a message from an ISONET queue;

- DELETEQ   to delete an ISONET queue.

Buffers are used within ISONET to contain protocol data units. Pointers to the buffers are passed between the layers to prevent data from being unnecessarily copied. Three routines are provided by the executive:

- ALLOCNORBUFF to allocate a normal data buffer;

- ALLOCEXPBUFF to allocata a small data buffer;

- RELBUFF   to release a buffer of any type.

The Timer Management routines are used by ISONET layers requiring time-out facilities. Two routines are supported:

- SETTIMER   to set up a timer;

- CANCELTIMER   to cancel a timer.

On expiry of a timer, a message is placed on the appropriate task's input queue.

The Inter-process Communication support routines (IIPC) provide the communication between an ISONET interface, linked in with a user program to the ISONET process. The routines are split into three groups as follows:-

- **User Process Procedures** - these procedures are called by a User Interface to pass events between the User process and the ISONET process. In this group the send procedures are synchronous, that is, they do not return until the receipt of the event is confirmed by the ISONET PROCESS.

- **ISONET Process Procedures** - these procedures are called by an ISONET interface to pass events from the ISONET process to a User process. These procedures operate asynchronously, that is, procedures passing events return immediately without awaiting confirmation. However, the ISONET process must not attempt to access any data passed to an IIPC procedure after that prodedure returns.

- **Environment Dependent Procedures** - these procedures provide the actual communications between a user process and the ISONET process. These procedures are called only by other procedures of IIPC.

Figure 2 shows the relationship between the various IIPC procedures and the User and ISONET processes and their interfaces.

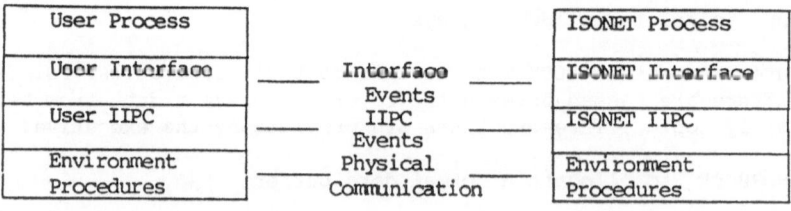

Figure 2 IIPC Usage

The ISONET executive is implemented almost exclusively in Pascal relying on the Pascal run-time library for heap management. The chief exception is the Timer Management routines which are written in Assembler
for some operating system environments.

To conclude, ISONET software has available to it all the executive
functions it requires. Porting from one environment to another is made
more easily since only the internal executive software needs modification.

As a final aid to portability, a common device driver interface
was defined in order that link layer tasks would not require to be
changed whenever a new communications device was to be supported.

ISONET
SOFTWARE STRUCTURE

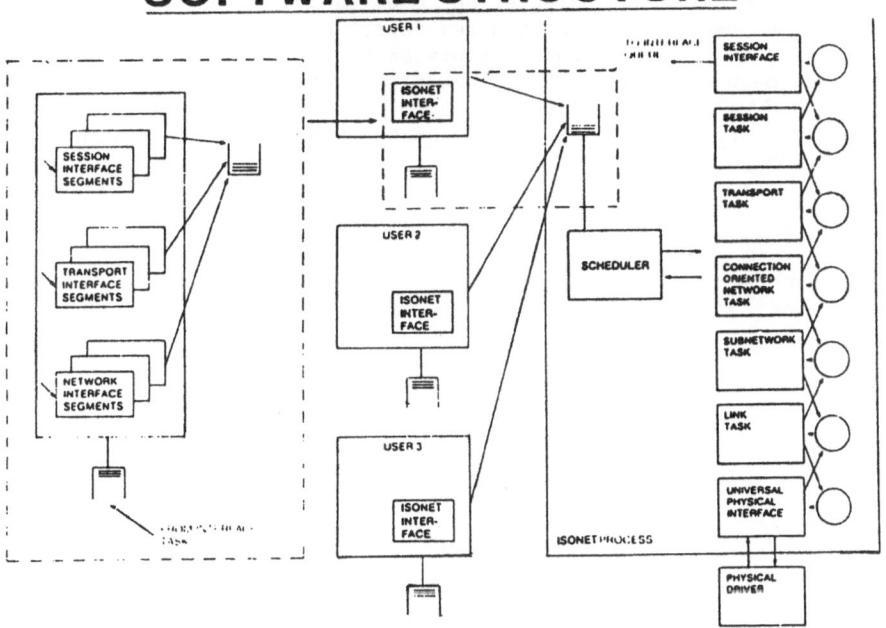

Figure 3 The ISONET-SXE Software Structure.

The ISONET-SE concept of one task per layer has been continued in this current ISONET phase. The exception to this is the Network layer of ISONET-SXE where two tasks have been implemented: an Upper-network Task handling routing and relaying and a Sub-network Task handling access to X.25 sub-networks. Figure 3 illustrates the design of ISONET. There is not Timer Task since all timer facilities hve been incorporated into the ISONET executive.

The priority order effective in ISONET-SE is maintained. The use of queues to pass between layers is also similar to ISONET-SE.

The management of data buffers is under the control of the ISONET executive. Again, the copying of data is kept to a minimum.

4. CONCLUSION

The migration to a portable ISONET has already proven to be a success. The essential goal, portability, has been achieved since the time taken to transfer to a different computer has been reduced to an acceptable level: in some cases as little as a few days, in most others less than three months. Additionally other advantages have arisen. Software testing time has been reduced since all but final system testing can take place on the development computer prior to porting. Also, the software maintenance effort has been minimised due to ISONET being held in a master version form.

Session 2

Distributed Databases

Session Chairman: Steven Oxman

DISTRIBUTED DATABASES, INTEROPERABILITY AND ACE ACCIS

Steven W. Oxman *
SHAPE Technical Centre
PO Box 174
NL-2101 CD The Hague
The Netherlands

The Allied Command Europe Automated Command and Control Information System (ACE ACCIS) will be one of NATO's foremost challenges in the interoperability of geographically distributed databases. The distribution of these ACE ACCIS databases extends through the entire European continent and beyond.

ACE ACCIS is the name of a system program that has as one of its goals the interoperability of in-place automated command and control information systems within ACE and future ACE ACCIS computer systems. Although many of the in-place computer systems are identical, many are different. With the present host nation structure and International Competitive Bid (ICB) procedures, it is expected that future computer systems that make up ACE ACCIS will be of different manufacture. This means that the geographically dispersed database of the ACE ACCIS will be supported on heterogeneous hardware that will employ heterogeneous operating systems and data management software. This heterogeneous environment adds complexity to a system design that has interoperability as one of its goals.

Another goal of ACE ACCIS is to maximize the use of common software. Towards this goal, a goal of the Data Management Subsystem Architecture Design work was to provide a homogeneous set of interfaces to the Information Exchange (IE), Man-Machine Interface (MMI), and Application Support (AS) subsystems of ACE ACCIS. This would prevent these subsystems from having to develop multiple interfaces with the Data Management Subsystem, depending on what the local computer systems provide in the way of data management services. The fifth subsystem that completes the ACE ACCIS framework is System Control (SC). The DM interface to SC is necessarily heterogeneous since we will utilize the vendor SC and DM packages. However, this is not a problem to ACE since the SC-DM interface will also be supplied by the commercial vendors.

----

* Author is now with: OXKO Corporation
                          PO Box 6674
                          Annapolis, MD 21401
                          U.S.A.

R. W. G. Herbers (ed), The Upper Layers of Open Systems Interconnection, 69–85.
© 1987 by D. Reidel Publishing Company.

To address our ACE ACCIS Data Management work, I would like to start by
presenting ACE ACCIS and Data Management Reference Models.

The Reference Model for ACE ACCIS presents the system as having
five subsystems: DM, MMI, IE, AS and SC. Each ACE ACCIS node incorporates these subsystems. System elements external to an ACE ACCIS node
communicate via the Information Exchange subsystem. Likewise, intranode
communications between subsystems utilize IE. All data is managed by
DM. All user interfaces are through MMI. AS provides application support software. SC provides the operating system software.

Now, concentrating on the Data Management Subsystem, we can provide a Subsystem Reference Model. The DM Subsystem Reference Model incorporates three layers, The Base Layer, the Translation Layer, and the
Information Layer.

The Base Layer includes commercial, off-the-shelf data management
products. It is strongly recommended that as a minimum, the following
software packages are utilized:

> Data Base Management System (DBMS)
> Data Dictionary (DD)
> Procedural Language Interface
> Report Generator

It is further recommended that a distributed DBMS support module be
utilized when commercially available in the future and that the following also be considered:

> On-Line Query Facility
> Application Generator
> Screen Generator

The system data is managed by the DBMS and the SC interface is at this
level in the model.

The Translation Layer provides a data conduit and a services
conduit between the first and third layers. Data reformatting and service commands translating activities will occur in this layer. These
data reformatting and command translation activities will provide the
interface between the Base Layer's formats and command and those of the
ACE standard data services provided by the third layer, the Information
Layer.

The Information Layer is to provide an ACE ACCIS standard set of
interfaces for AS, IE, and MMI. This layer will utilize the International Standards Organization (ISO) Relational Data Language (RDL).
This RDL is in the SQL form and is used extensively in the industry
today.

The ACE ACCIS Data Management Subsystem Reference Model provides
an architecture that should work in the ACE ACCIS environment and yet
meet the goals of interoperability and maximum reuse of software
throughout the system. This architecture also maximizes the use of
commercial, off-the-shelf software which should lower the technical
development risks and costs.

The ability to interoperate should be only part of the goal of an interoperability goal. To interoperate efficiently should also be considered. System performance is important to users. Although as yet untested, we have a data definition scheme that we believe will improve performance. This scheme is a data definition scheme that would be used by the system designer. It does not require explicit software support and it does not impact the manner in which the data can be used. We call this scheme Data Fragmentation. When first defining data, a data designer first identifies data elements. A data element is an elementary form of data; it is a single piece of information. An example is a security classification code. By itself, a data element seldom provides useful information to a user. Data elements are usually aggregated into data records. These data records are usually designed by computer system oriented data designer personnel. These data records are usually designed with only efficiency in mind. These data records are then aggregated into data files and data-bases. Oure data fragmentation scheme takes the user's view into more active consideration. After identifying the data elements and prior to aggregating them into data records, we suggest aggregating the data elements by groups that make operational sense to the user. This smallest grouping of data that makes operational sense is called a Data Fragment. An example of a Data Fragment (that includes the security classification code data element) is a message header. We postulate that by aggregating data by data fragments will not only assist users in understanding what is available in the systems, but will also assist in providing the most compact, self-sufficient data packages to the Information Exchange subsystem. We further postulate that this scheme will thereby improve system interoperability performance by placing the minimum amount of data on the communications lines that will get the requisite information to where it is needed.

The definition of databases in the individual ACE ACCIS computer systems should utilize this data fragment scheme. The definition of a single database should take into account the big picture of the ACE ACCIS data (top-down, Total organizational view) and should take into account the specific, and sometimes unique, view of the specific user group it is supporting (bottom-up view). The path towards defining a local database should begin by utilizing, to the greatest extent possible, the ACE standard database structure. At least two benefits are gained by following this recommendation. First, development costs in the area of data design will be less. This ACE standard database structure need only be defined once and then can be used by other groups in ACE without duplication of costs. As an example, the ACE Reporting System (ACEREPS) has a data design and definition requirement. The ACEREPS data design should be standard ACE wide. The second benefit supports interoperability. With all ACE ACCIS computers having this standard structure, all ACE users can rely on all systems having this much in common. This therefore defines the minimum, albeit not insignificant, amount of information that can be passed between any two ACE ACCIS computer systems and therefore ACE user groups.

Appended onto the NATO standard database structure would be the user group unique data structures. The standard database structure populated with all of the user group occurrences of data plus the populated user groups unique structures together make up the ACE global database. Taking the specific user group data plus scratchpad data sets for temporary computations and work plus data from other user groups for the purpose fo reference or back up, one would then define the database of that specific user group. This method provides a unified path to go from the ACE standard database structure through the ACE global database definition to the user group database definition. This method should save ACE labor time and support the interoperability goal.

A natural question to ask is how does the ACE ACCIS DMS Reference Model fit into the ISO Open Systems Interconnection (OSI) model. The OSI model is a communications model. The DMS would interface with the OSI application layer, number 7 of the IE. Also, it is presumed that DM will provide AS and MMI data services at this layer. It is not envisioned that DM will interface with layers one through six.

The Data Management Subsystem will provide the following operational functionality in all ACE ACCIS computer systems:

> Support Data Definition
> Perform Data Manipulation
> Support Data Security
> Perform Data Monitoring
> Maintain Data Integrity
> Manage Data Distribution
> Support Data Recovery
> Perform Data System Monitoring

All users can assume these functions to be operational in all ACE ACCIS computer systems. For additional information on these functions, I refer you to STC Technical Memorandum (TM) number 776.

In order to assume interoperability of heterogeneous computer system data management services, certain standards need to be developed and utilized. The DMS Reference Model, the use of SQL at Layer 3 of the DMS model, the ACE standard database structure and with it, its attendant standard data element naming conventions and data fragment scheme are examples of these standards. Beyond the standards, concepts need to be employed in order to view intersystem conformance to the defined interoperability standards. In order to provide interoperability between present and future systems, it is felt that the conformance concepts need to evolve. The most basic concept should insure interoperability of the systems in so far as the movement and use of data is concerned.

This first level of conformance can be defined as the ability to transfer data via ACE ACCIS IE communications means in the format as defined in a virtual (not necessarily explicitly coded) database definition. As a recommendation, the initial virtual database definition should be an ACEREPS schema. The cooperating computer systems would consider each other in an open system architecture view, not caring what is the internal architecture of each other, just black boxes that in some way produce and accept data in the ACEREPS format. In reality, the systems could accomplish this by either explicitly coding the virtual database definition within their DBMS or by having an application software module that formats outgoing data into ACEREPS format and accepts incoming ACEREPS data and formats it into the local database definition. This step brings forth interoperability to a limited degree and decreases the amount of data analysis and design work within ACE. However, back up facilities and common software usage are not supported.

The second level of conformance should extend the ACE virtual database definition to include data that is needed for database back up and recovery operations. This back up data would now reside at a back up computer where it is supported via automated updates. This back up data can not be altered by the back up computer system, but it could reference this data if need be.

The third and final conformance level would introduce a distributed ACE global database with distributed data control. At this point, an ACE standard distributed DBMS module should be utilized. The homogeneous data management services should then be available. This intersystem conformance approach should assist in moving ACE command and control information systems towards the interoperability goal and, at the same time, permit ACE to evolve its systems as the technology and industry allows.

I have presented a reference model for the ACE ACCIS DMS, a data aggregation scheme, a database definition methodology, a view towards connecting the DBMS with the ISO OSI based IE subsystem, the ACE ACCIS DMS functions, and concepts to view intersystem conformance by. These concepts should prove useful in obtaining the interoperability of geographically dispersed, heterogeneously configured computer systems from the standpoint of data management.

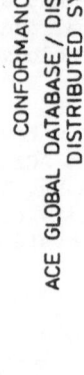

CONFORMANCE LEVEL 3 :
ACE GLOBAL DATABASE / DISTRIBUTED DATA MANAGEMENT
DISTRIBUTED SYSTEM SUPPORT

DATA

SYSTEM B

DISTRIBUTED ACE GLOBAL DATA
AND DISTRIBUTED DATA CONTROL
DDBMS COMPONENT

SYSTEM A

DATA

ASSUMPTIONS:

1. ALL ACE SITES WILL USE AN ACE STANDARD
   DDBMS COMPONENT

2. THE ACE STANDARD DDBMS COMPONENT WILL BE
   ACE DEVELOPED OR ACE WILL HAVE TO WAIT
   UNTIL (APPROXIMATILY) 1995 FOR A COMMERCIAL
   PACKAGE THAT WILL SUPPORT HETEROGENEOUS
   COMPUTER SYSTEMS

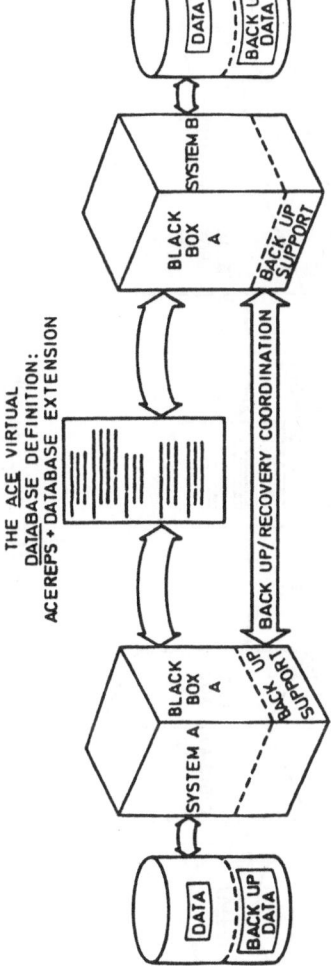

CONFORMANCE LEVEL 2:

VIRTUAL GLOBAL DATABASE / BACK UP + RECOVERY
EXTENDED INTER-SYSTEM COOPERATION

THE ACE VIRTUAL
DATABASE DEFINITION:
ACEREPS + DATABASE EXTENSION

ASSUMPTIONS:

1. THE ACE VIRTUAL DATABASE DEFINITION WILL EVOLVE
   FROM AN ACEREPS DEFINITION TO ACEREPS PLUS
   BACK UP/RECOVERY DATA DEFINITION TO FINALLY
   A COMPLETE ACE GLOBAL DATABASE DEFINITION

2. THE BACK UP/RECOVERY PAIRINGS WILL BE STATIC;
   THE BACK UP/RECOVERY ACTIONS WILL BE SUPPORTED
   BY SPECIFICALLY-WRITTEN SUPPORT SOFTWARE

CONFORMANCE (TO ACE ACCIS DM STANDARDS) LEVEL 1:
OPEN SYSTEM ARCHITECTURE / VIRTUAL DATABASE
INTER-SYSTEM EXCHANGE

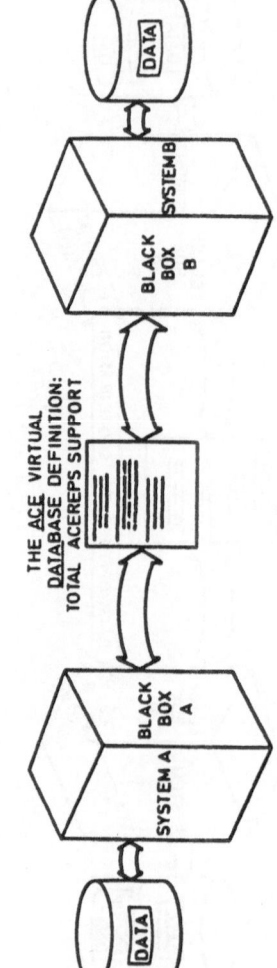

THE ACE VIRTUAL
DATABASE DEFINITION:
TOTAL ACEREPS SUPPORT

ASSUMPTIONS:

1. SYSTEMS A & B ARE INFORMATION SYSTEMS THAT
   ARE CAPABLE OF DEFINING SETS OF DATA AND
   CAN TRANSFER THE DATA EXTERNALLY

2. THERE EXISTS SOME ACE COMMUNICATION SYSTEM
   THAT CAN CONNECT THESE SYSTEMS' EXTERNAL
   DATA TRANSFER CAPABILITIES TOGETHER

 **DATA MANAGEMENT OPERATIONAL FUNCTIONS**

SUPPORT DATA DEFINITION

PERFORM DATA MANIPULATION

SUPPORT DATA SECURITY

PERFORM DATA MONITORING

MAINTAIN DATA INTEGRITY

MANAGE DATA DISTRIBUTION

SUPPORT DATA RECOVERY

PERFORM DATA SYSTEM MONITORING

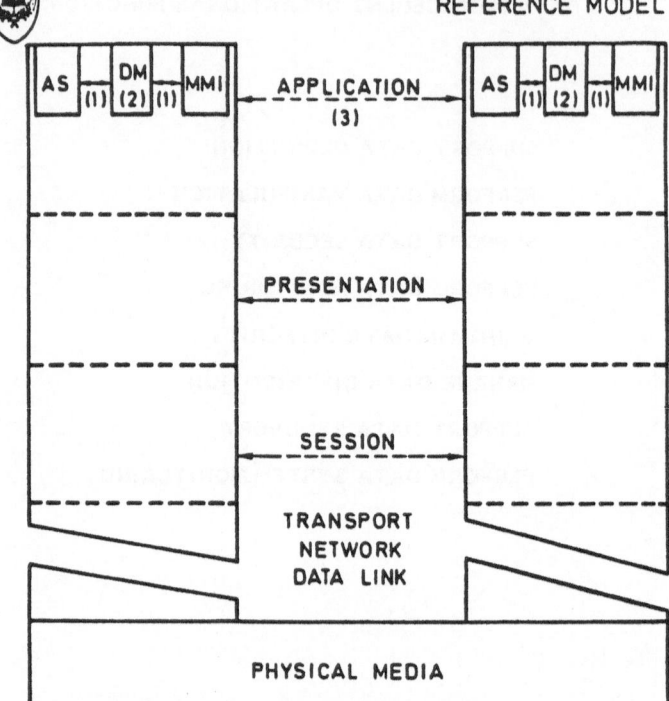

DM FUNCTION WITHIN THE ISO OSI REFERENCE MODEL

NOTES:

(1) AS AND MMI USE DM SERVICES FOR DATA ACCESS

(2) THESE BOXES DO NOT REPRESENT ALL DM FUNCTIONS BUT ONLY THE ASPECTS RELATED TO SYSTEMS INTER-CONNECTION (THE SAME APPLIES TO AS AND MMI)

(3) DM FUNCTIONS DIALOGUE WITH EACH OTHER BY USING PROTOCOLS ASSOCIATED TO THE APPLICATION LAYER

PATH TO THE DEFINITION OF A LOCAL DATABASE

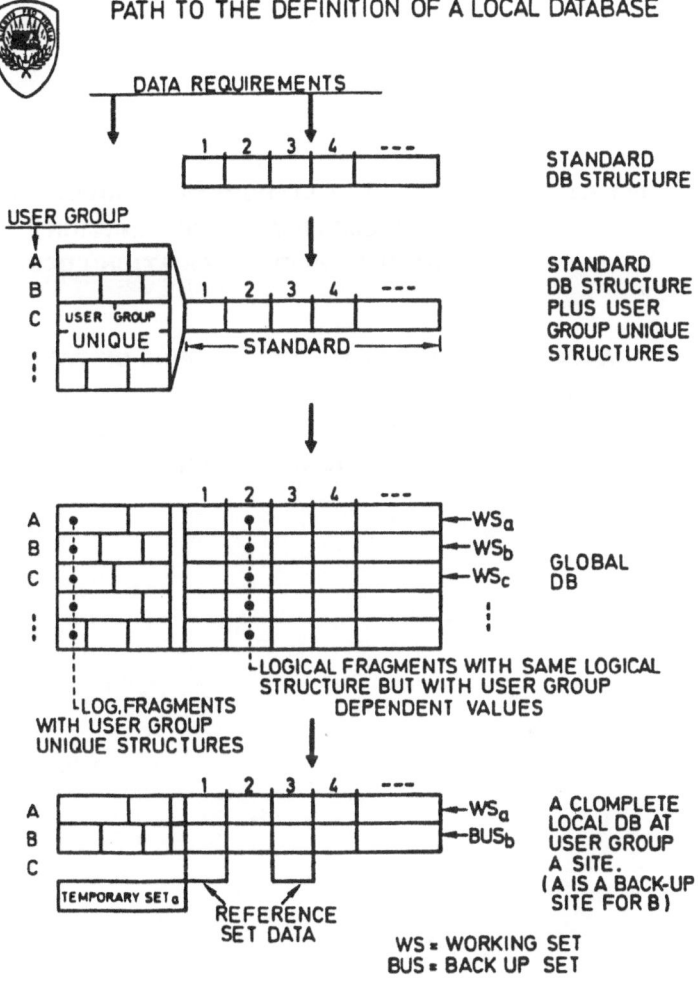

DATA REQUIREMENTS

STANDARD
DB STRUCTURE

USER GROUP

STANDARD
DB STRUCTURE
PLUS USER
GROUP UNIQUE
STRUCTURES

GLOBAL
DB

LOGICAL FRAGMENTS WITH SAME LOGICAL
STRUCTURE BUT WITH USER GROUP
DEPENDENT VALUES

LOG. FRAGMENTS
WITH USER GROUP
UNIQUE STRUCTURES

A CLOMPLETE
LOCAL DB AT
USER GROUP
A SITE.
(A IS A BACK-UP
SITE FOR B)

TEMPORARY SET a

REFERENCE
SET DATA

WS = WORKING SET
BUS = BACK UP SET

DATA FRAGMENT

DATA ELEMENT   –   THE MOST ELEMENTARY FORM OF DATA;
                       A SINGLE PIECE OF INFORMATION;
                       EXAMPLE IS CLASSIFICATION CODE.

DATA FRAGMENT   –   THE SMALLEST GROUPING OF DATA THAT
                       MAKES OPERATIONAL SENSE; EXAMPLE IS
                       MESSAGE HEADER (WHICH INCLUDES THE
                       CLASSIFICATION CODE).

A REFERENCE MODEL FOR THE TRANSLATION LAYER

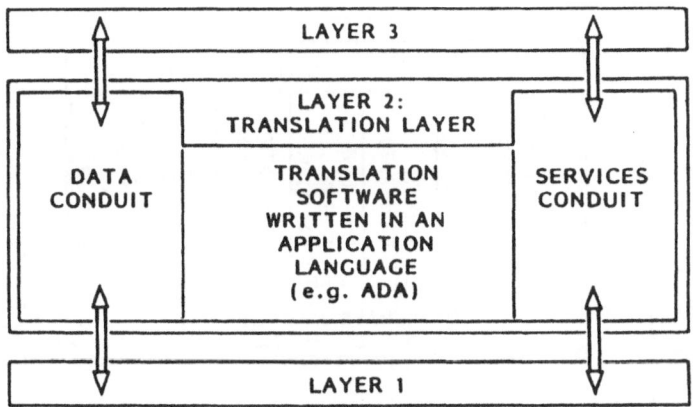

NOTE: LAYER 2 INTERFACES ONLY WITH
LAYER 1 AND LAYER 3; LAYER 2
HAS NO INTERFACES EXTERNAL TO
THE DATA MANAGEMENT SUBSYSTEM.

A REFERENCE MODEL FOR THE INFORMATION LAYER

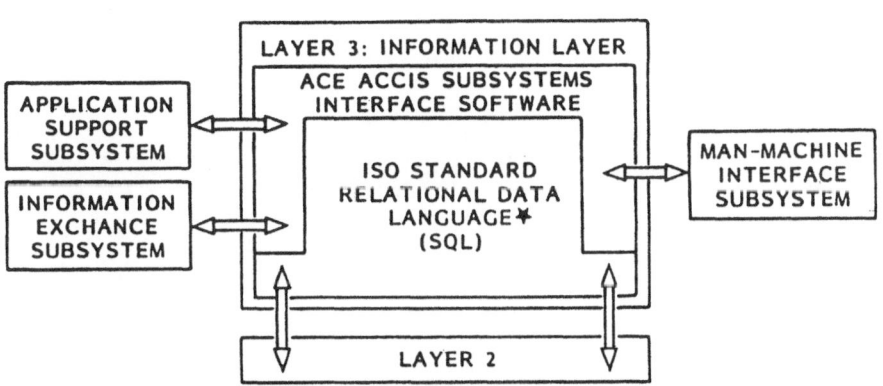

NOTE: ✶ IS PRESENTLY IN DRAFT FORM,
EXPECT STANDARD STATUS IN
1985 OR 1986

A REFERENCE MODEL FOR THE DBMS AND RELATED COMPONENTS

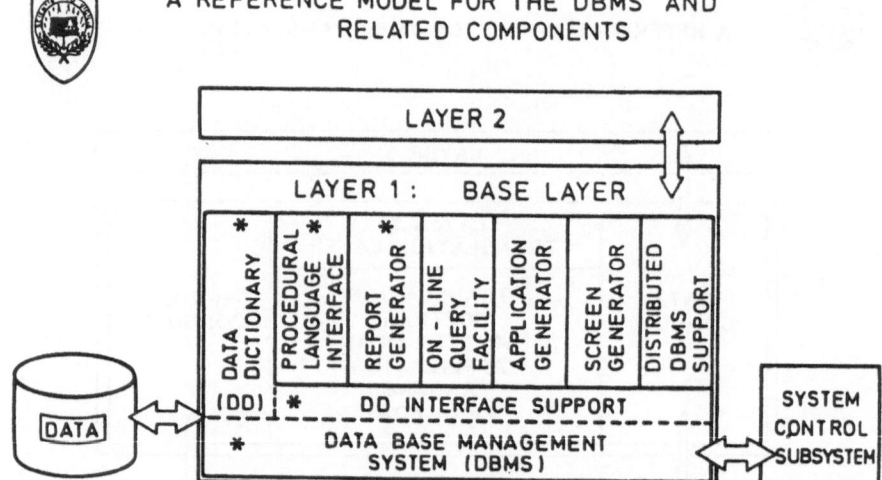

NOTES:
1. ONLY INTERFACES WITH THE DATA MANAGEMENT BASE LAYER ARE INCLUDED IN THIS DIAGRAM
2. * = MINIMUM BASE LAYER
3. THE DISTRIBUTED DBMS SUPPORT WILL LINK HETEROGENEOUS SYSTEMS; NOT YET COMMERCIALLY AVAILABLE

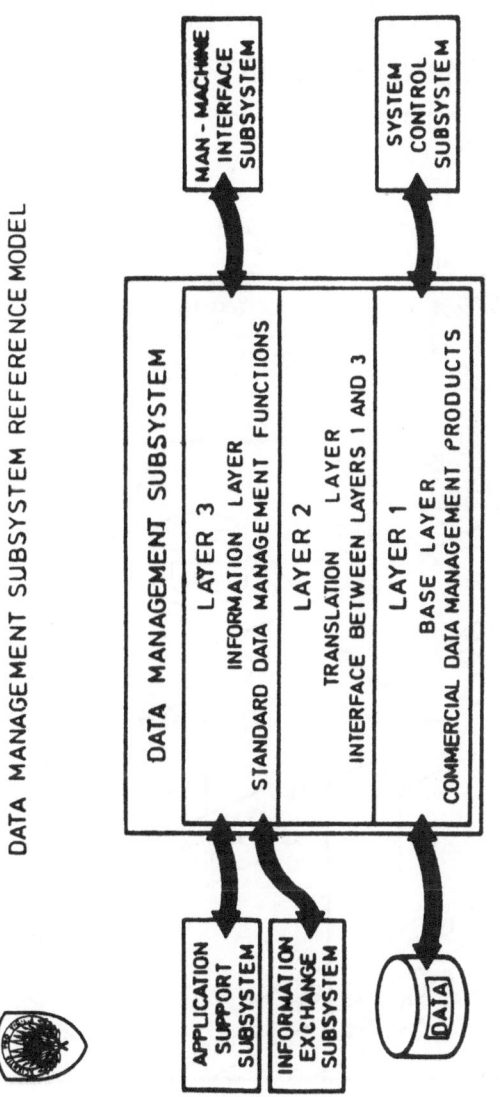

DATA MANAGEMENT SUBSYSTEM REFERENCE MODEL

ACE ACCIS ARCHITECTURE
COMMAND SUPPORT CONCEPT

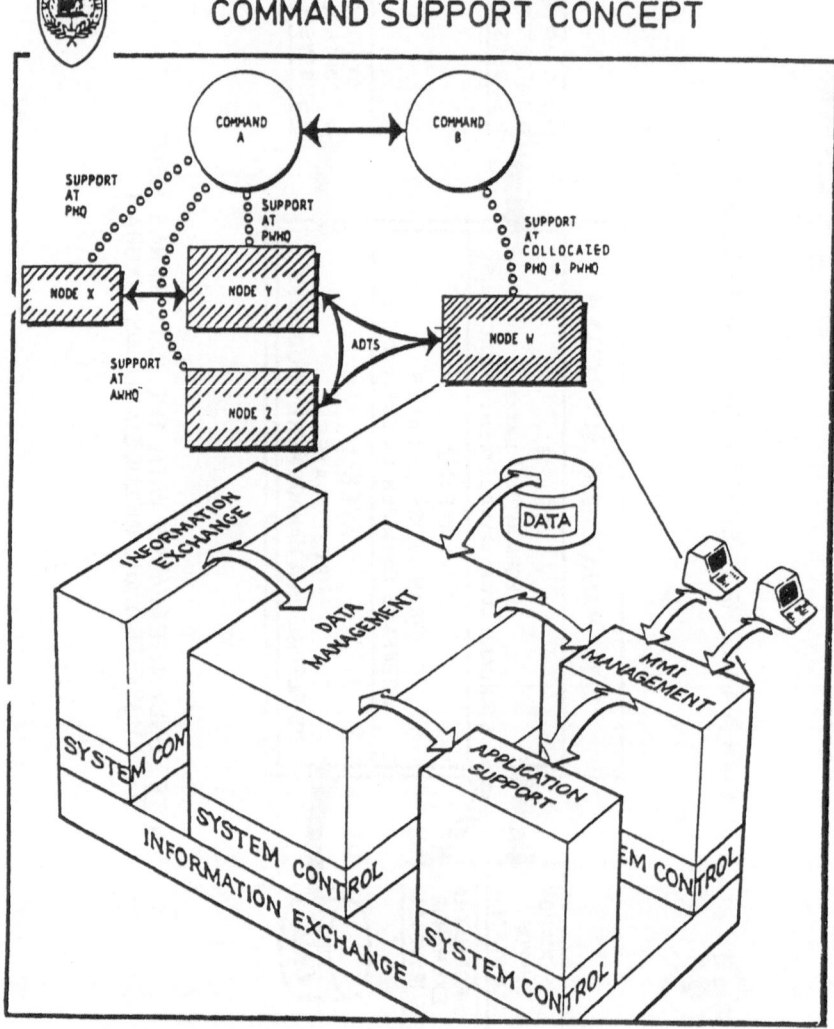

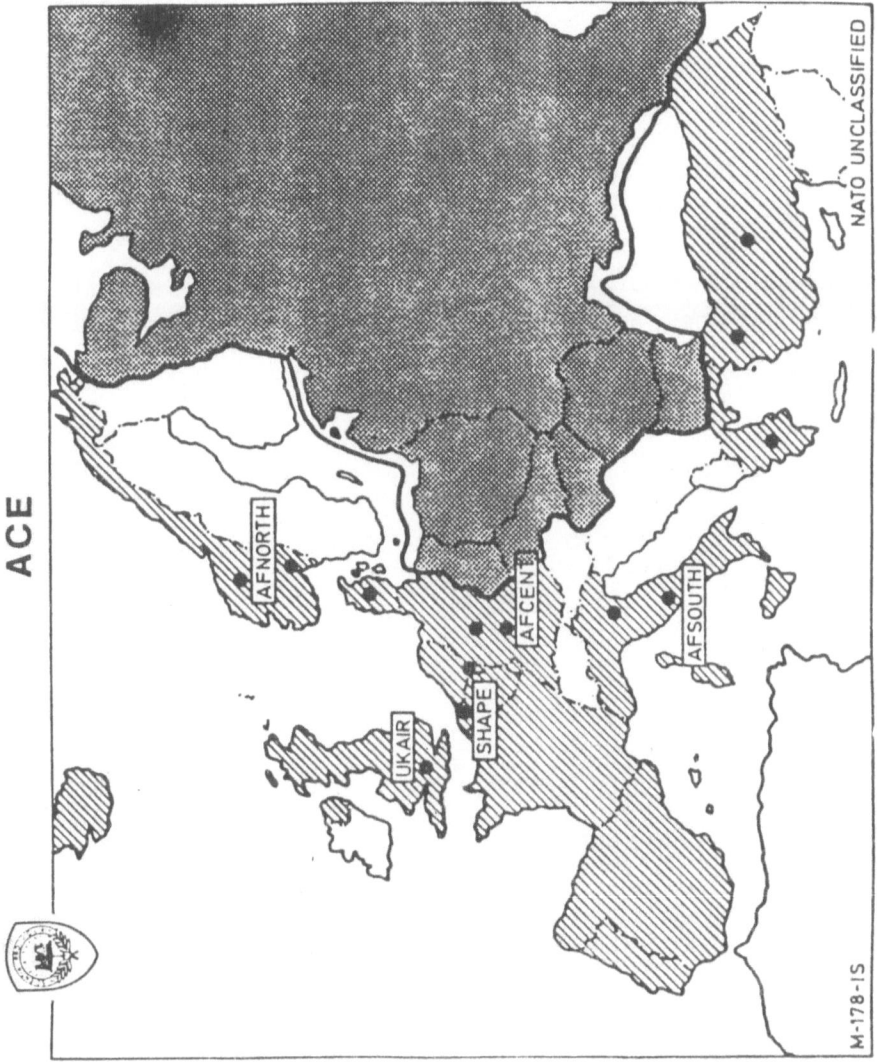

Session 3

Packet Radio

Session Chairman: Jon F. Wilkes

NOTE: No papers released for publication

Session 4

Graphics in the Presentation Layer

Session Chairman: Andrew J. Hill

STANDARDS UPDATE
WHAT HAPPENS NEXT?

C. D. Osland
Head of Computer Graphics Section
and
Prof F. R. A. Hopgood
Head of Informatics Division
Rutherford Appleton Laboratory
Atlas Centre, Childon
Oxfordshire OX11 0QX
United Kingdom

1. INTRODUCTION

From an enthusiastic start in 1974, work on standards for computer
graphics has developed into a growth industry in its own right.
Throughout the world, groups have been meeting to discuss and agree on
the specification of standards. More than 200 people are currently
involved. The standards cover several areas:

o programming interfaces;
o metafiles;
o device-level interfaces;
o both 2D and 3D.

This paper looks at these activities and traces the development of the
various standards from the past, through the present and into the
future.

Like any activity that involves communication between people, a
few terms are used so regularly that they become an extension to the
vocabulary - a jargon. While it is an attractive idea to avoid using
such terms, the various stages that a document goes through within ISO
(the international standards organization) before becoming an international standard recur so often that some definitions will make the
article clearer.

Workitem
An official project with agreed scope and goals. Workitem start
with one or more base documents which are reworked into a single
document until they are submitted for voting as a

R. W. G. Herbers (ed), The Upper Layers of Open Systems Interconnection, 91–99.

Draft Proposal (DP)

The first official stage towards becoming a standard. All ISO member nations concerned with the project comment and vote on the DP until is overwhelmingly agreed that no further technical changes are required, when it is submitted as a

Draft International Standard (DIS)

The DIS is then edited and amended until it is acceptably in ISO format and all known ambiguities in the document have been resolved, at which stage it can be voted as an

International Standard (IS)

At this stage, the document is published by ISO and it is generally left unaltered for about five years, at which time a review process may decide to endorse, revise or abandon it.

Within the national standards bodies, such as the American body ANSI, a similar process takes place, although the names of the stages are different.

2. PROGRAMMING INTERFACES (2D)

There are two ways in which users have tackled the problem of transporting programs that referenced graphics systems or devices. The first was to make one package emulate another. The second was to allow a programm to produce a file of graphics orders and to interpret them with a separate program. The first approach leads to the idea of a standard programming interface /1/ and is dealt with in this section and the next; the second is the starting point for a standard metafile and is dealt with later.

Both of the original developments for a graphics standard aimed at a programming interface. One was from ACM/SIGGRAPH - the GSPC "Core" system /2/ - and the other from DIN (the German standards body) - GKS /3/. There were technical differences between these documents, but under the ISO umbrella there evolved a version of GKS that covered much of the same area as Core, with the exception of 3D. ISO has been processing GKS for what may seem to an outsider as a long time. By October 1981, a document called GKS 6.8, which became GKS 7.0 after substantial editorial work, was submitted as a Draft Proposal.

This document was widely circulated. A number of substantial objections concerning omissions were raised. The next ISO meeting (June 1982) resolved these by including facilities for text alignment, for STROKE input and for "individual" as well as "bundled" attributes. The document that incorporated these - GKS 7.2 - was completed by the end of 1982 and circulated for voting as a Draft International Standard /4/. The result was general acceptance; two nations voted against the acceptance as a DIS unless some aspects of the document were clarified. These comments have been delt with. Other points had been noted as a result of the widespread availability of the GKS 7.2 document and the

ISO working group has been noting these and improving the document to
resolve all known ambiguities and errors.

The final document - tentatively called GKS 7.4 - is in the final
stages of preparation and will be forwarded to ISO for acceptance as an
International Standard during November this year.

3. PROGRAMMING INTERFACES (3D)

One obvious difference between GSPC Core and GKS in 1979 was that Core
allowed coordinate parameters to be specified in either 2D or 3D,
whereas GKS only provided for 2D. For Core, a 2D coordinate could be
regarded as a shorthand for a 3D coordinate where the Z component was
that of Core's Current Position.

Work has continued on the specification of graphics systems that
provide 3D coordinates to the user of the system. ISO is currently
reviewing two proposals which are seen as complementary rather than
competing: GKS-3D and PHIGS.

3.1. GKS-3D

This seeks to extend GKS to 3D by adding various capabilities,
as can be seen from the scope given in the latest working document:

a.   the definition and the display of 3D graphical primitives;

b.   mechanisms to control viewing transformations and associa-
     ted parameters;

c.   mechanisms to control the appearance of primitives inclu-
     ding light source, shading and shadow computation;

d.   mechanisms to obtain 3D input.

The aim is to specify the system in such a way that existing (2D) GKS
programs would run without any modifications and that the general style
of capabilities provided would match those included ·in GKS 7.4.

GKS-3D is an accepted workitem within ISO and the review process
to develop it is in hand. It is anticipated that a new document, incorporating all changes agreed at the last (June 1984) ISO meeting will be
prepared by September 1984 and will be forwarded to ISO for registration and then voting as a Draft Proposal.

3.2. PHIGS

The goals that have determined the development of PHIGS are very
differnt:

a.   definition, display and modification of either 2D or 3D
     graphical data;

b.   definition, display and manipulation of geometrically re-
      lated objects;

c.   rapid dynamic articulation of graphical entities.

It can be seen that in key areas PHIGS seeks to go far beyond the
scope of GKS or GKS-3D. Nevertheless, the main functionality of PHIGS
employs the same terminology and form as is used in GKS. The main
difference lies with PHIGS having a multi-level, hierarchical data
structure which can be modified. Because there is a need for an object
to be displayed more than once with different attributes in effect,
PHIGS allows the values of attributes to be inherited from the object's
context. This contrasts with GKS where the binding of primitives and
attributes is much more permanent.

ANSI have produced many revisions of the PHIGS document, responding to comments. ISO has asked ANSI to submit the latest document
as the basis for a workitem; this is likely to happen later this year.

4. LANGUAGE BINDINGS

In the early days of ISO work on graphics standards, it was realized
that the different languages from which people used graphics made it
necessary to define the programming interfaces in a way that was independent of any one language. For this reason, the GKS document does not
specify the interface from Fortran, Pascal or any other language. Instead, one subgroup deals with all language bindings for GKS.

Only some of the common languages are covered by standards:
Fortran 77, Pascal, COBOL, PL/I and BASIC have ISO or ANSI standards;
ISO work on ADA has just started. There is an intention to standardize
C, but this has not progressed far at present.

4.1. Language Bindings for GKS

The current status of the projects producing GKS bindings for these
languages is as follows.

Fortran 77   An agreed binding has been evolved and all changes to
               accomodate GKS 7.4 were agreed at the June '84
               meeting. The revised document is about to be forwarded
               to ISO for registration as a Draft Proposal.

Pascal   A binding has been evolved and changes are being made
               to accomodate GKS 7.4. The latest version of the docu-
               ment is about to be forwarded to ISO for registration
               as a Draft Proposal.

COBOL   A binding has been proposed within the USA but there
               is currently no ISO document.

PL/I   A binding has been proposed within the USA but there
is currently no ISO document.

BASIC   A self-consistent part of GKS level 0b has been added
to the latest BASIC document that is being circulated
for comment and vote within ANSI. The remainder of
level 0b is available by means of the routine facility that is also added in the latest document: this is
described in an appendix of the document.

ADA   A binding has been evolved and changes are being made
to accomodate GKS 7.4. The latest version of the document is about to be forwarded to ISO for registration
as a Draft Proposal. This work is likely to be held up
until ADA itself becomes an ISO Draft Proposal.

A language binding for C is being discussed within ANSI, but cannot be
processed by ISO until some indication of the way in which C itself
will be standardized emerges from ISO. The situation is not the same as
with ADA because of the existence of the official ADA specification
document.

4.2. Language Bindings for systems other than GKS

The language bindings subgroup has, to date, been mostly concerned with
language bindings for GKS. However, as other functional specifications
emerge (such as GKS-3D, PHIGS and CGI (see below), the subgroup will
also be involved in the development of language bindings for these
standards.

5. COMPUTER GRAPHICS METAFILE (CGM)

An alternative way of dealing with the transport of programs that use
graphics is to use a metafile. This is a file of more or less "device-
independent" graphics orders. A number of formats have been employed in
the past but no standards existed for the storage of graphical information.
     From the earliest days of efforts towards graphics standards,
there were people working to define a "metafile" standard. The GKS
document has, since October 1981, relegated the definition of a metafile format to a part of the document which is not formally a part of
the standard. It provides an example of a format suitable for the GKS
metafile interface. This was done to allow the correct relationship
between the GKS standard and a future metafile standard.
     Technically ISO started a workitem on a metafile standard in May
1983, although a great deal of work had already been done by then. The
base document had been produced by ANSI. Originally ANSI had worked on
the "Virtual Device Interface" and "Virtual Device Metafile" simul-

taneously: following their January 1982 meeting a self-contained
metafile proposal was produced.

The metafile document now consists of four parts. The first contains the functional specification of any conforming metafile. The
other three parts contain specifications of three methods of encoding,
each with its own particular goal.

Character Encoding

This is intended for use where it is important to minimize
the size of the metafile; where necessary, this is regarded as more important than processing speed. The encoding
conforms to the rules of ISO 646 and ISO 2022, making it
suitable for transmission through "ASCII" networks.

Binary Encoding

This encoding aims to minimize the processor effort required
to generate and/or interpret the metafile. It is therefore
highly suitable for storage and retrieval of graphical data
within a computer system.

Clear Text Encoding

This encoding is aimed at the requirement of having a metafile that can be read and edited by people. It is also very
safe to transport, even between systems with different native
character sets.

In addition, the document allows private encodings as long as they conform to the Functional Description and general rules of conformance in
Part 1. An example of this would be a binary encoding using word
lengths or representations other than those specified in Part 3.

The scope of the metafile standard is not only intended to deal
with program transportability: it also aims to provide a standard for:

o a data interface for graphics packages;

o a picture transfer mechanism between different devices,
   installations and systems;

o a means of retaining and transporting graphical data.

Within ISO, the metafile document /5/ is in the process of being voted
as a Draft Proposal; this vote finishes at the beginning of October
this year. There will be a major review of all comments concerning the
metafile at the next ANSI meeting (also October), the aim being to
produce a document that is mutually acceptable to ANSI and ISO. As long
as this proves possible, the document will be forwarded to ISO for
processing as a Draft International Standard in January or February
1985.

6. COMPUTER GRAPHICS INTERFACE (CGI)

It will be obvious to all users and package implementors that there is no particular standard for the interface between a graphics package and a device. Each manufacturer has felt free to define the interface for their own convenience. However, it will be obvious to the same people that, in a large number of cases, the functions provided by different devices are broadly similar.

In an effort to reduce the work required by package implementors - and as a way of encouraging standards for device manufacturers - there has been work in progress to define a standard interface for graphical devices. As was noted in the section above on metafiles, ANSI amalgamated their work on metafiles and interfaces while it was still convenient to do so. DIN have also been active in the development of CGI standards.

ISO has therefore asked ANSI and DIN to investigate the possibility of sponsoring a workitem for a computer graphics interface that addresses the following needs, amongst others:

o   a standard for implementors of graphics packages and device handlers;

o   a standard for transfer of graphical information between computer systems;

o   a standard mechanism for negotiation between graphical systems.

The difference between the way the CGI and CGM address the second of these requirements is that the CGI must provide for the transfer in real time, while the CGM has no such constraint.

Once again the document will consist of several parts (three this time); once again the first part will be the functional specification. The second part will be an encoding scheme suitable for use in "system to device" and "peer to peer" communication; this will be developed in collaboration with the appropriate ISO working groups. The third part will be a procedural encoding. Languages bindings will need to develop for this encoding. It will be of particular interest to package implementors, since it will provide a point at which their implementations can hand over to software provided by the device manufacturer.

If ANSI and DIN agree to sponsor such a workitem, there will be a great deal of work done during 1985 to develop the standard as quickly as possible; a number of documents, including the current ANSI VDI proposal and some DIN papers, are the most likely base documents for such an effort.

7. REGISTRATION

During the evolution of all these standards, it has become obvious that
it is not possible to standardize everything at once. In particular,
there are a number of graphical elements that can be found in a bewil-
dering number of varieties. An example would be the set of all "useful"
marker types. Any one person could probably think up a thousand in just
his own field.

Rather than delay the standards in progress by trying to get
agreement on extensive lists of such elements for each standard in
turn, the documents now just refer to a single registration mechanism
and mandate only a very small number of such elements. The registration
mechanism is being set up to deal with the standardization of the
following elements initially:

- o Generalized Drawing Primitives (GDPs)
- o Escapes
- o Line types
- o Hatch styles
- o Text font usage
- o Prompt/echo types
- o Error messages

This registration mechanism will, by default, provide for the extension
of each relevant graphics standard in each of these areas. Thus for an
extra marker type, it will define the appearance of the marker, allocate a marker type number for GKS, do the same for the CGM (including
each of the bindings) and so on for each standard. In some cases, the
element will not be appropriate (for example, Prompt/Echo types are not
relevant to the CGM).

By this means, it is expected that the requirement for extensions
to the standards in these areas will be met - without having to update
each standard - and also that all the standards will stay in step with
minimum effort and confusion.

8. SUMMARY

As recently as October 1981, the ISO working group was really only
concerned with one standard - GKS. With that document about to be
forwarded to ISO for adoption as a full International Standard, the
group's purpose might be thought to be fulfilled. Far from the work
being over, the group has responded to the pressure of demand for
standards in related areas and now has a large number of standards in
progress. They include -

- o GKS
- o GKS language bindings for Fortran 77, Pascal, ADA and BASIC
- o Computer Graphics Metafile (including three bindings)
- o GKS-3D
- o PHIGS
- o Registration mechanism for Graphical Elements

Waiting their turn behind these are standard for CGI, the language bindings for GKS-3D, PHIGS and CGI, metafiles for GKS-3D and PHIGS and bindings for the other standard languages.

There has been a definite increase in the awareness of the commercial value of adopting standards. This is already evident from the number of products quoting GKS and the numer of manufacturers who are joining the standards efforts themselves so they can know at first hand what is being developed and contribute to the effort.

Inevitably there are some who "jump the gun", guessing that a particular document will become "the standard". The apparent pace of standards work makes this understandable, but in the end it is only when everyone uses the same standard that the benefit is reaped.9.

REFERENCES

/1/ R.A. Guedj and H. Tucker, Seillac I, IFIP Workshop on Methodology in Computer Graphics, Seillac, France, May 1976. Proceedings published by North-Holland, 1979.

/2/ Status Report of the Graphic Standards Planning Committee of ACM/SIGGRAPH, Computer Graphics, 13(3), August 1979.

/3/ Functional Description of the Graphical Kernel System (GKS) (Preliminary version of the proposal for DIN standard 0066252).

/4/ Information Processing - Graphical Kernel System (GKS) - Functional Description, ISO/DIS 7942, ISO, Geneva, 1983

/5/ Information Processing - Computer Graphics - Metafile for storage and transfer of picture description information, ISO/DP 8632.

Session 5

The Application Layer

Session Chairman: Murray Kesselman

STATUS OF ISO PROTOCOLS IN
THE PRESENTATION AND APPLICATION LAYERS

Dr. H.J. Pearson
Smith Associates Consulting
System Engineers Limited
Cobham, Surrey, KT11 3DP
United Kingdom

1. INTRODUCTION

SG9 of the NATO Tri-Service Group on Communications and Electronic
Equipment is charged with developing a set of Technical Common Interface Standards defining the standards needed to provide the mechanisms
whereby the NATO Interoperability Management Plan (NIMP) may be implemented.

The NIMP is based on the adoption of the ISO Basic Reference Model
for Open Systems Interconnection (OSI) /1/, the "7-layer model".

Within SG9 the UK is taking the role of lead nation for the
Presentation and Application Layers (Layers 6 and 7) of the Basic
Reference Model. This paper is based on work carried out under contract
to the UK Ministry of Defence in support of the UK technical
representative to SG9. Overviews of the current status and technical
content of OSI Layers 6 and 7 have been given in /2/ and /3/.

The sub-committee (SC) structure of ISO Technical Committee (TC)
97 has recently been partially reorganised to bring together various
strands of work on OSI, particularly in the higher layers. Almost all
work relevant to the Presentation and Application Layers is being
carried out in the newly formed SC21 and in SC18.

This paper gives a broad overview of the architectures of the
Presentation and Application Layers and summarises the standards under
development within ISO.

It should be noted that none of the documents described here has
reached the stage of a published International Standard so they represent work still in progress, possibly subject to future changes of
direction.

2. PRESENTATION LAYER

The function of the Presentation is to coordinate the way in which information is encoded into octets (groups of 8 bits) for transfer between open systems. This coordination is carried out by providing
mechanisms for:

R. W. G. Herbers (ed), The Upper Layers of Open Systems Interconnection, 103–109.

a) negotiating the encodings to be used for transfer;

b) carrying out the encoding and decoding of information.

The Presentation Layer also "passes through" the services of the Session Layer (sometimes with added value) for use by the Application Layer.

Application Layer Standards need to specify the transfer of some form of datastructure on a connection. This datastructure may be a relatively small piece of application protocol (consisting of perhaps one or more optional parameters, some of which have an internal structure of optional sub-parameters), or may be a relatively large datastructure consisting of a lengthy report, part of a file or database, or some form of international or military document.

The definition of the meaning to be transferred (semantics) is recognised in OSI as an Application Layer matter - specific to individual applications.

The conversion of this requirement (to transfer these semantics) into the precise bit-pattern to be communicated is recognised in OSI as a Presentation Layer matter.

In general, there are many possible bit-patterns, or <u>concrete transfer syntaxes</u>, which (given agreement on the way they are to be used) can be used to convey the same semantics.

At the present time, there is not sufficiently rigorous notation available to enable an Application Standard to specify only the semantics to be conveyed, leaving all aspects of the transfer syntax for determination by algorithms forming part of the Presentation Layer standardisation.

Presently available techniques mean that when an application Standard specifies the semantics to be transferred, it is forced at the same time to <u>partially</u> determine the way that the semantics is to be represented. This partial determination of the representation is called an <u>abstract transfer syntax</u>.

ISO is developing a Standard for <u>abstract syntax notation one</u> (ASN.1), and for encoding rules which define the concrete transfer syntax for any datastructure whose abstract transfer syntax is defined using ASN.1.

This notation was originally developed by CCITT in order to define the fairly complex datastructures transferred as part of their message handling systems (electronic mail). It is recognised by ISO that ASN.1 may be the first of many such notations with others defined for applications with very different primitive elements and construction techniques. For instance, the primitives required to handle graphic information may be points, colours, shadings, line markings (dotted, dashed, full, etc.), point markings (triangle, cross, square, arcs, splines, infills, ellipses, and so on, together with overlaying, windowing, and notations.

Similarly, different concrete transfer syntaxes (encodings, representations) may be required at different times for the same datastructure (abstract transfer syntax). This may·be needed to, for example:

- use encryption algorithms when needed;

- use compression algorithms when needed;

- provide verbose but simple and human readable encodings
  when needed.

The Presentation Layer Standards require the allocation of unambigous
names to two sets of objects.

The first requirement is for an unambiguous name for a set of data
structures to be used on the connection. These datastructures will
typically (but not necessarily) be defined using an abstract syntax
notation. This set of datastructures is currently called a <u>presentation
context requirement</u>.

The second requirement is for unambiguous names for one or more
defined concrete transfer syntaxes capable of carrying the semantics of
a particular presentation context requirement. These concrete transfer
syntaxes will typically (but not necessarily) be defined by referencing
the algorithms of some encoding rules and applying them to the abstract
transfer syntax definitions.

The precise scope of the non-ambiguity of such names is not yet
determined, but it is likely that an ISO Registration Authority will be
established to allocate names for internationally recognised datastructure and concrete transfer syntaxes. Provision for enterprise-specific
naming, such as may be required for datastructures defined by banks,
airlines, NATO, or others is not yet clear. Also unclear is, whether
unambiguous names can be automatically constructed for these items when
they form part of an ISO Standard or a CCITT Recommendations, without
awaiting the establishment of an ISO Registration Authority.

The Presentation Service enables a service user to specify a list
of <u>presentation context requirements</u> for this connection by giving
their unambiguous names. The Presentation Layer Protocol then negoti-
ates which of the available concrete transfer syntaxes (using their
unambiguous names) is to be used for each presentation context requirement. The resulting combination of a single requirement and the agreed
concrete transfer syntax is called <u>a presentation context</u>; it is given
a local identification by the Presentation Service for the duration of
the connection.

Currently (February 1985) the Presentation Layer Standards:

- Presentation Service Definition;
- Presentation Protocol Specification;
- ASN.1 Definition;
- ASN.1 Encoding Rules;

all have Draft Proposal (DP) status, although the ASN.1 documents may
move to Draft International Standard (DIS) status shortly.

Work relevant to the Presentation Layer is also being carried out
within ISO ind the context of the Graphics Kernel System (see Section 3).

3. APPLICATION LAYER

The Application Layer contains Standards for many protocols, all using the services of the Presentation Layer to provide the functionality needed for specific areas.

The lower layers of OSI have a strictly hierarchical structure; in general there is precisely one protocol standard sitting above and using the services of a lower layer. The lower layer also have a well-defined upper boundary at which they offer their services.

These principles do not apply in the Application Layer. Many different standards will be produced, each using the Presentation Service and capable of operation on a Presentation connection.

These standards may, in general, be interrelated such that one Standard builds on, and uses the services of, another. This does not necessarily imply a strictly hierarchical relation. In some applications Standard A may use Standard B. In other applications, the reverse could hold. In some applications, A might use B which uses C, whilst in other applications A uses C direct.

Within a single presentation connection, we may conduct activity according to Standard A, then (on the same connection) conduct activity according to Standard B, then A again, and so on. An example might be file transfer, an electronic mail transmission, then another file transfer. This could be described as charging the "application context" for the connection, however there is no general agreement within ISO yet on the precise meaning of this term.

The "upper boundary" for Application Layer activity is also still unclear. All experts agree that the Application Layer is notionally unbounded. All specifications of bits on the line (ISO Standards or not) which are not part of Layers 1 to 6 are part of the Application layer.

In order to permit the specification of Application Layer Service primitives, some concept of the communicating parties is needed. Current architectural discussions include a broad recognition of terms and concepts as described below. There is, however, still unclearness and disagreement on detail.

The source or sink of data being communicated is an <u>application process</u> (computer program - within or outside the operating system).

The implementation-independent abstraction of those features of such a process which are concerned with OSI communication is called an <u>application entity</u>. Only application entities are discussed in OSI standards.

An application entity consists of a user element which exercises service primitives provided by OSI standards.

It has been recognised within ISO that some of the operations of different Standards are similar, and could usefully be standarised separately as a set of elements forming a "tool-kit" which can be referenced by other Standards. This led to the concept of Common Application Service Elements (CASE). The initial proposals in this area are called the CASE Kernel.

One issue still undecided in ISO is whether, in order to provide a simple protocol for such elements, it is necessary to enable CASE to

"police" all use of the Presentation Service, making it essentially
another (mandatory) sub-layer, with no use of the Presentation Layer
exept through CASE.

Standards are under development for the service primitives and for
the protocol for the CASE Kernel. This work is not yet at DP stage, and
is to some extent handicapped by lack of current understanding and
agreement on architectural issues.

The concept of an "application association" between two application entities is a key concept in CASE Kernel work. The idea is that
this association is maintained across loss of a presentation connection, and so corresponds, in some sense, to an application connection.

The present DP text for CASE consists of two multi-part documents,
one for Service Definition an one for Protocol Specificatiqn. In each
case, Part 1 is a two-page document listing the other Parts. Part 2 is
reserved for CASE Kernel, when this work matures sufficiently. Part 3
is the Commitment, Concurrency and Recovery (CCR) DP and Part 4 is
tentatively reliable bulk transfer service".

CCR Services and Protocols were developed by the Working Group
concerned with Management. Immediately prior to progression as a Draft
Proposal, it was agreed that these Standards should be seen as Part of
CASE, and the DPs are being issued as CASE Part 3.

CCR provides for the reliable completion of activity involving
several systems, no matter when crashes occur. It is exxential for the
management of distributed databases, and for most forms of activity
which proceed without hunman involvement. There is a relation between
CCR and CCITT X.400 (used in message handling) as a means of providing
reliable transfer.

Other Application Layer Standards currently being progressed in
ISO include the following:

File Transfer Access and Management (FTAM)

FTAM is concerned mainly with the negotiating the transfer of a file.

Job transfer and Manipulation (JTM)

JTM was designed to support remote off-line processing. It recognises
the need to transmit (transparent) documents to a system for
"processing", together with information which will enable that system
tö correctly dispose of documents resulting from the "processing". The
documents could be traditional JCL, program and data, and the "processing" could involve queueing for a "job-mill" style of activity. On the
other hand, the documents could be a letter with enclosures, and the
"processing" could be by a human being.

Virtual Terminal Protocols (VTP)

Work in ISO on protocols capable of supporting remote terminal access
to computers is taking a different approach to that adopted by CCITT in
its so-collad "triple-X" Recommendations X.3, X.28, X.29.

ISO has largely tried to avoid a model in which characteristics of
the device are evident. Rather it has adopted the "Virtual Terminal"
approach, in which the program and the teminal intelligence share a
common datastructure, (broadly modelling the screen). Both are able to
read it, and subject to access controls of the token variety, both can
write to it.

ISO recognises a number of "classes" of VT Standard which are
required to support simple text work, "forms-filling", graphics work,
and so on. These differ essentially in the nature of the advanced, and
future work is currently being reviewed to see whether it meets the
needs of the increasingly intelligent sophisticated terminals now
available.

Text Interchance

Standards for "text interchange", "electronic mail", "message handling
systems" (the terms are synonymous) are under development in ISO and in
CCITT. The work of the two groups is closely aligned, with the CCITT
work somewhat more fully developed (Recommendation X.400 onwards). The
ISO text is called "Message Oriented Text Interchange" - MOTIS. The
CCITT work is usually called "Message Handling Systems" MHS.

Document Structures

There is beginning to be a recognition within ISO of the need to
recognise and co-ordinate the definition of "documents". ISO SC15 has
produced a DIS for a "Data Descriptive File for Information Interchange" (DDF). This is a concrete transfer syntax for a document which
consists (in its simplest form) of a series of records, each record
consisting of a sequence of named fields, each of which may be present
or absent or multiply present in any particular record. In its most
complex form each record contains structuring information which con-
verts the simple sequence of fields into nodes of arbitrary hierarchical tree.

Another highly complex document definition is that of CCITT and
SC18 with the "Office Document Architecture" (ODA). This work provides
an abstract syntax definition (using ASN.1) for documents expected to
be useful for carrying business correspondence.

Database Work

Work on Standards for database is, at first sight, not directly concerned with OSI. It has, however, been placed with OSI work in the new
SC21. This reflects the recognition of the need for services and protocols to support:

- remote access to search or update a database;
- databases distributed across several systems;
- transfer of complete databases.

Present ISO work is heavily oriented towards ANSI work on the development of Standards for "Network Database Language" and "Relational Database Language". The ISO Working Group is monitoring the ANSI work, feeding its comments back to ANSI, with the hope that it will be possible to ratify the resulting documents as ISO DPs and ultimately standards.

Graphics Kernel System (GKS)

The importance of this work to OSI lies in two areas:

- the provision of protocols to support the ("off-line") transfer of graphic definitions (metafiles);

- the provision of protocols, probably as an extension of VTP work, to support the remote (interactive) control of a graphics device.

Operating System Command and Response Language (OSCRL)

ISO work on an OSCRL is still at a quite early stage. Extensive work has been done by IFIP and by ANSI, and some work by DIN.

4. REFERENCES

/1/ "Information Processing Systems - Open Systems Interconnection - Basic Reference Model", ISO IS 7498.

/2/ "An introduction to the current status of OSI Layers 6 and 7", Larmouth, J., G.E. Curtis and H.J. Pearson, D/DSLC/17/10/17, 25th June 1984.

/3/ "An introduction to the technical content of OSI Layers 6 and 7", Larmouth J., G.E. Curtis, H.J. Pearson, 11th September 1984.

THE MANAGEMENT OF COMMUNICATIONS-BASED SYSTEMS
AND
CURRENT WORK IN OSI MANAGEMENT

Chris Sluman
The CAP Group plc
233 High Holborn
London WCIV 7DJ
United Kingdom

ABSTRACT

This paper addresses the relationships between communications management and the management of distributed applications and goes on to
develop a discussion of the former. The general requirements of management are reviewed and a simple management architecture proposed. The
resultant management communications are categorised and a management
communications model constructed.

The paper concludes with a consideration of the current work of
ISO in the area of management in the OSI environment. It follows the
meeting of the ISO Management Group (ISO/TC97/SC21/16-4, now
ISO/TC97/SC21/WG4) in Paris, February 4-8 1985. A list of output
document from that meeting is included at Appendix C.

For the purposes of this paper, Communications-Based Systems are
defined as either those systems which basically provide communications
services, or those systems which provide services which themselves are
heavily dependent upon underlying communications facilities.

1. SCOPE OF MANAGEMENT OF COMMUNICATIONS-BASED SYSTEMS

In order to bound the discussion of the Management of communications-
based systems, it is useful to consider the nature of Information
Processing (IP). Where IP is not distributed across multiple systems,
its scope is limited to a single system environment, and is subject
only to the specific constraints of that system. This typically corresponds to a single operating system environment, in which the "management" capabilities for any IP activity are entirely dependent upon the
functions and facilities offered by the operating system.

Where IP is distributed across more than one system, there exists
the potential for the cooperation between a number of activities in
order to achieve the IP purpose. Each activity will be subject to the
constraints and capabilities imposed by its own host environment. However, coordination between acitivities will be required, as may coordination beween the systems.

111

R. W. G. Herbers (ed), The Upper Layers of Open Systems Interconnection, 111–124.
© *1987 by D. Reidel Publishing Company.*

In order to consider the nature of this coordination of distributed IP, it is useful to subdivide the activity into two parts. The first is the distributed application itself. The number of potential types of distributed application must be virtually unlimited. At this time, the study of the management of distributed applications is very much in its infancy, with programmes like COST 11 providing much of the early research.

The second part is the communications which support the distributed applications. This aspect is the subject of the OSI Basic Reference Model /1/, and therefore is the subject for OSI standardisation. The management of these communication aspects is considerably better understood, and is the primary subject of this paper.

2.   COMMUNICATIONS MANAGEMENT

This section develops the discussion of the various aspects of communications management, by considering the objects to be managed, the functions required of management and a general architecture to meet the requirements.

2.1 COMMUNICATIONS RESOURCES

It is necessary to identify the communication elements of distributed IP in order to discuss their management. These are termed "communication resources", and include the hardware and software elements which provide communication. Typical examples include:

- Individual Switches;
- Relay Equipment;
- Gateways;
- Physical Connectors and Bearer Systems;
- Cryptographic Equipment;
- Modems;
- etc.

Less obvious communications resources include:

- Complete Networks;
- Directories;
- Routing Tables and Configuration Databases;
- Status and Statistics Information;
- etc.

2.2 MANAGEMENT FUNCTIONS

In general, most (if not all) elements of a communications-based system can be considered as communications resources. It is necessary to examine the types of function required to manage those resources.

There is clearly a requirement to monitor the status of the resources. Requirements will vary from real time error/fault reporting, through performance measurement to long term statistics gathering. They will include security monitoring, event and alarm logging etc.

On the basis of the monitoring information, decisions might be taken resulting in controls being applied back to the communication resources. The requirement exists therefore to provide facilities for configuration updates, capability changes, startup/-closedown of resources, distribution of directories etc.

Higher level management functions (using the types of function already described) will include optimisation between resources, strategic planning, prioritisation of maintenance visits, distribution of encryption keys etc.

2.3 MANAGEMENT ARCHITECTURE

There are many possibilities for the structuring of a management architecture to meet the requirements outlined above. One such architecture that has proven useful to the author is presented here. It should be noted that this architecture does not represent any agreed UK or ISO position.

The functions of management can be grouped by timeframe of use. A useful partitioning is:

a. short term   -   real-time, up to a few seconds
b. medium term   -   seconds to hours
c. long term   -   days +

Typical short term activities include re-routing around failed equipment, the reporting of failures etc.

Medium term activities are generally concerned with resource optimisation and the day-to-day operation of communication services.

Typical long term activities are centred around strategic planning, using statistical analysis of traffic and performance.

This architecture has a number of implications:

a. management responsibilities:

   i)   short term management is clearly best suited to automated operation, performed by individual equipments. These include both simple equipments such as gateways, switches, modems etc. and complex equipments such as complete subnetworks;

   ii) medium term activities require decisions to be taken given as complete a picture of current status as possible. In many cases this implies human decisions based upon mechanised presentation of information, although automated decision-making will become increasingly evident;

iii) long term management activities are similar to those
found in the medium term, taken over a longer timeframe.
Decisions will therefore be based upon information gathered over a reasonable period, used to effect strategic
changes to total systems. This implies considerable human
involvement, perhaps with the aid of off-line computational
facilities for report generation etc.

b.   locational aspects:

i)   short term management is generally implemented within each
communication resource. It will be specific to each resource
whether a single resource, a subnetwork or a complete communication system;

ii)   medium term management considers the optimisation of resources
and hence logically exists external to each of the resources,
probably being best provided by one or more centralised services. This is not specific to any one resource;

iii) long term management is a human function performed externally
to any specific resource. It is also therefore best performed
at locations at which a total view of the communication system
is available.

c.   maintenance aspects:

i)   maintenance aspects of short term management are limited to
optimisation of the recovery of individual resources in the
event of errors or failures. In the case of simple equipments
this will probably involve failure with some form of indication. For complex resources, facilities will generally exist
to automatically isolate failed equipment and optimise the
use of the remainder. In both cases, failure notification
is required;

ii)   in the medium term, there is the concept of the maintainer
optimising his work by prioritising responses to maintenance
requests;

iii) long term maintencance is the strategic planning of maintenance activity, scheduling preventative maintenance etc.

Within the scope of the above activities are multe-purpose facilities,
which use a range of the monitoring and control functions to achieve
specific purposes which can be applied to all of the timeframes. An
example of this type of facilitiy is performance measurement, where
under some conditions on-line performance appraisal is required to
affect operating conditions and thresholds (short term), whilst under
other conditions degradationof performance may be symptomatic of a
more complex problem affecting a number of resources (medium term).

Statistical analyses of performance trends is also required for long term strategic planning.

3. MANAGEMENT COMMUNICATIONS

3.1 OVERVIEW

Having considered a basic architecture for management, a view of management communications can be presented. For each management timeframe, different management communications requirements exist.

For short term management there are two main possibilities; where the communications resource is a single (simple) element, any management functions are part of the local environment, thus no management communications are required. There the communication resource is a set of single elements (such as a subnetwork) then management communications between the element are required.

In the case of medium term management there are again two possibilities. To apply medium term management to a single resource (single element or combined multiple elements) facilities may be required locally or remotely. An example of local medium term management is a terminal connected to a machine which provides startup/closedown, error reporting, statistics reports, configuration controls etc. Remote medium term management would provide exactly the same services, at a position away from the equipment being managed.

For long term management, once the information has been gathered by medium term management, the mechanisms required by human planners will depend upon the type of planning performed. For the purpose of this discussion, no attempt is made to further speculate on communications to support this activity.

3.2 DETAILED MANAGEMENT COMMUNICATIONS

a.   short term management communication:

Short term management communications are required <u>within</u> specific communications resources. Practical considerations tend to dictate that such communications are vendor and/or technology specific. The methods by which competing vendors maintain market positions is by offering products with different internal management communications, providing different cost/performance benefits. An example of this is a packet switched subnetwork, where although the majority of vendors will offer a standard user service interface (such as X.25), the internal management of the subnetwork will determine its suitability for specific purposes. Some internal structures will limit the potential total size of the network, but might be highly reliable or fast. Others may provide for extensibility whilst sacrificing efficiency.

Therefore, short term management may in general be considered to be vendor specific, although as the ISDN concepts become firmer, the potential for standardised short term management communications will increase.

b)   medium term management communication:

The communication of medium term management information is only required for the transfer of information between communications resources and remote "users" of that information. As discussed in section 3.2, a wide range of information types may be required. In most cases, two (or more) communicating systems will wish to exchange medium term management information, such as accounting or fault reporting, as part of the normal use of each others services. In other cases, a centralised management service will wish to communicate medium term information to a nuber of different resources.

In order to achieve this interoperability for management purposes, standards for medium term management information exchanges are highly desirable. It is clear that the requirements for this type of standardisation fall within the scope of Open Systems Interconnection (OSI).

It is also important to consider the requirements for communications facilities to support the management information exchanges. For the information types outlined above, it is likely that the services of all the lower-layers of the 7-layer model will be required /2/.

c.   long term management communication:

There is no requirement for specific long term management information exchanges, as information gathering will be performed using medium term management services, as will subsequent control actions.

In summary, standards are required for medium term management information exchanges. Section 5 describes the progress of ISO in this area.

4.   THE WORK OF ISO IN OSI MANAGEMENT

4.1 HISTORY

ISO TC97/SC16 agreed to set up an OSI Management working group at its full plenary meeting in 1979 in London. The working group was designated TC97/SC16/WG4 and first met in April 1980. It has met every 6 to 8 months since that date:

- Paris   April 1980
- Berlin   November 1980
- Washington   June 1981
- Berlin   January 1982
- Tokyo   June 1982
- Paris   February 1983
- Ottawa   October 1983
- Copenhagen   June 1984
- Paris   January 1985

In addition to full plenary meetings, WG4 has sanctioned a small number of ad-hoc intermediary meetings, primarily in the areas of architecture and Commitment, Concurrency and Recovery (CCR).

Meetings are attended by representatives of national standards bodies (such as BSI, DIN, ANSI etc.), presenting a national viewpoint, but attending as individual experts. Early meetings of SC16/WG4 took the form of discussion groups, with each attendee contributing widely varying views on the subject. Little progress was made until the Washington meeting, at which Bachmann diagrams were first proposed as a means of representing the management architecture. A "Management Framework" was produced to provide the management group with a reference model. Also at Washington, the first attempt was made to properly prioritise the work of the group. This was refined considerably in Tokyo, and the project sub-divisions remained consistent until the recent startup of SC21 and its associated restructuring.

There are two main reasons why technical progress was initially slow:

a. There was confusion concerning the scope of the work. The interpretation of "Application and System Management" (the original title of the WG4 work item) can be taken in the narrow context of the communications medium relevant to OSI or it can be recognised that management of processing and information storage is also needed when systems are distributed. Only recently have experts agreed the need to separate these concerns.

b. The work item has covered many topics but until recently the sub-goals for each topic have not been well specified. The set of topics discussed by SC16/WG4 were:

   i) Management Framework - to complement the OSI Basic Reference Model, and provide a focal point for discussion of management architecture;

   ii) Management Information Services (MIS) e.g.

      - Fault management
      - Accounting management
      - Authorisation management
      - Directory management;

iii) Commitment, Concurrency and Recovery - providing a standard
     set of services to ensure the integrity of distributed appli-
     cations;

iv) Control of Application Process Groups - considering the func-
     tions required for the management of cooperating processes
     running on different systems.

4.2 ISO REORGANISATION

ISO TC97 has recently reorganised its work in the area of OSI and
distributed computing to improve the coordination between groups
working on similar subjects.

Discussion during the run-up period to the formation of
ISO/TC97/SC21 (titled "Open Systems", and bringing together OSI, OSCRL,
Graphics, Databases etc.) indicated that the new Sub-Committee would
provide an excellent opportunity to separate the concerns of communication management from those of processing and data storage management.

At the recent meeting in Paris, it was agreed that the manage
ment work item should be renamed "OSI Management", and should cover the
following topics:

a.   Management Framework;

b.   Management Information Services e.g.

     - Fault management
     - Accounting management
     - Configuration management
     - Performance management;

c.   Directory Services.

The work on Commitment, Concurrency and Recovery, having reached the
Draft Proposal (DP) stage, was assigned to SC21/WG6 for progression to
a full standard, along side other Common Application Service Element
(CASE) standards.

In the area of Control of Application Process Groups a document
was prepared /3/ setting out a revised model for developing management
standards relating to processing, data storage and the consequent OSI
communication of a distributed processing environment. The document is
seen as complementing the Management Framework. The confusion generated
by previous terminology was resolved and a detailed set of defined term
was prepared. As a result it is likely that the term "Control of Application Process Groups" will be dropped in favour of "Management of
Distributed Application Processing". The document identified many
questions for further study but gives pointers to the coherence of this
work with OSCRL (Operating System Command and Response Languages),
operating systems in distributed environments, distributed databases
and OSI services. In order to progress this new direction, the work in
this area has been assigned to SC21/WG5.

4.3 STATUS OF WORK IN SC21/WG4 AND TIMESCALES

The Paris meeting made considerable progress in all areas. A number of Member Bodies (including the UK) had prepared substantial contributions. These and a reasonable continuity of experts meant that most issues obtained a clear resolution.

a. Management Framework

This work area now provides only for an extension to the OSI Basic Reference Model for managing communication resources.

It was agreed that as no specific requirement for layer management had been identified (other than that which could be handled either totally within the protocols of a single layer or globally by system management at the application layer) the Framework would exclude layer management. However a mechanism for reintroducing the concept has been identified if a need can be proven. It is important that the needs of the lower-layer groups are met in this area, hence national and international liasons are required as a matter of priority.

It was decided that there was no constraint on the number of application entities within a system which could provide system management were provided, there would be at least one.

A joint meeting with the MIS group discussed the allocation of text to the Management Framework and MIS documents. It was agreed that the Framework should currently provide an overview of OSI Management, and specific architectural aspects of MIS should be handled by that group /4/, and contributed to the Framework when complete.

The framework document was revised /5/, and is being issued to Member Bodies and Liaison Organisations for review and comment.

The group identified the need to consider the requirement for minimal connection capability and have issued a short note requesting input on this topic /6/.

A number of other organisations, notably ECMA (in TC23/24), IEEE (in 802) and CCITT (in SG.VII) are actively engaged in work on own management architectures. Efforts are being made within all the groups to align their work and produce consistent output documents.

b. Management Information Sevices (MIS)

It was agreed that the Directory Service fell outside the scope of MIS, and should be progressed separately.

The group have used ASN.1 to specify syntax. In preparing their
output the group requested comments on the proposed syntax and requested input on the semantics for the current working drafts. They
also require input to further the protocol specifications and, as
no work was done on protocol specification at the Paris meeting, it
was considered appropriate to slip target dates by 9 months. The
objective is to have documents for issue as Draft Proposals by
June 1986.

c. Directory Services

The meeting agreed that a very close working relationship with
CCITT was desirable and instructed the Convenor to agree with
SC21 the formal ways in which this could be recognised. One recommended way was to seek accelerated status for the work leading
to joint meetings with CCITT. However, in spite of the need for
haste, it was noted that CCITT's meetings on this topic were unlikely to be restarted before September 1985. As a result the DP
target date of October 1985 was recognised as unrealistic and was
revised to June 1986.

In progressing the working draft it was agreed that all services
were to be specified (using ASN.1 notation) and that a basic subset
would also be defined. There will also be a simple Directory
Maintenance service. The document output from Paris specifies
only the protocols but contains sufficient material to enable a
service document to be prepared. This should be available in time
for the next SC21/WG4 meeting.

In summary, the following target dates for developing standards (to DP)
were agreed in Paris:

- Basic Management Framework   July 1986
- *Management Information Services   June 1986
- Directory Services   June 1986

* - MIS will be published as a set of standards. The date given is for
the architecture part of the set, plus one or more of the individual
standards.

Assuming that there are no major problems with the drafts, it will take
an additional year for each document to become an International
Standard.

4.4 IMPLICATIONS ON MANAGEMENT OF COMMUNICATIONS-BASED SYSTEMS

It is clear that there is a very strong alignment between the management architecture discussed in sections 3 and 4 of this paper and the
work of ISO in OSI. ISO is not concerning itself with either short term
management issues or with the specific areas of the processing of

management information. Thus the MIS work corrresponds directly to medium term management, providing facilities for the exchange of medium
term management information between systems.

The general structure for OSI management information exchanges
considers the interacting processes to be "normal" applications, using
the services of the presentation layer and below for communication. The
applications have to be uniquely identified for naming/addressing
purposes, but they are not intrinsically different to ordinary application processes.

The ISO management architecture group have also considered the
subject of layer management (see section 5.3 a.) The discussion here
centres around the question as to whether or not specific (additional)
protocols are required within the lower layers to perform specific
management functions. In considering the requirements for communicating
management information (i.e. MIS), it appears that in general, the services of the bottom six layers are required.

Therefore an architecture has been developed which does not permit
specific management protocols outside the application layer. This
raises a number of potential problems, especially in the case of mal-
functioning or incomplete systems which do not have the full set of
lower-layer services available. It is for this reason that "minimum
functionality" is being addressed at present, in order to determine the
minimum set of facilities required to meet the management communication
needs.

Directory Services are seen by many in the OSI community as
general system services, with Directory Management as part of the total
service. It is important at this time to ensure that this work is
aligned with that in the areas of Naming and Addressing.

4.5 MILITARY INVOLVEMENT

Military involvement in the area of OSI Management has to date been
limited. With the military emphasis on security and survivability of
communications networks, proper control and monitoring of those systems
is essential. Multi-vendor procurements and evolutionary designs dictate that the OSI approach is essential, as long as all military requirements are met. This can only be assured by military participation
in the work at this cirtical stage, to identify specific requirements
and to consider specific methods of meeting them.

In the UK, Project UNITER is adopting the OSI Architecture and
standards, and sees Management as a critically important area of work.

5. REFERENCES

/1/ ISO 7498 Basic Reference Model for OSI.

/2/ Introduction to the Current Status of OSI Layers 6 and 7,
     Larmouth, Curtis and Pearson, June/August 1984.

/3/ Management of Distributed Application Processing, SC21/N389

/4/ Structure for Management Information, SC21/N387.

/5/ OSI Basic Management Framework, 6th Working Draft, SC21/N391.

/6/ Request for Comment concerning Minimal Connection Capability,
     SC21/N395.

6. LIST OF ABBREVIATIONS

ANSI   American National Standards Institute
ASN.1   Abstract Syntax Notation One

BSI   British Standards Institution

CASE   Common Application Service Elements
CCITT   Consultative Committee on International Telephones and Telegraph
CCR   Commitment, Concurrency and Recovery

DBMS   Data Base Management System
DIN   Deutsches Institut für Normung
DIS   Draft International Standard
DP   ISO Draft Proposal

ECMA   European Computer Manufacturers'Association

FTAM   File Transfer, Access and Management

GKS   Graphical Kernel System

IFIP   International Federation for Information Processing
IS   International Standard
ISDN   Integrated Service Digital Network
ISO   International Organisation for Standardisation

JCL   Job Control Language
JTM   Job Transfer and Manipulation

MIS   Management Information Services

NATO   North Atlantic Treaty Organisation

OSI   Open Systems Interconnection

SC   ISO Sub-Committee

TC   ISO Technical Committee
TR   ISO Technical Report

VT   Virtual Terminal
VTP   Virtual Terminal Services and Protocols

WG   ISO Working Group

7. DOCUMENTS ISSUED AT PARIS MEETING

SC 21

Number   Title

382   Procedures for Management Information Service Standardisation
383   Fault Management Requirements
384   Accounting Management Requirements
385   Configuration Management Requirements
386   Performance Management Requirements
387   Structure of Management Information
388   Management Information Service Definition
389   Management of Distributed Application Processing
390   Directory Access Protocol
391   OSI Basic Management Framework 6th Working Draft
392   Decision on Layer Management Information Exchanges
393   Liaison Statement to ISO/TC97/SC6
394   Response to Questions Raised in SC16 N1838
395   Request for Comment concerning Minimal Connection Capability
396   Liaison statement to CCITT SG.VII
397   Disposition of Member Body Comments on DP 8649/3 and DP 8650/3
398   Addendum to CCR on Global Restart Points
399   Liaison statement to IEEE 802 on System Management Protocols
400   Recommendations of the ninth SC21/WG16-4 Meeting
401   Proposal for New Work Item: OSI Management Information Services
402   Proposal for New Work Item: OSI Directory Services and Protocols

MESSAGE HANDLING IN THE NORWEGIAN
DEFENCE DIGITAL NETWORK
(NDDN)

Tor Gjertsen and Ole-Erik Hedenstad
Norwegian Defence Research Establishment (NDRE)
P.O. Box 25
N - 2007 Kjeller
Norway

ABSTRACT

A message handling system has been specified for the Norwegian Defence
Digital Network, NDDN. The paper gives a survey of the architecture,
functions and implementation strategy for the message handling system.
It has been decided to use the principles and protocols specified in
the CCITT X.400 series of recommendations. The paper deals with how the
X.400 series can be applied to a military system, and presents enhancements to the CCITT recommendations required by the NDDN application.
Which role should existing military procedures like ACP127 play in the
future? The paper explains how requirements for compatibility with the
past can be met in an X.400 based message handling system.

1. INTRODUCTION

The Norwegian Defence has under implementation the Norwegian Defence
Digital Network (NDDN), a service integrated network offering telephone
services and circuit- and packet-switched data services. The network is
based on civil telecommunication standards with a few enhancements to
meet the military requirements. In particular the data services which
are based on the CCITT recommendations X.21 and X.25 respectively.

R. W. G. Herbers (ed), The Upper Layers of Open Systems Interconnection, 125–151.

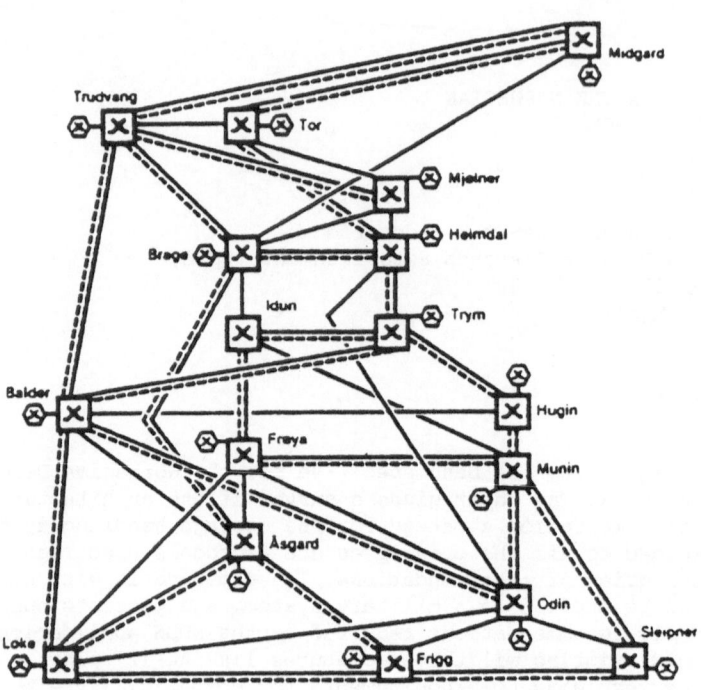

Fig. 1. The NDDN backbone network

Key features of the NDDN are:

SECURITY   -   bulk encryption
                  -   TEMPEST proof
                  -   traffic flow security

SURVIVABILITY   -   physical protection
                  -   EMPP
                  -   redundancy
                  -   autonomy
                  -   three-level network control structure

NODECA (Norwegian Defence Communication Administration) is responsible
for the procurement and operation of NDDN, and Standard Telefon og
Kabelfabrik (STK) is contractor. The specification of NDDN was a colla-
borative effort between NODECA and Norwegian Defence Research
Establishment (NDRE), and carried out in 1980-81. The contract was
signed in 1982. The two first switching nodes of NDDN were installed
late 1984, and the entire backbone network will be operational and
accepted early 1987, including all features.

As a value added service in NDDN, NODECA will offer a formal military message handling service. This will replace the existing ACP127 based teleprinter service which has to rely on a manual torn-tape relay system. This paper gives an overview of the planned message system, and describes how special military requirements are handled in a system based on the new CCITT recommendations for message handling services, the X.400 series.

2. SYSTEM SURVEY

2.1 ARCHITECTURE

The NDDN Message Handling System (NDDN MHS) will consist of geographically separated individual systems, which have to communicate with each other. The communicating part of the system is constructed inaccordance with the ISO Open Systems Interconnection (OSI) architecture, as described in IS 7498, Basic Reference Model. The OSI-architecture has also been adopted by CCITT in recommendation X.200.

The CCITT study group VII has produced 8 recommendations on Message Handling Systems in the X.400 series, which form the base for the NDDN MHS. Along with the CCITT documents, a model has been worked out for the description of the message handling system for the Norwegian Defence.

Figure 2 gives a functional description of the message handling system, which for the purpose of the model, is divided into two parts, the User Agents (UA), and the Message Transfer Agents (MTA).

The UA contains functions for the composition, reading, writing and storage of messages. A UA is controlled by traffic operators at the signal office (it is one UA per signal office), and the UA serves one or more organizational entities. These organizational entities are the addressees in the message handling system. The distribution of received messages to the addressees' staff cells is performed by the UA. On this particular point, the NDDN MHS deviates from the Interpersonal Messaging Service described in X.400. The reason for this deviation is that in a formal military message system, the addressee is an organization and not an individual.

The MTA contains functions for the transfer of messages between UAs, from the originating UA to the recipient UAs. That is to say that it serves the UA regarding the transmission of a message, and assumes responsibilty for the transfer of the message to all the recipients (in the case of a multi addressed message). It routes the message to other MTAs by switching, and delivers the message to attached User Agents. Note that the MTA transfers messages to recipient UAs, the distribution of the message to addressees is performed by the UA.

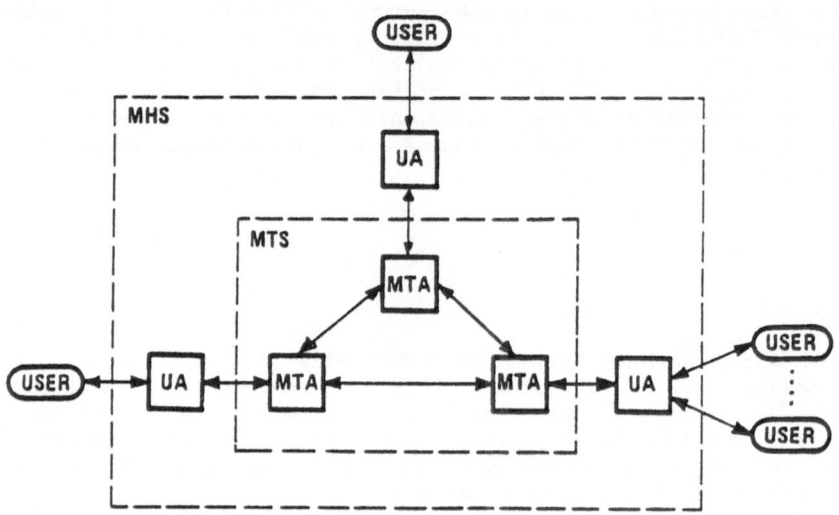

Fig. 2. Model for the NDDN MHS - functional description

The NDDN MHS may also be described in a layered structure, and
specifically in terms of the layers as per the OSI Basic Reference
Model. This is illustrated in Figure 3. The protocols in the various
layers may then be expounded, as well as the services between the
layers. Each layer will contain one or more functional entities. The
message handling system is itself located at the Application Layer, and
is again partitioned into two sublayers, the User Agent Layer (UAL),
and the Message Transfer Layer (MTL).

The OSI model describes solely the particular part of the system
which is "open", ie dependent of communications with other systems.
Figure 3 shows the User Agent in the functional description, paritioned
into a User Environment (UE) and a User Agent Entity (UAE). The former
is external to the OSI environment, while the latter exists in the User
Agent Layer. The User Environment contains purely local functions
necessary to realize the required user services, and to achieve the
required man/machine interface.

The User Agent Entity in the User Agent Layer contains functions
that require interworking with User Agent Entities in other systems.
This will take place primarily as described in the CCITT rec.
X.400/X.420.

The Message Transfer Agents are contained in the Message Transfer Layer (MTL), which consists of Message Transfer Agent Entities (MTAE) and Submission and Delivery Entities (SDE). These are primarily according to CCITT rec. X.410/X.411. Submission and Delivery Entities are always co-located with User Agent Entities.

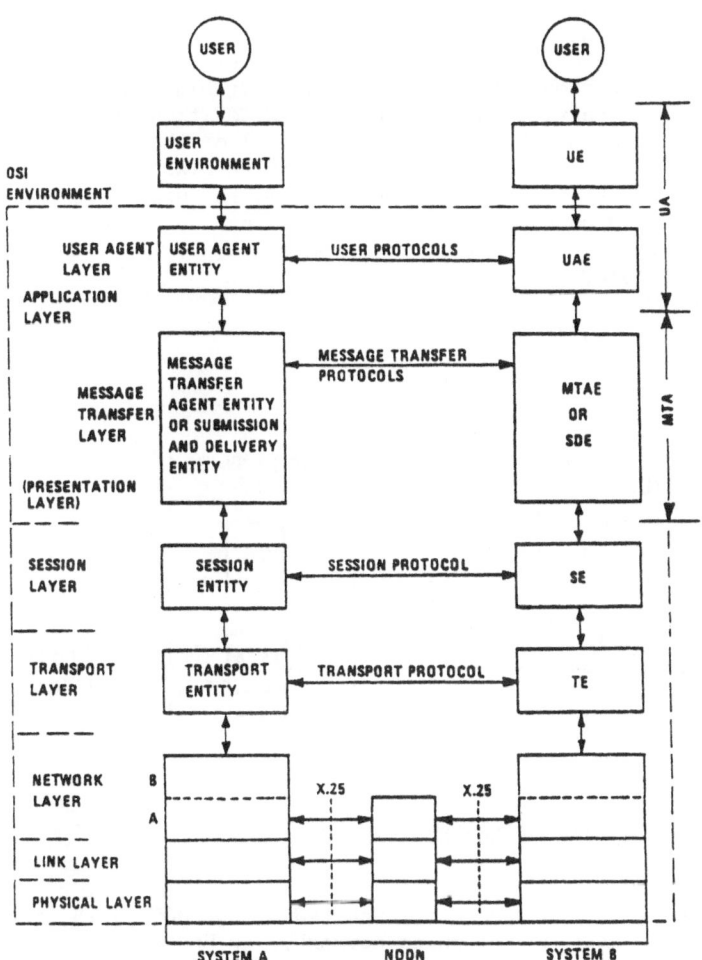

Fig. 3. Model for the NDDN MHS - layered description

2.2 THE NDDN MHS CONCEPT

In NDDN the message handling system will be constructed from two main
components, the User System (US) and the Message Switch (MS). Figure 4
shows the physical mapping of the architectural elements.

The User System will serve the local users of the message system,
and will typically be located at a signal office. It contains one or
more UAs, each serving one or more addressees. The UAs give access to
the message services and local utilities as editing, message storage
and retrieval functions.

The primary task of the Message Switch is the execution of the
message transfer functions including message switching and multi
addressing. This is carried out by the MTA. In addition the Message
Switch contains a UA for the operational control of the MS from the
Traffic Control Terminals (TC-terminals). This UA also will exist as a
recipient and originator in the message system, and will have the
capability of providing simple services for accessing the message
system as a user. That means ordinary messages may be read or written
from the TC-terminals.

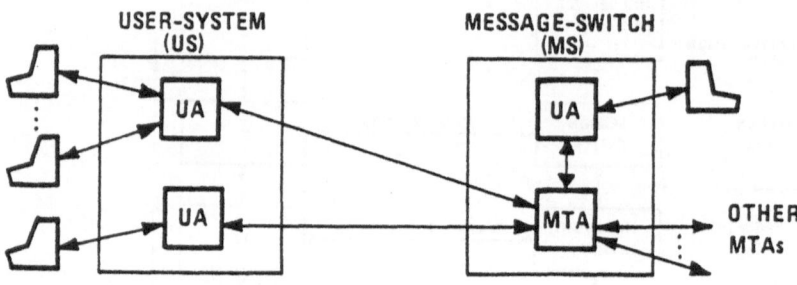

Fig. 4. Physical mapping of the NDDN MHS elements

The Message Switches are interconnected by the NDDN X.25 network
service, to form a message switching network, the Message Transfer
System (MTS). Each of the Message Switches are serving a group of User
Systems giving them access to the Message Transfer System. The user
terminals are connected to the User Systems, which provides the common
user access to the message handling services. Also the User Systems
make use of the X.25 service in their communications with their Message
Switch. Figure 5 gives a layered view of the NDDN MHS concept and the
components of the system.

The NDDN/X.25 has been enhanced to meet the security and priority requirements in a military environment. Further the NDDN MHS will utilize the multi homing capability of the network, i.e. the Message Switches and main User Systems will be connected to two different packet switches to increase the survivability. For the same purpose every User System may be served by a back-up Message Switch, a facility that is simplified by the use of the X.25 network service.

Smaller signal offices, which are to small to be equipped with a User System, shall in principle be capable of accessing a neighbouring User System via a dedicated circuit in the NDDN. They will use simple terminals, and share resources in the serving User System. However, this will not be the normal solution for a small signal office. Remote sites have to rely on their own equipment, i.e. the Small User Systems.

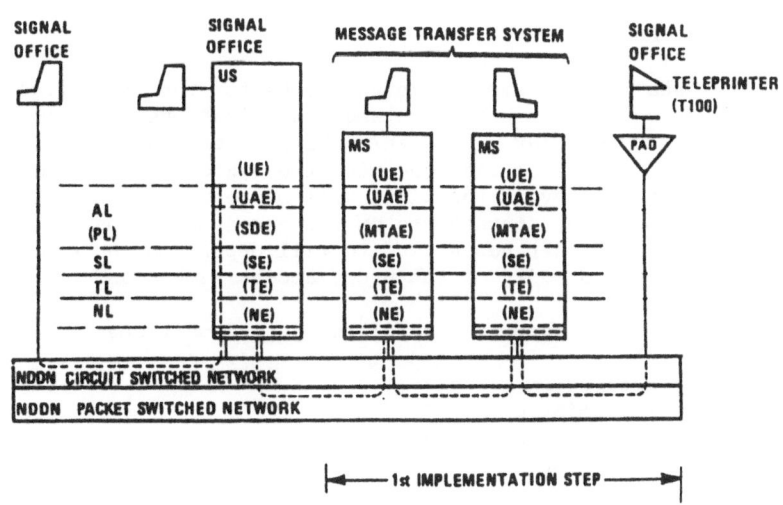

Fig. 5. Concept for the NDDN MHS - layered description

A stepwise implementation strategy has been chosen for the NDDN MHS. In the first step the Message Transfer System will be put in place, ie the Message Switches and their Traffic Control Terminals. They will replace the existing manual tape relay network, and could well be called a national TARE. During this stage the signal offices will utilize existing equipment and procedures. As a consequence the Message Switch has to support the ACP127 procedure as an access method for teleprinter based signal offices. Logically they are treated as "user systems" by the Message Switch. The chosen strategy makes it possible to introduce the Message Switches one by one, and they are able to co-operate with the remaining tape relay centers.

The ACP127 procedure will be partially automated, such that manual intervention will be necessary only on limited occasions. Fault conditions will be corrected from the Traffic Control Terminal by instructing the system or by service messages according to ACP127.

The next implementation step will be to upgrade the main signal offices by the installation of the User Systems. The smaller signal offices have to stay with the teleprinters still for some time.

In the long term the teleprinters will be replaced by the introduction of the Small User System, ie single user equipment, simpler than the ordinary User System, but with local processing and storage capability. TELETEX based equipment might be a candidate.

Access for teleprinters to the Message Switches may best be achieved by the use of PADs (Packet Assembly Disassembly) or a similar concentrator unit to be able to go packetwise to/from the Message Switch.

2.3 USER SERVICES

The NDDN MHS shall primarily provide services for formal message handling, i.e. official messages between organizations. The user has access to the services through a man/machine interface, and the user will typically engage in a dialogue with the system. In contrast to a manual system, a variety of functions will be performed automatically, such that the users may concentrate on the essentials. The services which the individual user has access to will depend on the profile of the user, i.e. the category of the user, access rights and his level of authorization.

The system shall support the following user services:

- message generation
- message transmission
- internal message co-ordination
- message reception
- storing of messages
- message retrieval from storage

Message generation
The system shall provide user assistance for message composition in the form of word processing functions. It shall be possible to utilize standard formats or existing messages and develope these further to produce a new message.

Message transmission
The message may be transmitted to the addressees after having been accepted and released by an authority. The releasing officer will evaluate the content of the message before it is confirmed as an official message. The message is transferred from the User System to the Message

Switch by means of an access protocol. The message transfer system, i.e. the Message Switches, will then assume responsibility for the further handling of the message.

Internal message co-ordination
It may also be required to transmit a message internally between staff cells or within the same staff cell before the message is released, to obtain comments from interested parties. Thus the User System will have the capability of circulating messages.

Message reception
A User System will be capable of receiving messages and may support several addressees. An addressee is either a department, military unit or organization. For further distribution of the message to the staff cells concerned, and to the actual terminals within the staff cells, the system will require an internal distribution service. The message will be automatically distributed according to a locally maintained distribution list. Manual intervention may be done in exceptional circumstances. The main criteria for internal distribution are the message addressee and the Subject Indicator Code (SIC) of the message. An operator in a staff cell will have the capability of transferring a received message to a position in another staff cell in the same system. Further services will exist for forwarding of received messages.

Storing of messages
The User System will hold a Message Store in a hard disc unit. Both incoming and outgoing messages for a period will be stored, and the corresponding message journal will be maintained, even for a longer period. It will be possible to partition the storage logically, so that each department or staff cell is able to operate within it's own logical store, separated from the other ones.

Message retrieval from storage
The User System will provide the services required to enable the various categories of users to retrieve the messages for which they have authorization, from the Message Store.

The NDDN MHS will also provide services for informal message handling, i.e. transfer of inofficial notes between individuals, without any releasing control. They will be marked as informal, and recognized as such in the presentation format. They will be stored in the users private mailbox, separated from the formal Message Store.

2.4 OPERATION AND MAINTENANCE

Operation and maintenance (O&M) of the NDDN MHS are partitioned into a technical and a traffic oriented part. Technical O&M has as its main purpose the proper functioning of the equipment. Functions and aids to allow technical personnel to maintain a comprehensive monitoring, fault locating and restoral capability, are initiated from the O&M-terminal of the system unit (User System or Message Switch).

Traffic oriented O&M is intended to control the system such that a satisfactory message traffic flow is achieved at all times and circumstances. These functions are carried out by Traffic Operators from the TC-terminals. Concerning the Message Switches, traffic control will always be maintained from the co-located Communication Center.

Figure 6 shows a typical configuration of a Communication Center which is equipped with a User System, and has a co-located Message Switch. The different types of terminals are the O&M-terminals at the system units, the Traffic Control Terminals for the User System and the Message Switch respectively. The Traffic Terminals at the signal office and the common user terminals in the Staff Cells give access to the ordinary message handling services.

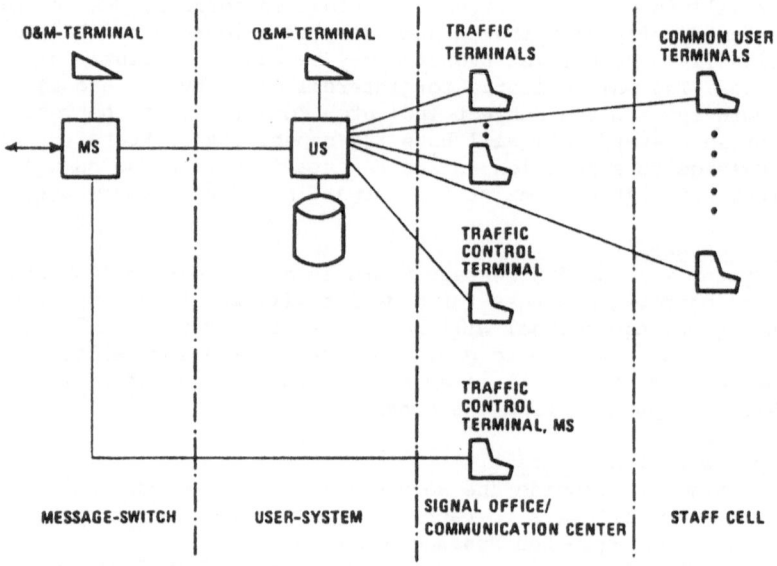

Fig. 6. Typical configuration of a Communication Center

The operational control of the NDDN MHS is strongly based on local functions and processing capabilities, and the fact that the Communication Centers will always be manned. In principle each Message Switch and User system may be operated autonomously. There is, however, a requirement for central co-ordination and support of certain network functions. For this purpose, two Message Control Centres (MCC) will be established, one of these being a hot stand by.

The MCC shall be capable of supervising the NDDN MHS status, produce routing tables and distribute these to the Message Switches.
Further the MCC will collect statistical data and trouble reports from
Message Switches. The MCC will also maintain the Central Address Regi-
ster, and up-date notices may be sent to the User Systems. Depending on
the local decision, the up-date notices may be taken into account for
the local address registers in the User Systems.

Since the message handling system is overlayed a network (NDDN)
with a powerful O&M capability, the O&M-functions of the network level
will be utilized in co-operation with the centralized management of the
NDDN MHS.

3. THE CRITICAL CHOICE - X.400 vs ACP127

3.1 CCITT X.400 CHARACTERISTICS

In the CCITT MHS model the Application layer is divided into two sub-
layers, the User Agent Layer (UAL) and the Message Transfer Layer (MTL)
(see figure 7). At the Message Transfer Layer the message is divided
into two parts, the message envelope and the message content. The message envelope contains the information needed by the MTA to transfer

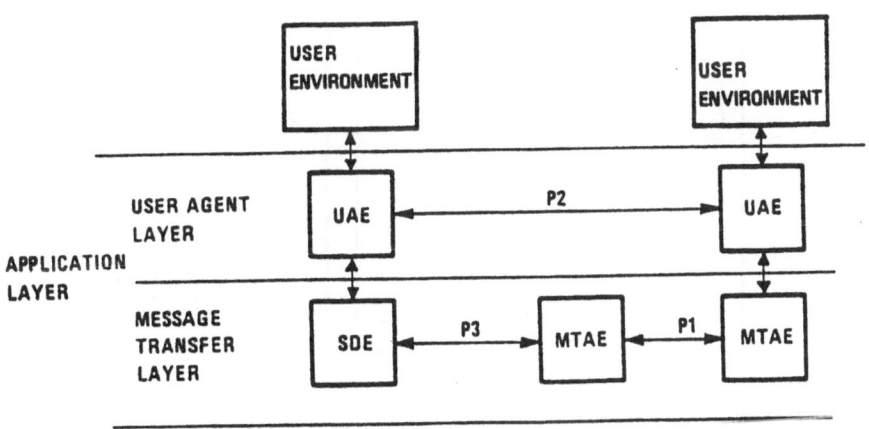

Fig. 7. The MHS model

the message to its recipients. The message content is the information
the originator wants to give the recipients (see figure 8). The information in the message content is of no interest to the MTA. The main
task of the MTA is to transfer the message content to the recipient
User Agents.

The message content is interpreted at the User Agent Layer. The
Message Transfer Layer provides means to identify which User Agent
protocol is actually used in the content. This means that a range of
User Agent protocols may be specified, and that messages of all these
types may be transferred using the same Message Transfer Protocol.

The User Agent protocol

So far one User Agent protocol have been specified. This protocol is
denoted P2 (in the X.400 series it is also called the Interpersonal
Messaging User Agent protocol). This protocol divides the message into
two parts, the message heading and the message body. This is illustrated in figure 8. The message heading consists of a set of heading
components. Typically heading components are message identification,
originator, primary and copy recipients, priority (importance) and
security classification (sensitivity).

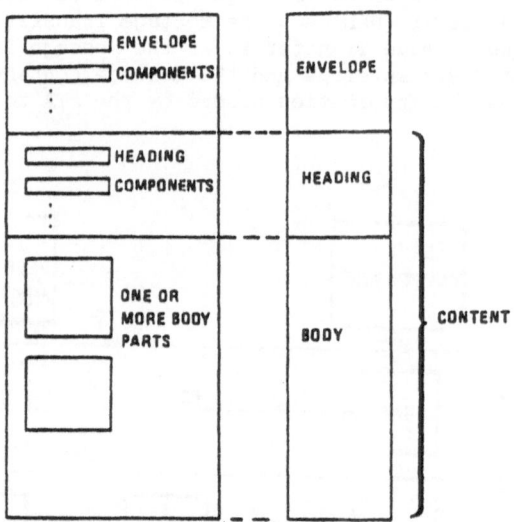

Fig. 8. The message structure

The message identification is a unique identifier of a message. The
identification may be used by the users of the message system. The
priority component gives information to the recipient UA's about the
importance of the message and thus in what order the received messages
should be processed. The User Agent Layer also provides functions to
forward messages. When a message is forwarded, a new message heading is
put in front of the old message.

The message body may consist of one or more parts, each of which may be of different types. One type is text coded according to IA5. Another body type is Teletex pages. Facsimile images and voice information are also defined as body types.

The Message Transfer protocol

Between two cooperating Message Transfer Agent Entities (MTAE) there is defined a Message Transfer protocol denoted P1. The P1 protocol provides functions such as message identification, priority handling, multiaddressing and message relaying. The message identification is used by the MTAE's to distinguish messages within the Message Transfer Layer. The priority tells the Message Transfer Agent Entity in what order the messages are to be transferred.

A message may be addressed to more than one recipient, (called a multiaddressed message). The Message Transfer Agent Entities take care of the necessary administration to route the message to all the recipients. As few message copies as possible are transferred. It only sends one copy of the message to each MTAE that takes part in the actual message transfer. All the copies have the same message identification, but in addition each of the copies has an extension identifier. The message envelope in these copies is a little different. In the message envelope it is marked which User Agents this copy is intended for. This information instructs the Message Transfer Agent to which User Agents it is responsible to deliver the message. This prevents message duplication.

The P1 protocol also provides means to handle a situation where the MTAE is not able to relay the message any further. The MTAE may then send a non-delivery notification to the message originator's User Agent.

The submission and delivery protocol

A Submission and Delivery protocol denoted P3 is defined between the MTAE and the Submission and Delivery Entity (SDE). The SDE is co-located with a User Agent. This protocol defines the submission operation and the delivery operation.

In the submission operation the SDE sends a message to the MTAE and asks the MTAE to take the responsibility of transferring this message to the recipients. If the MTAE is able to take the responsibility for this message, then MTAE gives a confirmation to the SDE together with a submission time stamp. The time stamp is the time when MTAE accepted the responsibility.

In the delivery operation the MTAE transfers a message to the SDE and then gives the responsiblity for the message to this SDE. In the delivery envelope of this message it is given a delivery time stamp. This time stamp is the time when MTAE started the delivery operation.

3.2 WHY NOT ACP 127?

ACP127 is the tape relay procedures specified for use in tape relay
systems. The procedure is well suited for teleprinters.
    Table 1 shows the format lines in ACP127 and the corresponding
functions on layers in the NDDN MHS model. The main functions of the
ACP127 procedure is located at the session and application layer. Note
that the ACP127 procedure is not in conformance with the OSI architecture.

Session functions of ACP127
 ACP127 provides the following session functions:

-    Message separation.
     The function marks the start of the message (format line 1 in
     ACP127) and the end of the message (format line 16 in ACP127).

-    Message control.
     The function controls that all messages sent over the ACP127
     channel actually are received at the receiving end of the
     channel. The method used in ACP127 is that each message sent is
     given a channel number (in format line 1). The channel number is
     increased with one for each message.

-    Message interrupt.
     The transfer of a message may be interrupted when an error occurs
     or a higher priority message is to be transferred. At a later
     time the whole message has to be transferred once more.

    The X.400 MHS uses the CCITT specified session service and session
protocol (X.215 and X.225).
    The "message separation" function in ACP127 has the disadvantage
that a sequence of graphics characters (human readable) are used to
mark start and end of message. It implies that the same character sequence is not allowed to occur in the message text. The X.225 session
protocol provides another technique to separate messages. This technique gives a unique start and end of the message and does not put any
restrictions on the information you may have in the message content.
    The "message control" function in ACP127 does not confirm receipt
of each message. Only when a message is lost, an error report is given
to the sender of the message. The X.225 session protocol gives a more
reliable message control by providing a positive confirmation of each
message.

FORMAT LINE	ELEMENTS	REFERENCE TO NDDN MHS MODEL
1	START OF TRANSMISSION SEQUENCE	SESSION LAYER
2	PRECEDENCE AND CALLED STATION(S)	MESSAGE TRANSFER LAYER
3	CALLING STATION AND .MESSAGE IDENTIFICATION	USER AGENT LAYER
4	SECURITY WARNING AND HANDLING INSTRUCTIONS	MESSAGE TRANSFER LAYER
5	PRECEDENCE	USER AGENT LAYER
6	ORIGINATOR	USER AGENT LAYER
7	ACTION ADDRESSEE(S)	USER AGENT LAYER
8	INFORMATION ADDRESSEE(S)	USER AGENT LAYER
9	EXEMPT ADDRESSEE(S)	USER AGENT LAYER
10	GROUP COUNT	USER AGENT LAYER
11	SEPARATION	USER AGENT LAYER
12	MESSAGE TEXT	USER AGENT LAYER
13	SEPARATION	USER AGENT LAYER
14	CORRECTIONS	TRANSPORT LAYER
15/16	END OF TRANSMISSION SEQUENCE	SESSION LAYER

Table 1: ACP127 and the NDDN MHS Model.

The ACP127 does not provide a function for resumption of an earlier interrupted message. The whole message has to be retransfered. In the X.225 session protocol you may resume the transfer of an earlier interrupted activity at the point the interruption happened.

The X.215 session service is superior to the session functions of the ACP127. Still it is possible to keep the application functions of the ACP127 and combine ACP127 application layer with X.225 session protocol at the session layer. In the following the discussion of ACP127 is made on this background.

Application functions
ACP127 provides the following application functions:

-   Message envelope (format lines 2 and 4 of ACP127).
-   Message identification (format line 3 of ACP127).
-   Message heading (format lines 5 to 11).
-   Text body.
-   Message forwarding or readdressing.
    A new message envelope and a new message heading is put in front
    of the old message heading. The old message envelope is removed.
-   Rerouting (a ACP127 pilot is put in front of the message
    envelope).

The ACP127 message consists of a sequence of lines, separated by the
end of line function. Some of the components of the ACP127 message
envelope and message heading do not have a unique identification. The
interpretation of these are determined by the ordering of the
components. The other components are identified by readable text
symbols (for instance the TO symbol that identifies the line containing
the addressees of the message). A text symbol is also used to mark the
start and end of the text body of the ACP127 message, and this text
symbol must not be present in the text body.
     The X.400 protocols gives an unambigiuous identification of the
envelope and heading components. Each component is encoded using the
presentation transfer syntax specified in X.409. The component has a
type and a value. The value is encoded together with its type and
length.
     The ACP127 is only able to transfer 5 bits characters in the body.
It is possible to transfer binary data, but then the data has to be
formatted into 5 bits characters. The X.400 User Agent protocol encodes
the body and the body parts in the same way as the envelope and heading
components. This means that the body may include a variety of information types (for instance text, facsimile images, graphics data and
binary data). More than one body part may also be put into the same
message body, and these parts may be of different types, i.e. a multi-
media message.
     ACP127 provides some applications functions not specified in
X.400. As a minimum the NDDN MHS has to provide all the ACP127 functions. Thus some enhancements to X.400 have been made in the NDDN MHS.

3.3 NDDN MHS USE OF X.400

The NDDN Message Handling System is based upon the CCITT MHS. The NDDN
MHS gives two types of message services, a formal and an informal
message service. In the formal service the User Agent serves one or
more addressees. Each User Agent is controlled by traffic operators,
and the traffic operators may also assist the end users at the staff
cells. The same User Agent also serves one or more informal addressees.
In the informal service the addressee is one specific user or a group
of users. The traffic operators are not supposed to assist these
addressees.

CCITT MHS adaptions

 Most of the CCITT specified MHS functions are used in the NDDN MHS.
The NDDN specified MHS functions are summarized in section 4.4 and 4.5.
However, the use of some of these functions deviates to some extent
from the use specified in the CCITT MHS. The intention of the following
is to describe these deviations.

 In the formal message service the "non-delivery notification"
function is only used when the message envelope is damaged. In the
CCITT MHS it is specified that this function also may be used if the
MTA is not able to deliver the message to the intended recipient. In
the NDDN MHS an alternate recipient will always be available. As the
last possibility, the message may be printed out at the MTA and the
paper may be delivered to the recipient, for instance by courier. All
the MTA's are manned with one or more traffic operators.

 However, informal messages are not allowed to be delivered to an
alternate recipient. Thus in the informal message service the non-
delivery notification will be used when the User Agent is not available.

 The "non-receipt notification" function will only be used for the
informal message service. The recipient User Agent uses this function
to deny receipt of a message when the specified informal addressee does
not exist at this User Agent.

 The "receipt notification" function will be used to explicitly
inform the originator that the message is received by the addressee and
that the purpose of the message is understood. (this is message acknowledgement as defined in ACP121). The notification is generated and sent
to the originator when an end user (serving the addressee) instructs
the User Agent to acknowledge the message.

 The sensitivity indication function and the precedence function
defined in CCITT MHS will have more levels in NDDN MHS. The levels will
be according to the security classifications and precedence levels defined in ACP121.

Additional functions

 The requirements for a military message handling system are specified
in ACP121 and ACP127. To fulfil the military requirements some enhancements to the X.400 have been specified in the NDDN MHS.

 Some new message heading components have been defined, for instance the Subject Indicator Code component to be used by the User
Agent for message distribution. Official addresslists have also been
introduced together with exempt addressees.

 In the NDDN MHS the User Agent may receive a message addressed to
an addressee not served by this User Agent (the addressee may have
moved). Then the traffic operator must be able to route this message to
the User Agent he believes serves the addressee. The mechanism used in
ACP127 to handle this situation, is placing a pilot in front of the
message. A similar function is also specified in the NDDN MHS.

Another new function in the NDDN MHS at the User Agent Layer, is
the message type indication. The User Agent uses this function to distinguish between four types of messages.:

- formal messages
- service messages (a part of the formal message service)
- exercise messages (a part of the formal message service)
- informal messages

Based on this information the User Agent may process these types of
messages in a different way.

At the Message Transfer Layer only one additional function has
been specified. This is an indication whether the message needs secured
(encrypted) message transfer or not.

X.400 functions not used

There are also functions specified in the X.400 which will not be used
in the NDDN MHS.

For instance the delivery notification function is not used. In
the formal message service the User System and the Message Switch will
be manned with traffic operators. If a message can not be delivered to
a recipient User Agent, the traffic operator will take care of the
message. The originator may trust to the system.

4. THE NDDN MESSAGE HANDLING PROTOCOLS

4.1 STANDARD ACCESS

The computer based User Systems will gain access to the Message Transfer System via the Submission and Delivery protocol denoted P3'. This
protocol is based on the P3 protocol specified in X.411.

The P3' protocol is defined between a Submission and Delivery
Entity (SDE) and a Message Transfer Agent Entity (MTAE). Either of
these entities may initiate an interaction and request that an operation is performed. Then the other entity tries to execute that operation and reports the result to the initiator of the operation. The
result may be of three types. These are success, failure or rejection.
The reject result reports that the malformed message has been received.
The failure result reports that the operation could not be completed.
The P3' makes use of the procedures and formats for remote operations
as defined in X.410.

The following operations are defined in P3':

- submit
  The submit operation allows the SDE to request that the MTAE
  transfers a message to the recipients.

- delivery
  The delivery operation allows the MTAE to deliver a message to
  the SDE. The SDE may reject to receive the message if the message
  is malformed or the access control is violated. The SDE is not
  allowed to reject the reception of a message if it is wellformed
  and the access control is not violated.

- notify
  The notify operation allows the MTAE to transfer non-delivery
  notifications to the SDE.

- control
  This operation controls the access to the Message Transfer
  System.

The submission or the delivery operation may fail because the submitted
or delivered message is malformed. In both cases the operation has to
be repeated.

4.2 TELETEX ACCESS

Another possible access method is the Teletex access protocol denoted
P5'. This protocol is based upon the P5 protocl specified in the recommendation X.430. It has not been decided whether the P5' protocol actually will be implemented in the Message Switch. This will be evaluated.

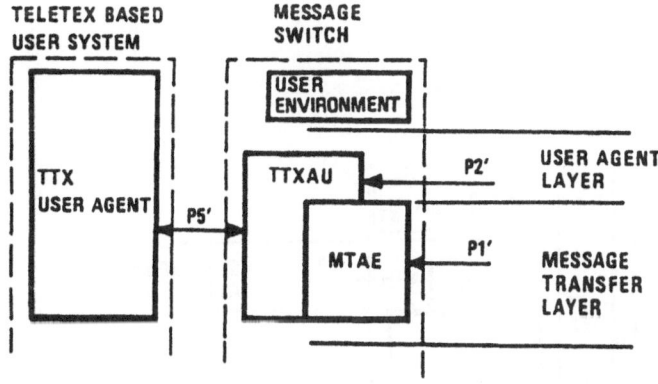

Fig. 9: Teletex access.

The P5' protocol is defined between the Teletex terminal and the TTXAU
(Teletex access unit) in the Message Switch (see figure 9). Either the
Teletex terminal or the TTXAU may initiate operations or actions as it
is called in X.430. The P5' protocol gives the same types of operations
as the P5' protocol.

An action is composed of one or more Teletex documents. The first
document contains the components of the message envelope and the message heading. This document also contains information about the number
of documents that is associated with this one and together form a message. The message body is put into the next documents. This mechanism
gives an unambiguous separation of the message heading/envelope and the
message body.

The P5' protocol uses humanreadable encoding. It means that the
components of the message envelope and the message heading are identified by text symbols. For instance the action addressee component of
the message heading is identified by the text symbol "TO:". This encoding is similar to the method used in the ACP127 procedure.

One disadvantage of the P5' protocol is that the Teletex terminal
is not able to interrupt an action, start another action and then resume the first one. The Teletex terminal are allowed to interrupt an
action, but then it must resume this action as the first thing when the
Teletex terminal continues the interaction with the TTXAU. Otherwise
the Teletex terminal have to discard the interrupted action and perform
the whole action once more at a later time.

4.3 ACP 127 ACCESS

Existing teleprinter equipment will gain access to the Message Transfer
Service via the ACP127 procedure.

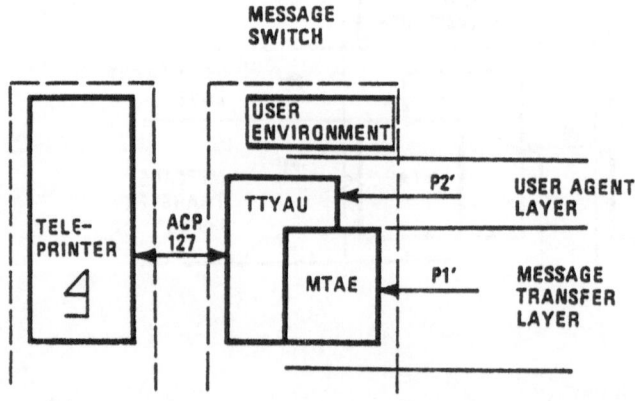

Fig. 10: ACP127 access.

The ACP127 procedure is defined between the teleprinter and the TTYAU
(Teletype access unit) in the Message Switch. This is illustrated in
figure 10.

No changes has been made in the ACP127 procedure, so the
teleprinters may be operated in the same way as in the existing Tape
Relay System.

4.4 USER AGENT LAYER

4.4.1 Service elements specified in X.400. The service provided by the
User Agent Layer (UAL) is described by a set of service elements. Most
of the UAL service elements specified in X.400 are also specified in
the NDDN MHS. This section summarizes the X.400 specified UAL service
elements provided in NDDN MHS.

The UAL service elements are divided into four service groups in
the NDDN MHS. The first group consists of those service elements provided by the Message Transfer Layer (see section 4.5) In the second group
you find the basic service elements at the User Agent Layer. The third
group consists of elements that require actions by the originating or
the recipient User Agent Entities in order to provide the service elements. As opposite to the group 3 service elements, the group 4 service
elements only convey information from the originating to the recipient
User Agents. No action is performed at the User Agent Layer to provide
group 4 service elements.

The service elements in group 2 are the Typed Body and the Message
Identification. The Typed Body conveys information about the body type
together with the body itself. The Message Identification is generated
by the User Agent. It is composed of three elements:

-    the name of the originating User Agent
-    the date and time the identification was generated
-    the serial number.

The serial number combined with the date and time gives a unique
identification of the message within the originating User Agent. The
name of the User Agent makes this identification global.

The service elements in the group 3 are the Receipt Notification
and the Non-receipt Notification.

Table 2 gives a short description of the group 4 service elements.
Table 2 also shows whether a similar function is provided in today's
system based on ACP121 and ACP127.

4.4.2 NDDN enhancements.

To fulfil the military requirements, the X.400 specified set of UAL
service elements has been enhanced in NDDN MHS. Table 3 summarizes
these service elements.

SERVICE ELEMENT DEFINED IN X.400	DESCRIPTION OF THE SERVICE ELEMENT	ACP121 FUNCTION?
ORIGINATOR INDICIATION	THE MILITARY ORGANIZATION THAT THE MESSAGE IS SENT ON BEHALF OF.	YES
AUTHORIZING USERS INDICATION	THE NAME OF THE PERSON(S) THAT AUTHORIZED THE SENDING OF THE MESSAGE.	
PRIMARY AND COPY ADDRESSEE INDICIATION	PRIMARY ADDRESSEES MUST TAKE ACTION ON THE RECEIVED MESSAGE. COPY ADDRESSEES RECEIVE THE MESSAGE FOR INFORMATION.	YES
EXPIRY DATE INDICATION	THE TIME AND DATE AFTER WHICH THE MESSAGE IS OF NO VALUE.	
CROSS-REFERENCING INDICATION	THE REFERENCE TO ONE OR MORE MESSAGES ASSOCIATED WITH THIS MESSAGE.	
IMPORTANCE INDICATION	THE PRECEDENCE (PRIORITY) OF THE MESSAGE BEING SENT.	YES
SENSITIVITY INDICATION	THE SECURITY CLASSIFI-CATION OF THE MESSAGE BEING SENT.	YES
SUBJECT INDICIATION	A SUBJECT DESCRIPTION OF THE MESSAGE BEING SENT.	YES
BODY PART ENCRYPTION INDICATION	A BODY PART MAY BE MARKED TO INDICATE THAT IT IS ENCRYPTED.	
MULTI-PART BODY	THE MESSAGE BODY MAY BE PARTITIONED INTO SEVERAL PARTS.	
REPLY REQUEST INDICATION	THE ORIGINATOR WANTS A REPLY FROM THE ADDRESSEE.	
REPLYING MESSAGE INDICATION	THE MESSAGE IS MARKED AS BEING THE REPLY TO ANOTHER MESSAGE.	
FORWARDED MESSAGE INDICATION	THE BODY OF THE MESSAGE BEING SENT CONTAINS A FORWARDED MESSAGE.	YES

Table 2: Information conveying UAL Service Elements.

SERVICE ELEMENT	REFERENCE TO SIMILAR FUNCTION IN ACP121/ACP127.
ADDRESSLISTS AND EXEMPT ADDRESSEES	COLLECTIVE ADDRESS GROUPS, ADDRESS INDICATION GROUPS AND EXEMPT ADDRESSEES
DTG INDICATION	THE DATE-TIME GROUP OF THE MESSAGE
COPY PRIORITY	PRECEDENCE FOR INFOR- MATION ADDRESSEES
SIC INDICATION	SUBJECT INDICATOR CODE FOR MESSAGE DISTRIBUTION
SPECIAL HANDLING INDICATION	SPECIAL HANDLING DESIGNATION
ORIGINATOR'S REFERENCE NUMBER	ORIGINATOR'S REFERENCE NUMBER
CODRESS ENCRYPTED BODY INDICATION	GROUP COUNT
REROUTED INDICATION	PILOT
TRANSMISSION INSTRUCTIONS	TRANSMISSION INSTRUCTIONS
MESSAGE INSTRUCTIONS	MESSAGE INSTRUCTIONS
MESSAGE TYPE INDICIATION	

Table 3: NDDN enhancements at UAL.

The enhancements make the NDDN MHS capable of cooperating with today's
message system based on ACP121 and ACP127. The service elements are
similar to the group 4 service elements, they only convey information
from the originator to the recipients.

The Message type Indication service element is introduced to make
it possible to distinguish between four types of message. These four
types are formal, service, exercise and informal messages.

4.5 THE MESSAGE TRANSFER LAYER

4.5.1 Service elements specified in X.400.

The service provided by the Message Transfer Layer (MTL) is described by a set of service elements. Most of the MTL service elements specified in X.400 at the Message Transfer Layer are also specified in the NDDN MHS. Table 4 summarizes the X.400 specified MTL service elements provided in NDDN MHS.

SERVICE ELEMENT DEFINED IN X.400	DESCRIPTION OF THE SERVICE ELEMENT
ACCESS MANAGEMENT	AUTHENTICATION BETWEEN UA AND MTA.
CONTENT TYPE INDICATION	THE TYPE OF PROTOCOL USED AT THE USER AGENT LAYER.
CONVERTED INDICATION	A CONVERSION OF THE CONTENT HAS BEEN PERFORMED BY MTS.
DELIVERY TIME STAMP INDICATION	THE DATE AND TIME THE MTS DELIVERED THE MESSAGE TO THE RECIPIENT UA.
MESSAGE IDENTIFICATION	UNIQUE IDENTIFIER OF THE MESSAGE WITHIN THE MTS.
NON-DELIVERY NOTIFICATION	NOTIFICATION TO THE ORIGINATING UA THAT THE MESSAGE WAS NOT DELIVERED.
ORIGINAL ENCODED INFORMATION TYPES INDICATION	AN INDICATION OF WHICH INFORMATION TYPES THAT ARE PRESENT IN THE CONTENT OF THE MESSAGE.
REGISTERED ENCODED INFORMATION TYPES	THE ENCODED INFORMATION TYPES THAT THAT THE UA IS ABLE TO HANDLE.
SUBMISSION TIME STAMP INDICATION	THE DATE AND TIME THE MESSAGE WAS SUBMITTED TO THE MTS.
ALTERNATE RECIPIENT ALLOWED	IF NECESSARY, THE MESSAGE MAY BE DELIVERED TO AN ALTERNATE RECIPIENT.
GRADE OF DELIVERY SELECTION	THE PRECEDENCE OF THE MESSAGE.
MULTI-DESTINATION DELIVERY	THE MESSAGE IS DELIVERED TO SEVERAL RECIPIENTS.
IMPLICIT CONVERSION	THE MTS MAY PERFORM ANY NECESSARY CONVERSION.
HOLD FOR DELIVERY	THE MTS MAY HOLD MESSAGES FOR DELIVERY UNTIL A LATER TIME.

Table 4: MTL service elements.

4.5.2 NDDN enhancements

At the Message Transfer Layer only one additional service element has been specified. This is the Security Warning service element. This service element is used when the message has to be transmitted on a secure (encrypted) connection.

5. GATEWAY TO OTHER SYSTEMS

There is a requirement for interoperation between the national strategic message handling system, NDDN MHS, and the strategic NATO systems. NDDN MHS also have to interoperate with various tactical systems.

The gateways to other systems will be implemented in two different ways, either in the Message Switch or as separate system units. The latter probably could benefit from a development based on the User System hardware and software. If the capacity requirements can be met, this might well lead to an integration of this type of gateways in ordinary User Systems. However, this has not yet been decided.

The Message Switches will contain the following gateways to other systems as part of the first implementation step:

- national Tape Relay network (existing teleprinter system)
- NICS TARE

Other gateways will be specified later, as separate units, among them gateways to the following systems:

- NORCCIS
- TADKOM (national tactical delta system)
- maritime communication systems
- radiosystems for land

5.1 GATEWAY TO NATIONAL TAPE RELAY SYSTEM

The stepwise implementation strategy leads to the requirement for this gateway, and ACP127 is the required procedure. This is equivalent to the handling of teleprinter access to the Message Switch, which already have been described in section 4.3, "ACP127 access".

5.2 GATEWAY TO NICS TARE

NICS TARE is NATO's message transfer network, and is based on the use of ACP127 both as access method and internodal procedure. On the link level NICS have defined an error detection and control procedure, EDC, that have to be implemented in the NDDN Message Switch. NICS TARE specifies different channel operations. Synchronous full duplex operation with EDC is the one selected for the gateway. On the higher levels, the ACP127 procedure will be implemented in a way that will be understood by the NICS TARE.

6. IMPLEMENTATION SCHEDULE

Figure 11 shows the planned time schedule for the NDDN Message Handling System. It reflects a realistic implementation plan from the technical point of view, but it may be changed for financial reasons, in particular the latest implementation steps. The invitation for tender will be sent to interested industrial parties at the end of march this year, after a specification period of more than two years.

NDDN MHS	1983	1984	1985	1986	1987	1988	1989
SPECIFICATIONS	———						
INDUSTRIAL COMMENTS		– – –					
1ST IMPLEMENTATION STEP:							
INVITATION FOR TENDER			X				
CONTRACT			X				
INSTALLATION						———	
IMPLEMENTATION OF USER SYSTEMS:							
INVITATION FOR TENDER				X			
CONTRACT				X			
INSTALLATION							———
IMPLEMENTATION OF SMALL USER SYSTEMS:							
SPECIFICATION				– – –			
INVITATION FOR TENDER					X		
CONTRACT					X		
INSTALLATION							———

Fig. 11: NDDN MHS - implementation schedule.

7. CONCLUSIONS

The Message Handling System for the Norwegian Defence Digital Network
has been designed to meet the military requirements set by the Chief of
Defence. One of the design criteria has been to use standard protocols
and technology from the civil community as far as possible. The CCITT
recommendation X.400 was selected, and we are aware of that this decision will lead to development of a new product class deviating from
existing equipment for message handling. However, we have received
signals that the industry are willing to take that risk because they
believe this is the technology of the near future in the civil marketplace. The indicated time schedule fits well into the implementation
schedule of the NDDN network, and the CCITT X.400 matured in time to be
taken into account in the specification of the NDDN MHS.

Session 6

Security and Validation

Session Chairman: Christian Köhler

COMPUTER NETWORKING, INTERNETWORKING, AND SECURITY

Howard S. Weiss
Network Security Division
Office of Research and Development
U.S. Department of Defense Computer Security Center

ABSTRACT

This paper will present the concepts of computer networking, internetworking, and security as applied to networks. The paper will cover
various networking techniques and the U.S. Department of Defense (DoD)
concept of internetting - that is, the interconnection of independent
and different technology networks. Also, current concepts in
network/internetwork security will be discussed.

1. INTRODUCTION

The U.S. Department of Defense (DoD) is a very strong proponent of
computer networking and internetworking. There are thousands of
computers under the aegis of the DoD which are geographically dispersed
and have the need to communicate with one another. Even more critical,
these computers need to communicate with each other in a secure
fashion. DoD has and is sponsoring a great deal of network and
internetworking research. The DoD Computer Security Center, as well as
other DoD agencies, is sponsoring and performing research to provide
secure networking and internetworking. This paper will examine, from a
background standpoint, how networking came to be, where internetworking
is taking us, and what the means are for providing security in such an
environment.

2. NETWORKING AND PACKET SWITCHING

The networking technology currently being utilized throughout the
networking community is packet switching. The concept of packet
switching was first developed in the early 1960's. (1) Early work on
defining the packet-switching concept was done at the RAND Corporation.
The RAND study described a distributed network that was both survivable
and broke up its digital transmission of data into entities called
packets. The National Physical Laboratory (NPL), in the United Kingdom,
was also studying computer networking during the same period of time.

R. W. G. Herbers (ed), The Upper Layers of Open Systems Interconnection, 155–167.
© 1987 by D. Reidel Publishing Company.

The NPL work proposed a network architecture similar to the one proposed by RAND. The NPL work went a bit farther though, proposing not
only packet transmission of data but also interface computers between
the hosts and the network and switching nodes on the network backbone.

The U.S. DoD was an early sponsor of research in computer networking and packet switching. Throughout the mid-1960's, the Defense
Advanced Research Projects Agency (DARPA) heralded packet switching as
the networking technology of the future. DARPA had generated enough
interest in the concept of packet switching by 1969 to fund the
development of a packet-switching network that came to be known as the
ARPANET.

DARPA awarded the ARPANET contract to Bolt, Beranek, and Newman
(BBN) of Cambridge, Massachusetts in January 1969. (1) The contract
required BBN to build several packet-switching nodes, install them, and
test them with several host computers connected. The first ARPANET
packet switching node, called an Interface Message Processor (IMP), was
installed in December 1969 at the University of California at Los
Angeles (UCLA). The next three packet switches were installed at the
University of California Santa Barbara (UCSB), the Stanford Research
Institute (SRI), and the University of Utah. The packet switches were
linked by wideband telephone circuits. By june 1970, five more packet
switches were added to the network: System Development Corporation
(SDC) and the RAND Corporation, both in Santa Monica, California; Bolt
Beranek, and Newman (BBN), Massachusetts Institute of Technology (MIT),
and Harvard University, all in Cambridge, Massachusetts.

The ARPANET has undergone a continual evolution since the first
installations. The routing algorithms have undergone several revisions,
bugs have been worked out, the network protocols have undergone revisions and have been completely changed, and the network has grown
significantly. These will be discussed in the next section on internetworking.

Over the years, networking has grown tremendously. In the U.S.,
there are two public, packet-switching networks, TELENET and TYMNET,
which provide network access for subscribers. Interestingly, TELENET
was a direct spinoff from the development of the ARPANET with BBN
providing the startup financing as well as the technical expertise.
TYMNET grew into a public network after originally being built to
support the Tymshare Corporation's computer time-sharing business.

Local area networking has exploded in the last few years with the
introduction of the Xerox ETHERNET (5). Many vendors now sell-off-the-
shelf local area network (LAN) products and several more sell custom
local networks to support their office automation or distributed
processing systems. The agreement between Xerox, Intel, and Digital
Equipment Corporation to support a standard ETHERNET product has
provided even more impact in the LAN market.

Although the ETHERNET has become a de facto standard, several
other LAN technologies have been introduced and have been catching on
in the market place. Broadband and ring networks, in competiton with
the baseband ETHERNET, have been gaining popularity among users and

many systems have been installed. LAN has become so popular and widespread that the Institute for Electrical and Electronics Engineers
(IEEE) has adopted a standards document for LANs. The IEEE 802 document
provides standards for manufacturers for bulding LAN. The IEEE document
specifies standards for three technologies - baseband, broadband, and
ring.

3. INTERNETWORKING

The explosións in computer networking technology quickly created a need
to interconnect networks. Packet switching has come of age and has
become understandable, affordable, and available. The concept of the
"internet" (interconnected networks) was developed.

There were several reasons for the move towards interconnection.
For example, within laboratories, various sections having their own
computers might need to be networked together. LAN technology provides
the solution. Taking this a step further, it might be necessary to
exchange information between various sections in the same lab facility,
each having their own separate LAN. It might also be necessary for
sections in different laboratories, geographically dispersed, to
exchange data. The need for individual LANs capable of communicating
with one another, as well as with long-haul networks, demanded action.
In addition, the geographically distributed laboratories might be
connected to different long haul networks. This created a requirement
for long haul networks to communicate with one another. Requirements
such as these created the environment for the investigation of how to
interconnect and interoperate networks based on differing technologies
and operating in different manners.

For the U.S. DoD, internetworking provides maximum interoperability between the various laboratories and agencies, allows alternate
routing to create a more robust and dependable communications system,
and allows for the reconstitution of broken network pieces.

DARPA has sponsored the bulk of the research in internetworking
within the U.S. and has entered into agreements with foreign government
research agencies to perform additional cooperative internet research.
The DARPA experimental INTERNET is made up of many independent networks
interconnected by a system of internet gateways. Currently, 185
networks are listed in the DARPA Internet Host Table (7) and there are
over 3000 uniquely assigned networks numbers. (9)

The U.S. Defense Communications Agency (DCA) is now operationally
charged with operating the DoD's internetwork system, the Defense Data
Network (DDN). The DDN has encapsulated the strategic digital
networking capabilities within the DoD. The original ARPANET has become
a part of the DDN and has been split into two independent networks, the
operational MILNET, and the research-oriented ARPANET. The MILNET and
ARPANET are linked together via a set of internet gateways and are run
as completely unclassified networks. Although part of the DDN system,
several other networks are not interconnected, for security reasons, to
the unclassified DDN networks.

The concept of the internet gateway has allowed the
interconnection of differing networks based on the premise that all the
networks run a common set of high-level protocols. The entity known as
the gateway can be thought of as a network host which is connected to
more than one network. It is the job of the gateway to forward packets
from one network to another by interpreting the address information
resident in the packet. The gateway is a smart device that knows how to
communicate with the networks it connects and also knows how to interpret addressing conventions for the different networks. It also knows
about the existence of other gateways in order to route data to networks to which it is not directly attached. A pictorial view of networks connected by internet gateways is shown in Figure 1.

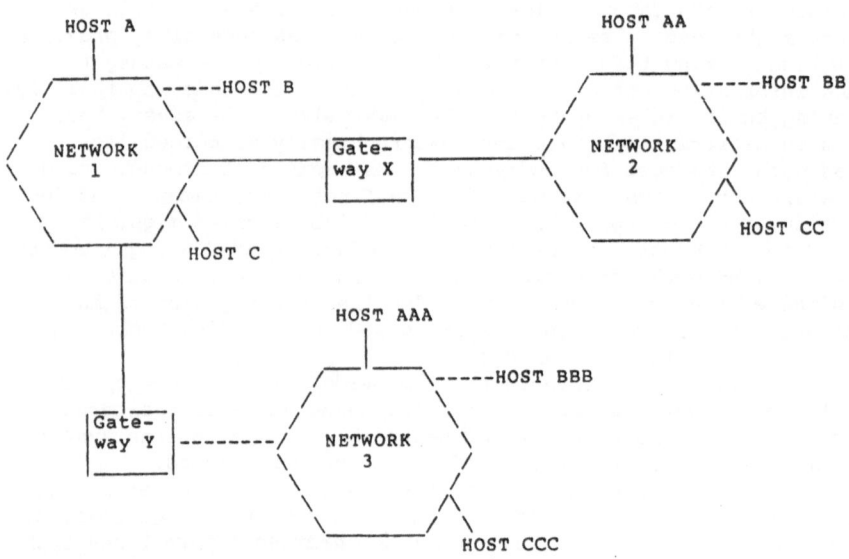

Figure 1: INTERNET gateways interconnecting networks.

The common set of protocols assumed to be running on the various
networks are the DoD standard protocol suite, TCP/IP (transmission
control protocol/internet protocol). The various networks can be based
on radically different technologies at their lowest levels, but they
can communicate if they support the standard higher-level protocols
(TCP/IP). As will be discussed in later sections, the gateway system is
dependent only on the common usage of the internet protocol (IP) while

various hosts may make use of different protocols, common to themselves, which run on top of the IP. The concept of protocol layering
allows for this layer independence of protocols.

Protocol layering plays a very important role in the design and
implementation of the internet system. The DoD has defined its own
protocol layering model which resembles the International Standards
Organizations's Open Systems Interconnect (ISO OSI) model but has been
specifically adapted for the DoD. The model has not been officially
adopted as a standard as of this writing. The proposed DoD model is
shown in Figure 2.

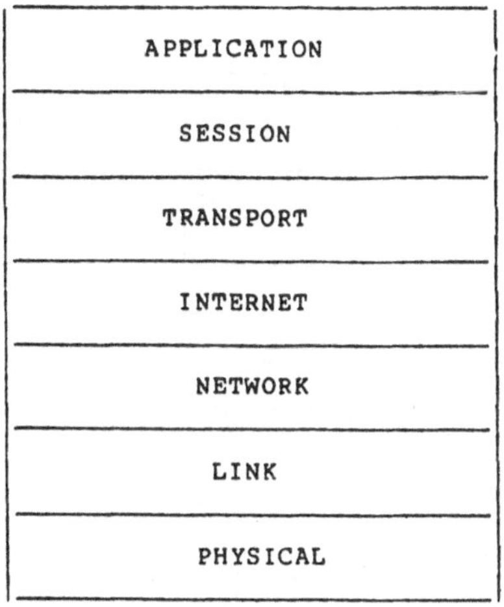

| APPLICATION |
| SESSION |
| TRANSPORT |
| INTERNET |
| NETWORK |
| LINK |
| PHYSICAL |

Figure 2: The proposed DoD protocol reference model.

To digress for a moment, an explanation of the makeup of the various
protocol layers of the proposed DoD model would be in order. The lowest
levels of a network's specific protocol implementation would encompass
the physical, link, and network layers. (See fig. 2.) The physical
layer could be an electrical interface such as RS-232 (V.24), RS-449
(V.11), or ARPANET 1822. (2) The link level could be a framing protocol
such as HDLC (hierarcical data link control), or the ARPANET 1822. The
network level could be the X.25 level three, packet protocol or the
ARPANET 1822 host-to-IMP protocol.

The protocol hierarchy layering of the DoD standard protocol suite appears in Figure 3. This figure is meant only to be illustrative, not exhaustive, in its display of the different protocols which can operate at the various levels of the proposed DoD Reference Model.

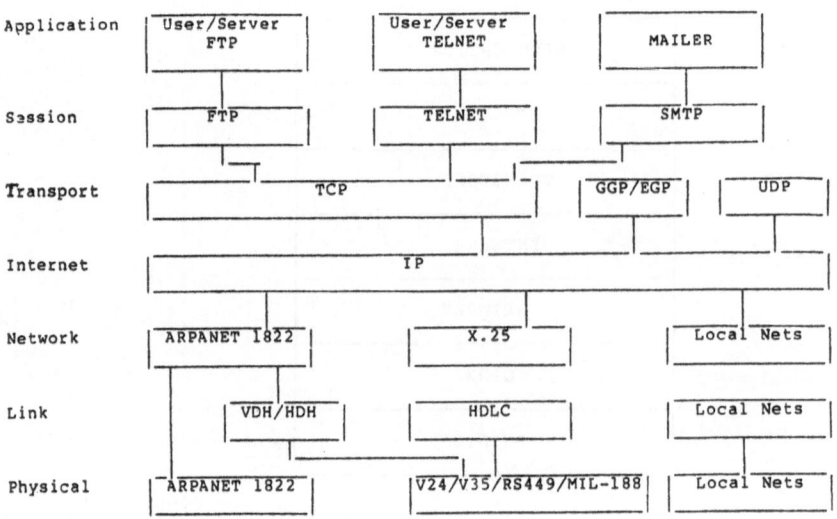

Figure 3: DoD protocol layering hierarchy.

The operation of the internet gateway is based on the use of IP in the internet layer. As is shown in Figure 3, all the protocol layers, except the internet layer, allow various, alternative protocols to be used. The internet layer specifies one, and only one protocol, IP. IP can be thought of as the common protocol that all systems use if they want to communicate via the DoD INTERNET. The host computers attached to the various networks are only interested in the transport layer and the layers running above transport (session and utility). Each level of

protocol has a specific purpose. The following paragraphs will help to
refine the concept of protocol layering and how it is used within the
DoD INTERNET system.

A good analogy to the protocol-layering hierarchy is the peeling
off of onion skins. When one peels an onion, layers of skin must
successively be removed to reach the bare onion. Now think of the
various layers of protocol as layers of onion skin and the actual data
being sent on the network as the underlying onion. The various network
devices peel off layers of protocol in order to eventually reach the
actual data. In the world of the ARPANET, the layers of protocol within
the network header appear as illustrated in Figure 4.

1822 Network Header	Internet Protocol Header	TCP or other Transport Protocol Header	..... D A T A .....

Figure 4: ARPANET header protocol layering.

In the ARPANET, the physical and link layers are combined in the
ARPANET 1822 electrical level interface. This hardware interface
consists of ten signal wire pairs which perform a bit serial handshake
to transfer data from the host to the packet switch. What is shown as
the 1822 network header in Figure 4 is the network layer. This is the
protocol layer that the ARPANET packet switches examine to perform
their packet delivery and routing function. The internet protocol
header shown in Figure 4 is the internet protocol layer and is simply
passed on as data by the packet switch. The internet header is examined
only when or if the packet is passed to an internet gateway. If the
packet does not go through a gateway, it is essentially ignored. The
TCP header shown is also passed as data by the packet switch and is
examined by the host receiving the packet. This header contains packet
sequence numbers, flow control information, and port numbers to identify the higher-level protocol services required by the packet. TCP is
the transport-level protocol used by hosts to communicate in a reliable
fashion. If the host does not need reliable communications, other
protocols can be used (e.g., the user datagram protocol). The internet
gateways communicate amongst themselves for routing purposes using the
gateway-to-gateway protocol (GGP) or the external gateway protocol
(EGP), both of which run in the transport layer above the IP.

Each host computer on the ARPANET has established an internal
table of gateways which can be used to address packets to "foreign"
networks. In essence, if a user on a host sends packets from his host
(i.e., host A on network number 1) to another host (i.e., host BB on
network number 2), the sending host checks the network number in the
packet address. It knows its home network is number 1 and sees that the
packet is being addressed to another network, namely number 2. To
accomplish this task, the host looks in its table of gateways to see
what path is defined to move packets from network 1 to network 2. When
it finds a gateway, it routes the packet to that gateway by placing the
gateway's address on network 1 into the network specific header (i.e.,
1822 network header) of the packet. Meanwhile, the true destination
address is retained in the internetwork header. The following example
will further illustrate this concept.

The host has looked in it's gateway table and determined that the
host known as X - which is actually a gateway - is the place to send
the packet. Host (gateway) X is attached to both network number 1 and
2. When X receives the packet from host A on network 1, it examines the
internet header, sees that the final destination of the packet is on
network 2 (to which it is directly attached), builds a new network
specific header, and sends the packet off for final delivery. The new
network specific header might be an ARPANET header but could just as
well be an ETHERNET or some other network specific type of header. In
cases where there are intermediate networks which must be traversed
before the packet is finally delivered, the gateway must decide what
other gateway to route the packet to and insert that gateway's address
into the network specific header. A system of interconnected networks
is illustrated in Figure 1.

4. SECURITY

The increasing use of computer networking and the continuing
interconnection of networks creates the need for network security.
There is a need to protect the data which resides on the various
computers which are attached to the interconnected networks as well as
the data which traverses the networks.

In network and internetwork security there is a basic dividing
line between work being performed to provide solutions for today's
"real world" problems and research meant to provide payoffs in the long
term. Historically, much of the network security work has involved
encryption. Research is now examining methods in which encryption may
not be needed and, also where computer security technology can be
combined with encryption. The following paragraphs will discuss these
two areas in order to give more insight into the currrent problems, how
they can be fixed with today's technology, and the research that will
prevent problems in the future.

4.1. THE RESEARCH WORLD

The DoD Computer Security Center is performing research on network and internetwork security from several different aspects - from writing a quantifiying document which will allow a security rating to be assigned to a network, to researching secure network protocols, to designing and building trusted network interface devices for a multilevel secure network.

A major task of the Center is to perform system analysis and to rate computer systems with respect to the DoD Trusted Computer System Evaluation Criteria. (4) Many commercial networks, especially LAMs, are being offered for sale by vendors as off-the-shelf systems. Many of these vendors have added what they call "network security" features to their networks and would like these networks to be evaluated by the Center. The Criteria, however, only addresses computer systems and not networks.

The Criteria specifies security classes which can be assigned to computer systems - from A, which is the highest, to D, which is the lowest. The Criteria requires that specific mechanisms must be incorporated in a system in order for it to obtain a specific security class. These required mechanisms differ, depending upon the security class desired. Many of the requirements of the Criteria are meaningless when applied to a computer network.

An example of this is where the Criteria requires that a system implement a discretionary access mechanism to obtain at least a class C rating. This means the system supports user and data separation based on access permissions. It is not clear how this requirement would map onto a computer network when the network is being evaluated without any attached hosts. This leads to the question - how do you evaluate the security of a network? Is it examined by itself or only in the environment in which it will be running (i.e., with hosts attached)? To answer these questions and provide a document against which networks can be analyzed and evaluated, the Center is in the process of writing a criteria which is specifically targeted at networking.

Security with respect to network protocols is an area of great activity. The current DoD standard protocols provide for reliable communications and offer some security protection. TCP, for example, provides a means of placing sequence numbers on each packet. The sequence numbers are placed on each packet transmitted by the sending TCP and are checked by the receiving TCP. The receiving TCP must acknowledge the receipt of each packet using the sequence numbers. This feature allows the protocol to make sure that all packets of a message are sent and received properly and that no packets have been inserted or deleted from the message. If any transmitted packets are not acknowledged within a preset time, they are retransmitted until either an acknowledgement is received or a preset number of retransmission is reached. If the retransmission fails, the sending protocol marks the receiver as not responding and notifies the user. The acknowledgement and retransmission scheme allows for the reliable transmission and reception of data across all types of underlying networks, without regard to their reliability.

Formal, software verification techniques are being examined for application in the building of secure networks or secure network components. Work at several universities and laboratories on network protocol specification verification attempts to formally examine the potential operation of protocols with respect to their correctness. (10) In its fullest form, a formal, mathematical security model of the network is built and then a formal specification of the protocol is written in a specification language. The formal security model would display the security policy of the network. Verification tools such as verification condition generators and theorem provers would then be used to check the correctness of the formal specification with respect to the formal model. The protocol would then be implemented based on the formally proven specification. The ultimate challenge pushing the current state-of-the-art in program verification is to use verification technology to prove the actual software implementation of the protocol. This has been done in very limited form on small systems (i.e., less than 2,000 lines).

Research is also in progress in using formal verification technology to build secure network components. This research is being based on the concept of the Trusted Computing Base (TCB). The TCB is heavily referenced in the DoD Trusted Computer System Evaluation Criteria. The Criteria given defines a TCB as: "The totality of protection mechanisms within a computer system - including hardware, firmware, and software - the combination of which is responsible for enforcing a security policy. It creates a basic protection environment and provides additional user services required for a trusted computer system." (4) Various network components have tasks that are security critical. For example, on a LAN using packet broadcast as its means of transmission trusts each of the network interface units to accept only those packets specifically addressed to that unit. The only assurances built into the interface units of commercially-available LANs are based on best commercial software practices. This means that the hardware and software has been checked out by the manufacturer, but one is usually not surprised if implementation or design bugs appear in the early deliveries of the system. By basing network components on formally-verified TCBs, it is hoped that the various devices can be built securely and proven to be secure.

A secure network device can imply that it is trusted to perform a specific task at a specific security level or imply that it can perform a number of tasks at different security levels. A single-level secure device is easier to design, prove, and build than a multilevel device. This can be seen upon reexamination of the previously discussed LAN. Suppose all of the network interface units on the LAN are single-level secure devices preset, in some secure manner, for a single level of transmission and reception. The basic task of these devices, then, is to add a fixed label specifying the security level of the packet being transmitted and making sure that any packet addressed for reception carries the specific classification level. Of course, this may cause problems in a real-world situation where there are network users at various classification levels. The paper world allows users with higher levels of classification access to come down to a lower level but not

vice-versa. For example, a classified user can access unclassified data
but an unclassified user cannot access any classified data. The single-
level LAN would not allow a higher-classification user to access lower-
level data or even communicate with a lower-level user. A specific
level could only communicate with that specific level. Doing anything
else would violate the single classification level rule that was
designed into the system.

The multilevel problem causes a much higher degree of checks to be
performed in the interface unit. The unit may be able to change its
level based on who a user is or may be resettable by a security officer. It may know its maximum level but also know that it can communicate with levels lower than its maximum. This hierarchy complicates the
design of the device but is the direction in which the world is moving.
Segregation of data with controlled sharing is what is needed and is
the area being addressed by research.

Securing an internet is a problem for the research world as well
as the real world. The internet exists today, and security is needed.
Some of the programs for providing security will be discussed in the
next section.

4.2. THE "REAL WORLD" SOLUTIONS

The work being performed in order to solve current problems is based on
earlier research. Much of the work revolves around protecting data
through the use of encryption techniques. Several projects are using
borrowed "computer security" technology to build secure network
devices.

To provide transmission security, encryption equipment can be used
on communications lines in a point-to-point fashion. Two computers
linked in a simple, telephone line fashion can be secured by using
encryption devices on each end of the telephone line. This concept is
termed "link encryption." Commercial encryption devices are being
manufacured by several U.S. companies. Several semiconductor
manufacurers are selling chips which implement various encryption
algorithms in hardware. The commercial availability of such products
effectively gives everyone the ability to use encryption to protect
data.

To secure a full network using link encryption techniques is very
expensive because of the number of encryption devices involved. The
numbers can grow quickly because the data routed through the network
packet switches must be decrypted on entrance into the switch and then
reencrypted upon exit. Since the packet switch itself does not know how
to deal with encrypted data, an encryption device must be attached to
every communications line connected to every packet switch on the
network. These techniques can be used to build a secure network where
all the packet switches are installed in secure facilites. One network
currently being built in such a manner is the DDN DISNET (Defense
Integrated Secure Network), an ARPANET technology network which is
secured to the DoD SECRET level. DISNET supplies a SECRET-level network

which allows host computers in at least SECRET-level facilities (whose
users are cleared to at least the SECRET level) to communicate with one
another at the SECRET level.

The Private Line Interface (PLI) is a network security device that
provides secure networking across otherwise unsecured networks. The PLI
was developed about ten years ago and is certified to provide secure
communications on the ARPANET. The PLI is a very expensive device consisting of two mini-computers and an encryption device that are inserted between the host computer and the network switch. A host interfaced
to a network in this manner only communicates with other hosts interfaced in the same way. The PLI, based on the use of the old ARPANET
protocol NCP (network control program), cannot operate in an internet
environment. A new device, the Internet Private Line Interface (IPLI)
is currently under development and will provide PLI-like security in an
internet environment. The IPLI uses the DoD standard protocol suite and
it's hardware is based on microprocessor technology. Modern technology
allows the device to be smaller and cheaper than its predecessor.

An internetwork security program aimed at providing a multilevel
secure internet is known as BLACKER. This project also uses the DoD
standard protocols and is implementing the concept of end-to-end
security. End-to-end security implies that data is secured from
terminal-to-terminal, host-to-host, terminal-to-host, and host-to-
terminal, regardless of the underlying network environment. BLACKER
uses the concept of access control to determine network access. Using
what is called an access controller, decisions can be made whether
network entities are allowed to communicate with one another or access
information. In addition, encryption is used on a connection-by-
connection basis with the encryption key for each connection different.
Also, the various BLACKER devices being built are employing such
computer security technology as formal, mathematical definitions of
program specifications and the proof of the formal specifications using
verification tools.

5. SUMMARY

This paper has presented the reader with a brief historical view of
networking and packet switching, the growth of internetworking, and
what is presently being done and being contemplated to secure networks
and interconnected networks. It is hoped that the information in this
paper was informative to those who are not familiar with the DoD
approach to internetting as well as those who are not familiar with DoD
approaches to network security. It should be realized that this paper,
because of classification constraints, is by no means a total
description of network security research and development.

6. REFERENCES

1.   Bolt, Beranek, and Newman; "A History of the ARPANET: The First
      Decade," Report #4799;Defense Advanced Research Projects Agency;
      April, 1981.

2.   Bolt, Beranek, and Newman; "Interface Message Processor -
      Specifications for the Interconnection of a Host and an IMP;"
      Report #1822; December 1981 Revision.

3.   Cerf, V.S., and Cain, E.A.; "The DoD Internet Architecture Model;"
      Computer Networks, Vol. 7, No. 5, North-Holland, October, 1983.

4.   Department of Defense Computer Security Center, "DoD Trusted
      Computer System Evaluation Criteria," CSC-STD-001-83; Aug., 1982.

5.   Digital, Intel, Xerox Corporations; The ETHERNET -A Local Area
      Network - Data Link Layer and Physical Layer Specifications;
      Version 2.0; Nov., 1982.

6.   Network Information Center; "Internet Protocol Transition
      Workbook;" SRI International! March, 1982.

7.   Network Information Center; On-line file "<netinfo>hosts.txt;" SRI
      International; December, 1984.

8.   Postel, J.; "Internet Protocol - DARPA Internet Program Protocol
      Specification;" RFC 791; Sept., 1981.

9.   Reynolds, J., and Postel, J.; "Assigned Numbers;" RFC 923;
      University of Southern California Information Sciences Institute;
      Oct. 1984.

10.   Shotting, K.; "On the Formal Specifications of Computer
      Communication Protocols;" TR-973; University of Maryland Master's
      Thesis; Dec. 1980.

11.   System Development Corporation; "DoD Protocol Reference Model
      (Draft);" TM-7172/201/00; Febr., 1982.x

SECURITY PROBLEMS IN DISTRIBUTED SYSTEMS

CH. Jahl
N. Ramsperger
IABG
Einsteinstr. 20
D-8012 Ottobrunn
FRG

ABSTRACT. From the short history of data processing it is known that
guaranteeing security in an ADP-system is a serious challenge. At the
present time, only a few centralized systems are emerging which seem to
meet this challenge to a certain extent. The demand becomes an even
more serious one if the systems are distributed. This paper considers
security problems in distributed systems from a general point of view.
To that end, it first clarifies the notions of security policy, security model, and security mechanisms as well as their relationships. It
then develops a set of generic security functions which seem necessary
and adequate in order to guarantee security for distributed systems.
These functions can be realized in different ways by appropriate combinations of organizational and technical measures. The generic security
functions are considered in the light of possible security threats
against different classes of distributed systems. A framework is developed which allows the classification of distributed systems with
regard to possible security threats. Applying this framework enables
one to draw conclusions concerning the security achieved of distributed
systems and the modifications which are necessary to make them more
secure.

CONTENT:

1. Introduction
2. Generic Security Functions
3. Classification Scheme
4. Application of the Classification Scheme
5. Discussion of the Generic Security Functions
6. Summary and Conclusions

R. W. G. Herbers (ed), The Upper Layers of Open Systems Interconnection, 169–194.
© 1987 by D. Reidel Publishing Company.

1. INTRODUCTION.

There has been a long debate concerning distributed computing to
support data processing needs of enterprises and large organizations.
In the recent past, two important factors have been evolved for the
reinstatment of this debate: first, it has become easier to connect
existing systems by means of new communication media. Thus, a compound
system consisting of interoperable subsystems is able to provide its
users with the union of services offered by the single systems. Second,
medium and small sized processing systems and especially the ubiquitous
micro processor make a rethink of the proper division of data processing support necessary. In order to arrive at a solution for a proper
division one has to be aware of the problems encountered therein, of
their importance, and of the possibilities to overcome them. One of the
major problems is concerned with security. Distributing a system adds a
new dimension to the security problem. In order to consider security
problems in distributed systems some notions will first be introduced
and explained.
        In a data processing system and its environment two kinds of
entities can be dinstinguished: active entities and passive entities
henceforth called **subjects** and **objects** respectively. Simple examples
are users and programs as subjects and data files as objects. A subject
can act or operate on an object. This can be done by reading, writing,
changing, or deleting it. In addition, there may be objects which can
be executed on behalf of a subject. Such an object temporarily becomes
a subject which itself may act on other objects. A simple example is a
data file containing an executable program. On the one hand, it is just
an object used by a subject "file system", on the other, after loading
and starting it becomes a subject. Another example is a utility program
invoked by a user in order to edit a certain file. Still another
example is a database system which handles a user's request to query
certain relations. Looking at the latter example from another point of
view, the database system can be conceived as being a subject which
temporarily becomes an object the execution of which takes place by
handling a message which contains the user's request.
        The database example gives reason to refine the notion of an
object: named results of predefined queries can be considered as being
abstract objects which are derived from basic objects namely the
relations. These abstract objects are called **views**. A view can, again,
be addressed by a query. Views are examples of the general concept of
implementing abstract objects by subjects and less abstract objects,
where subjects by acting on objects provide the higher level objects.
        In order to avoid potential chaos, rules have to be set up which
regulate the operations of subjects on objects. To that end, sets of
operations are defined which a certain subject is allowed to perform on
a certain object under certain conditions. This leads by itself to the
general rule that only those activities are allowed to be carried out
in the system which are explicitly defined. These definitions are
called **rights**. Somewhere in the system there must be mechanisms which
ensure this. In order to do so, the identities of the subjects and

objects involved must be determinned without any uncertainty. The
identity can be defined as the fulfillment of a set of provable
criteria established for that entity. E.g., for the subject "user" it
is quite common practice to prove only one criterium namely whether the
user knows his password. However, the same user may act in different
roles: e.g. as a member of a project team or as a person who is in
charge of certain administrative affairs. Dependent on the role he is
in, he possesses different rights. Thus, the role becomes an additional
criterium for the determination of the identity. The concept of roles
can, of course, be applied to programs also. E.g., an editor is in the
role of working on behalf of a certain user: the files it is then
allowed to act on are dependent on the user's rights.

After the user has been correctly identified, how can he be sure
that it is the correct subject inside the system he is interacting
with? How can he be sure that it is not a program which behaves like
the system but whose only intention is to spy out the user`s passwords?
This shows that, in principle, identification is mutual.

Up to now, only identities of subjects have been considered. This
still leaves the question of how to prove the identity of an object. If
the object is administered by a subject - as is a relation by a
database system - the subject has to take care of that. If, however,
the object is an independent entity - as is a private data storage
medium - its identifying criteria are eventually given by its content.
If the system is able to guarantee the integrity of this content a
small part of it - the so-called header information - will suffice.

Rights can be administered at several places in a system: e.g., a
certain subject's right to direct queries to a database system can be
controlled by the underlying operating system whereas the subject's
right to query certain relations should obviously be controlled in the
database system itself.

Even if it can be assured that only existing rights are exercised
there still remains the possibility that information can be inferred by
combining preexisting knowledge with the results of different read
accesses to data. This is a well-known problem in the area of
statistical databases. There are still other ways to gain information:
the observation of certain system states or of flow of data at a
certain point in time can mean valuable information to an expert.
Gaining information in these ways or by exercising rights is here
called **general information gaining**.

Now **data security** can informally be defined as the fulfillment of
well established requirements concerning the admissibility of general
information gaining as well as of performing operations on data. Also
the availability of services is often subsumed unter data security.

In order to achieve data security it has to be guaranteed that
only rights are exercised which are known to the system. To that end
technical and organizational measures have to be combined properly.
This can be illustrated by some simple examples: As a first example,
the rights have to be defined. This is the responsibility of a system
administrator who does so in accordance with the policies of his
organization. If, as another example, the organization guarantees that
only a certain user has access to a certain terminal there will be no

need for the system to further identify the user. If, as still another example, the organization guarantees that no undue replacement of programs can take place there is no need for their identification. These examples already show that overall security is composed of two parts complementing each other:

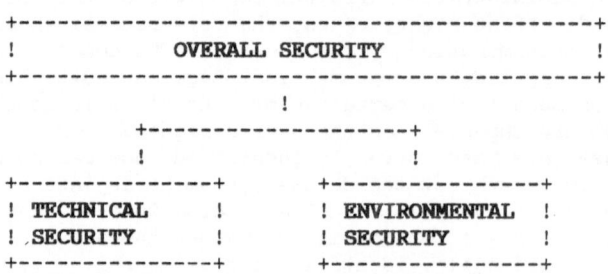

Figure 1.1; Overall Security

A proper functional division for the cooperation of technical and environmental security measures is not an easy task. It strongly depends on the progress on the technical side and on the treats expected on the environmental side.

The considerations above are valid for centralized as well as distributed systems. Clearly, the achievement of data security in distributed systems is a bigger challenge. Because of the lack of a generally accepted definition, what is understood by a **distributed system** is now defined in this paper.

A system is called distributed if
-    it consists of a not necessarily fixed number of autonomous subsystems (AS)
-    there are services offered by the system as a whole which are provided only in cooperation with several AS,
-    the AS are connected by a medium, the communication through which can be delayed in a non-deterministic way.

Figure 1.2 shows some activities in a distributed system: subject S1 of system AS1 wants to act upon object O which is administered by subject S2 in AS2. A potential additional load on the communication medium caused by AS3 may attribute to the non-deterministic communication delays.

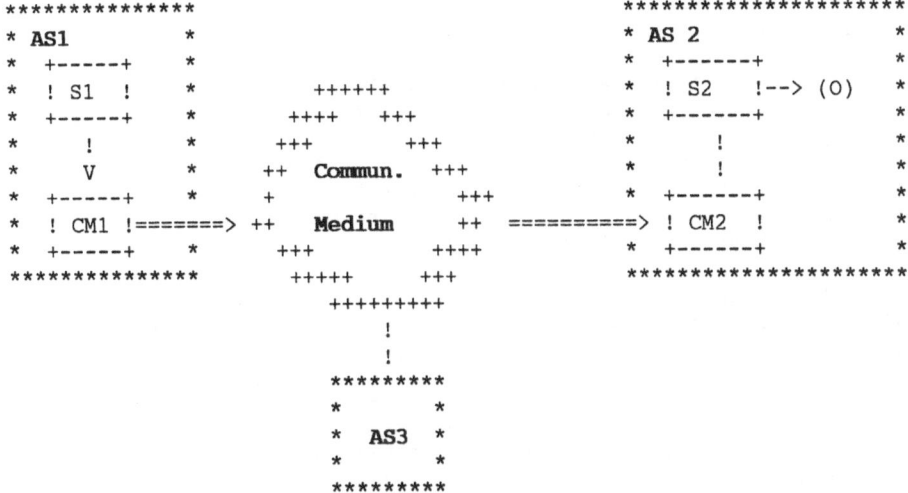

```
ASi: autonomous subsystem i
Si:  subject i
CMi: communication mechanism i
O:   object
```

Figure 1.2: Example of Distributred System

Figure 1.2 raises some additional distribution related questions: The
right for S1 to act on object O refers to entities in different
systems. Ensuring that this right is properly exercised makes a
cooperation between the two systems involved necessary. However, these
systems may belong to different organizations. Can it be guaranteed
that their respective security policies are not in conflict? Finally,
the communication medium might falsify transferred data and thus
influence the cooperation of the system in an undesired way.

2. GENERIC SECURITY FUNCTIONS

It is the purpose of this chapter to develop a set of generic security
functions (GSF). The GSF have to be implemented throughout the system
and its environment in such a way that they in joint operation
guarantee data security.

    At the very beginning of the development of a data processing
system **requirements** are established which describe in general what the
system is expected to do. Making these requirements more precise and
specific, results in a **specification** of the system. The specification
can be considered as being some kind of a model which precisely

describes the behavior of the system. Following the well known maxim "Divide and rule", the **construction** of the system is carried out by decomposing it into several components or functional units (FU) which in cooperation perform the tasks of the system. The result of this step is a description of the cooperation and the requirements which are to be met by the FUs. Thereafter, for every FU the construction process is recursively continued. After it has come to an end - no further decompositions are necessary - the FUs have to be realized and integrated into the higher level FUs. The integration process continues until the highest level - the system level - is reached.

Security aspects can be integrated into this classical construction method. Overall **security policies** be they dictated by legislation, by regulations of an enterprise, or by basic service regulations of a military organization - become part of the general system requirements. Making them more precise ideally leads to a formalized **security model** of the system. When the system is decomposed, decisions concerning the next lower level security policies have to be made which in turn lead to security models of the FUs. These models can be considered as being the **security mechanisms** of the system and are expected to implement the security policies which, on the one hand, the system itself has to obey, and which, on the other, it has to enforce upon the user.

There are some problems associated with this construction process: First, high level security policies often have a tendency to be ambiguous: e.g. if they, on the one hand, allow things to be done unless explicitly forbidden and, on the other, allow them to be done only in case of an explicit authorization, an unsolvable conflict may arise. Second, it can be difficult to express the intentions of a policy by means of a formal model: for example, if a booking-clerk has the right to make airline reservations only if asked for by a customer and if she performs a booking without being asked for, then she misuses her/his right. The irregularity of such an action can often only be recognized afterwards. Third, sometimes components already existing have to be taken into account by the construction process. The security mechanisms they offer may restrict the overall policy which can be implemented. Not least, policies are conceivable which are impossible to implement in a tolerably efficient way.

The integration of security aspects in a step of the construction process is depicted in figure 2.1 where an FU is decomposed into FUs'.

As was shown in fig. 1.1 overall security is achieved by a proper combination of technical security and environmental or organizational security. Environmental security has to be enforced by an overall authority. Technical security can be refined as in fig. 2.1. A corresponding refinement is possible for environmental security: there again policies describe the requirements to be fulfilled by the organization, organizational models make them more precise, and proper measures implement the policies. This leads to figure 2.2.

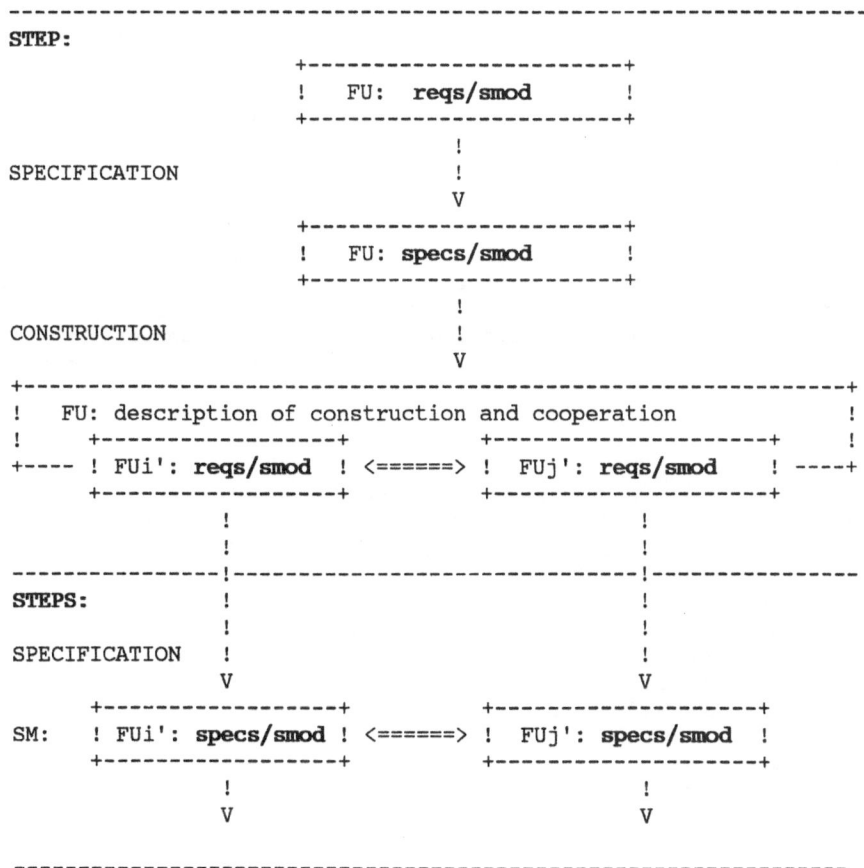

```
STEP:
                        +------------------------+
                        !   FU:  reqs/smod       !
                        +------------------------+

                                    !
SPECIFICATION                       !
                                    V
                        +------------------------+
                        !   FU:  specs/smod      !
                        +------------------------+

                                    !
CONSTRUCTION                        !
                                    V
+---------------------------------------------------------------------+
!   FU: description of construction and cooperation                   !
!      +------------------+          +---------------------+          !
+----  ! FUi': reqs/smod  ! <======> !  FUj': reqs/smod    ! ----+
       +------------------+          +---------------------+
                  !                             !
                  !                             !
-----------------!-----------------------------!-----------------
STEPS:            !                             !
                  !                             !
SPECIFICATION     !                             !
                  V                             V
       +------------------+          +---------------------+
SM:    ! FUi': specs/smod ! <======> !  FUj': specs/smod   !
       +------------------+          +---------------------+
                  !                             !
                  V                             V

       -------------------------------------------------------
```

```
        reqs: requirements                specs: specifications
        spol: security policy             smod: security model
        <==>: cooperation
        SM  : security mechanisms of FU
```

Figure 2.1 Steps of Construction Proces

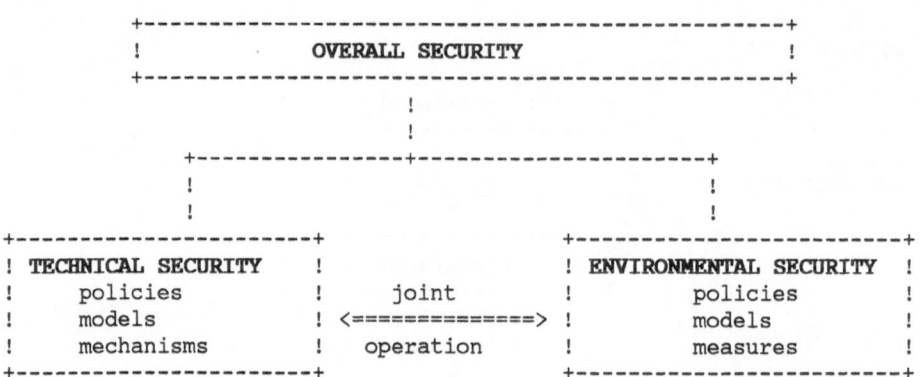

Figure 2.2 Refined Overall Security

Figure 2.2 can again be refined in the style of the construction
process. This will be done in fig. 2.3 for a distributed system (DS)
consisting of two autonomous subsystems AS.

So far a framework has been outlined which consists of
-     the **definition of a distributed system** an example of which is
      given in fig. 1.2,
-     **rights** which are under certain conditions exercised on **objects** by
      subjects, and related notions.
-     the general construction process with the notions of **security**
      policies, models, and mechanisms integrated,
-     considerations of the **technical and organizational aspects of**
      overall security.

Given this framework, **generic security functions** (GSF) are developed
the technical and organizational realization of which shall guarantee
overall security. The GSF will first be defined and the justified.

Management of Rights (MR). This GSF deals with keeping all the data
which describe the rights. MR offers services for defining, deleting,
changing, informing about, and, if necessary, passing on of rights.
Furthermore, MR has to take care that different rights are not in
conflict.

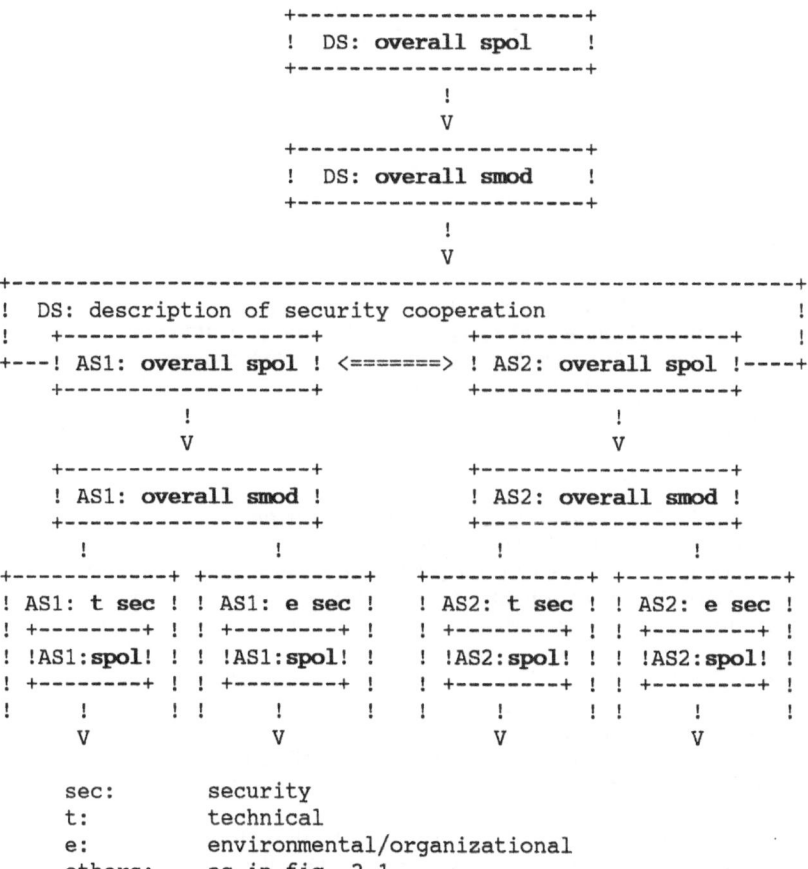

```
                    +----------------------+
                    !  DS: overall spol    !
                    +----------------------+
                               !
                               V
                    +----------------------+
                    !  DS: overall smod    !
                    +----------------------+
                               !
                               V
+-------------------------------------------------------------------+
!  DS: description of security cooperation                          !
!     +-------------------+          +-------------------+          !
+---! AS1: overall spol ! <=======> ! AS2: overall spol !----+
      +-------------------+          +-------------------+
               !                              !
               V                              V
      +-------------------+          +-------------------+
      ! AS1: overall smod !          ! AS2: overall smod !
      +-------------------+          +-------------------+
          !         !                    !          !
+-----------+ +-----------+    +-----------+ +-----------+
! AS1: t sec ! ! AS1: e sec !    ! AS2: t sec ! ! AS2: e sec !
! +--------+ ! ! +--------+ !    ! +--------+ ! ! +--------+ !
! !AS1:spol! ! ! !AS1:spol! !    ! !AS2:spol! ! ! !AS2:spol! !
! +--------+ ! ! +--------+ !    ! +--------+ ! ! +--------+ !
!     !      ! !     !      !    !     !      ! !     !      !
      V            V                  V            V
```

sec: security
t: technical
e: environmental/organizational
others: as in fig. 2.1

(The process is to be continued especially for the technical part as is
shown in fig. 2.1)

Figure 2.3: Security Related Construction Process

<u>Verification of Admissible Exercise of Rights (VR).</u> This GSF deals with
testing whether a subject is allowed to exercise a right if it intends
to do so.

<u>Verification of Identity (VI).</u> This GSF deals with verifying the
identity of subjects which want to exercise rights, and, if necessary,
the identity of objects.

Evidence Provision (EP). This GSF provides information concerning the
intended or completed exercise of rights in order to make possible to
subsequently decide whether violations of security policies have
ocurred.

Reinstantiation (RI). This GSF deals with reusable resources (e.g.
containers for data). RI has to prepare them in such a way that no
conclusions can be drawn concerning their former use.

Error Recovery (ER). This GSF deals with handling system errors.

Communication Security. This GSF shall guarantee that data to be
transferred are received only and only by that receiver who was
addressed by the sender, and that the identity of the sender is made
known to the receiver. Furthermore, CS shall guarantee that the data
are not forged, and that no other subject can get any knowledge either
of the data or of the transfer itself.

Now that the GSF have been introduced they still have to be
justified. To that end, a subject is considered which needs to exercise
a right. In order to be able to check whether it is authorized to do so
there must be some data - here called **protection data** (PD) - in the
system which contain information about all rights. Keeping these data
is the task of the **MR function.** The former example of a subject's
access to relations or views of a database system shows that MR
functions have to be realized at different places in the system. It is
up to the organization to define rights in accordance with its policies
by using the services offered by the MR functions. The organization has
to take into account the granularity of rights. If the granularity is
not fine enough, compensating organizational measures have to be
implemented.

The protection data are the basis on which decisions are made
about the admissibility of the exercise of rights. Here the **VR** and **VI**
functions come into being. Both functions have to intervene when a
subject is going to exercise a right. The VI function has to verify who
or what the subject is and what role it is in. Then the VR function has
to verify whether the subject is allowed to perform or to have
performed the intended operation. The reason for differentiating
between these functions is that the same subject may want to exercise
several rights in succession. Then it may be sufficient to involve the
VI function at the beginning only. Another reason is that the
implementation of the VR function should in the same way be spread out
in the system as the protection data are whereas the implementation of
the VI function could rather be centralized.

Several attempts to exercise a non-appointed right can simply be a
mistake. It can, however, also mean that a subject tried to circumvent
the VR function. Exercising several rights in turn can simply be
correct, however, it can also mean that a subject tried to derive
information which it is not allowed to gain. Or other things may happen
which were not intended by the original overall security policy. It is
the task of the **EP function** to provide information about these things

which allow their true nature to be recognized at least afterwards. To
that end, the EP function must have knowledge of all rights which can
be exercised. The idea behind this is that the existence of such a
function defeats intentions to misuse rights. It is up to the
organization to evaluate the information collected by the EP function
and to react in an appropriate way.

So far, the necessity of that GSF has, hopefully, been
demonstrated which is a direct consequence of the notions of right and
security policy. Now, GSF will be considered which has to do with the
reality of implementations.

If an object is implemented by a subject acting on lower level
objects - as e.g. a file system which provides files by means of disc
storage - and if the object is deleted the question arises what shall
happen to the lower level objects. The answer is that these reusable
objects must be put into a state as if they had never been used before.
Achieving this is the task of the **RI function**.

In reality errors are possible. For example, a program may contain
a fault which under certain circumstances causes undesired effects.
Also, malfunctions of the hardware are possible from time to time. For
recognizing and handling errors the **ER function** becomes necessary. ER
functions are very desirable even if no security requirements have been
laid down for the system. For example, database systems demonstrate
that there should be ways to recover from data losses due to hardware
malfunctions. If, however, security requirements are to be fulfilled,
ER functions become a necessity in order to make the other GSF
reliable. The least that has to be done by the ER function in the case
of an error is to notify the organization which has to take care, on
the one hand, to improve or replace erroneous programs and, on the
other, compensate for potential consequences of faults. Notification of
the organization and relying on its proper reactions often is the only
activity which the ER function is capable of carrying out.

The GSF considered so far are necessary even for a centralized
system. Therefore, they are also necessary for the local AS of a
distributed system. In the case of cooperation between two AS - as e.g.
in the example outlined in fig. 1.2 - the GSF have to cooperate too. To
support this the **CS function** becomes necessary which is considered to
be already justified by its very definition. It is tacitly assumed that
the communication medium contains an ER function in order to make it
reliable and permanently available. Problems encountered in the
cooperation of distributed GSF are discussed further in chapter 5.

To conclude this chapter, fig. 2.4 depicts an overview of the GSF
and their relationships as well.

The MR and VR functions together precisely describe the behavior
of the system as far as security is concerned. Thus, they can be
considered as building up the security model of the local system. In a
distributed system the functions MR, VR, EP, and ER have to cooperate
with their corresponding counterparts. The communication is carried out
with the help of a local communication mechanism CM as in fig. 1.2. CMs
in different AS also have to cooperate in making use of the CS
function. The functions VI, EP, and ER can be realized by combinations
of technical and organizational measures.

3. CLASSIFICATION SCHEME

Overall security can only be achieved by the appropriate combination of
technical and environmental measures. In order to assess the effect of
these measures on distributed systems it is advantageous to classify
the systems first. This can be done by considering
-    the **potential threats** to a system, and
-    the **overall organization** in which a system is embedded.
These two aspects can be understood as two different dimensions of a
classification scheme. Locating a given system in this scheme leads to
further general considerations how the GSF can defeat the corresponding
potential threats to the overall organization in question.

```
-------------------------------------------------------------------------
admin.     CHANGING                                     SUBSEQUENT
activ.     RIGHTS                                       VERIFICATION
-------------!----------------------------------------------!------------
system       !                        EXERCISING            !  commu-
activ.       !                        RIGHTS                 !  nication
------------ ! ---------------------- ! -------------- ! ---- ! ----
             !                        !                !      !
      ::: ! :::::::::::::::::::::::::: ! :::::::         !      !
      :  !       security model       !        :        !      !
      :  V       ::::::::::::::        V        :        V      !
right :  +----+   :    *****   :    +----+   :    +----+ !
relat.:  ! MR !<=====>*   *========>! VR !<---------! EP ! !
GSF   :  +----+   :  * P *   :    +----+   :    +----+ !
      ::::::::::::::   *    *   :::::::: ! :::::        !      !
                      * D *            V               !      !
                      *    *        +----+             !      !
                      *   *========>! VI !<-------------+      !
                      *****         +----+                     !
                                                              !
-------------------------------------------------------------- ! ---
implementation     +----+           +----+                     !
related            ! RI !           ! ER !                     !
GSF                +----+           +----+                     !
-------------------------------------------------------------- V ---
communication                                      +----+
related                                            ! CS !
GSF                                                +----+
-------------------------------------------------------------------------

        x --> y: x"needs something from y
        ==>:     data flow
        PD:      protection data
```

Figure 2.4: Overview of Generic Security Functions.

The threats possible can be deduced from the tasks performed by the
system. It is in the nature of a distributed system - as is expressed
in its informal definition in chapter 1 - that some of its tasks are
performed in cooperation with some of its autonomous subsystems (AS).
Such a task can be conceived as consisting of subtasks which complement
each other and are carried out in the AS involved. A prerequisite for
cooperation is the exchange of data objects. This leads to cycles of
data transfers between the AS. Threats to cooperations can be reduced
to threats to or caused by single data transfers examples of which are
listed in table 3.1. Thus, it suffices to consider the different
categories of transfers of data objects. These categories are:

- genuine data (D),
- programs (P),
- requests for performing certain activities (A).

TRANSFERS		EXAMPLE
Init(AS1)	Resp(AS2)	
A	nil	Update a data base
A	d	Query a data base
A	p	Deliver a program
A,D	nil	Deliver mail
A,D	d=A(D)	Process transferred data
A,D	d=p(D)	Crosscompile with compiler at the responder's site
A,P	d=P(d)	Run a transferred program (data reside at the responder's site)
A;P;D	d=P(D)	Run a transferred job consisting of program and data (load sharing)

A: Activity,   D/d: Data,   P/p: Program
Capital letters indicate that initiator (Init), small letters
that responder (Resp) is the source

Table 3.1 Transfer Cycles.

From the categories of data transfer in table 3.1 typical threats can
be deduced. With fig. 1.2 in mind the threats will be made more
specific in the following list.

Threat URA: **unauthorized request to perform an activity.** AS1 requests
an activity to be executed in AS2 which it has not the right to do. AS1

pretends to be AS3 which may be allowed to initiate this specific
activity.

Threat RDT: **received data tampered.** AS2 receives data origination from
AS1 which have been tampered with. Either AS3 has tampered with the
data while they were transferred or AS1 has intentionally sent the
wrong data. These data can be a threat to AS2 itself or to another
subsystem which requested a service from AS2.

Threat PMR: **program misuses rights.** AS1 transfers a program to AS2.
This program shall perform accesses to data of a database residing at
AS2. The threat exists that the transferred program not only delivers
the expected result, but also tries to send back original data. These
data could be encoded in different forms, e.g. in the results sent back
to AS1.

Threat PUA: **program performs access unauthorized under the global
policy.** A program can try to access data objects to which according to
the global policy, it has no right. In most cases, the granularity of
the access rights provided by the local MR function is too coarse in
comparison to the necessities of the global policy.

Threat PER: **program is erroneous.** A program made available by AS1 to
AS2 can be erroneous. Neither does it misuse its rights nor does it
perform an unauthorized access, it simply delivers wrong results. If
these results are further processed by AS2 they can be a threat to AS2.

Threat MRI: **misuse of results.** AS1 receives data from AS2. These data
represent information which is intended for private use by AS1 only.
Two threats are possible:
> - to AS2 if AS1 forwards these data to AS3,
> - to AS1 if AS2 also delivers these data to AS3.

Threat UPR: **unauthorized profiling of user bahavior.** AS2 can keep
statistics concerning the activities initiated by AS1. On the one hand,
this information can be used to improve services; on the other, it can
be misused. Thus, keeping statistics is a potential threat.

These threats build up the first dimension of the classification
scheme. Its second dimension is established by the form of the overall
organization. Criteria have to be found to characterize the different
forms. Since AS are the building blocks of a distributed system, their
specific qualities, the way they are organized, and the environment
they are embedded in, lead by themselves to the following attributes:

OP/CL: open versus closed system. A closed system is characterized by a
fixed number of AS. For such a system it is in principle possible that

every AS knows about all other ones especially about the security policies they obey. This is not true in an open system to which, at each point of time, new AS can be connected.

WTS/NTS: with versus without trusted AS. If a system contains at least one trusted AS this one can be made responsible for carrying out certain security related tasks, e.g. checking the identity of subjects.

WCA/NCA: with versus without a common authority. Only a common authority can guarantee that security policies of different AS are not in conflict. It can enforce actions that are deemed appropriate to be carried out, in all AS.

WCT/NCT: with versus without complete mutual trust. Mutual trust is given if each AS can trust all other AS as far as security aspects are concerned.

To complete these descriptions of the organizational attributes the notion of trust needs some explanations. Trust can be gained in three ways:
>   (1) observation,
>   (2) mediation,
>   (3) verification.

Three examples will help in understanding the specific differences:
(1) After many **observations** of an action which each time triggered the same reaction, one trusts the fact that this action triggers the specific reaction always.
(2) If other people's experiences about reactions on actions are believed trust is gained by **mediation.** This is not independent of how the other people gained their trust.
(3) If a thorough evaluation - taking all possible conditions into account - is performed of why and how an action triggers a corresponding reaction, trust is gained by **verification.**

The three types of gaining trust exhibit an increasing quality. When classifying a system, absolutely reliable results can only be expected if trust is gained by verification. On the other hand, a thorough verification of a system is a task which, due to its complexity, cannot be expected to be carried out with mathematical precision within a reasonable time. Thus, in real life trust is mainly gained in the less strict other two ways.

For a given system it can be determined whether each organizational attribute holds or not. This leads to 16 combinations of which, however, only eight are reasonable. Obvious examples of contradictory combinations are:
>   open system <---> common authority
>   open system <---> complete mutual trust
>   without trusted AS <---> complete mutual trust.

It is left to the reader to figure out the other nonreasonable combinations. The remaining reasonable combinations are the elements of the organizational dimension. The combination of both dimensions is **represented as a threat matrix** in table 3.2.

```
-----------------------------------------------------------------------
                                  THREATS
-----------------------------------------------------------------------
Organization      URA    RDT    PMR    PUA    PER    MRI    UPR
-----------------------------------------------------------------------
NCT NCA NTS OP     .      .      .      .      .      .      .
NCT NCA NTS CL     .      .      .      .      .      .      .
NCT NCA WTS OP     .      .      .      .      .      .      .
N CT NCA WTS CL    .      .      .      .      .      .      .
NCT WCA NTS CL     .      .      .      .      .      .      .
NCT WCA WTS CL     .      .      .      .      .      .      .
WCT NCA NTS CL     .      .      .      .      .      .      .
WCT WCA WTS CL     .      .      .      .      .      .      .
-----------------------------------------------------------------------
```

Table 3.2: Threat Matrix

For each entry in the threat matrix an evaluation must take place
to see how the threat manifests itself in the different system
organizations. System organizations with complete trust need not be
evaluated: by definition there are no threats. The results of this
evaluation are depicted in tables 3.3 and 3.4. In table 3.3 entries
show the kind of countermeasures which must be applied. There are some
entries which indicate that no effective countermeasure exists. Entries
with an additional question mark indicate that the countermeasure
cannot be expected to completely defeat the threat.

```
-----------------------------------------------------------------------
                                  THREATS
-----------------------------------------------------------------------
ORGANIZATION      URA    RDT    PMR    PUA    PER    MRI    UPR
-----------------------------------------------------------------------
NCT NCA NTS OP    lg      -      l      l      l      -      -
NCT NCA NTS CL    lg      -      l      l      l      -      -
NCT NCA WTS OP    g/lg    -      l      l      l      -      g
NCT NCA WTS CL    g/lg    -      l      l      l      -      g
NCT WCA NTS CL    lg     lg?    lg      l     lg     g?     g?
NCT WCA WTS CL    g/lg   lg?    lg      l     lg     lg?    g?
WCT NCA NTS CL     0      0      0      0      0      0      0
WCT WCA WTS CL     0      0      0      0      0      0      0
-----------------------------------------------------------------------
```

```
   /:    or
   l:    local
   g:    global
   lg:   local and global
   -:    no contermeasure possible
   0:    no threat
```

Table 3.3 Threat Matrix with Kind of Countermeasure.

Each column of table 3.3 shows one or two different entries besides the entry 0 (no threat). In the case of two entries, the change from one to the other corresponds to a change in the attributes NTS/WTS (trusted AS) of the organizational form. This observation gives rise to distinguish for each threat in table 3.4 whether it exists in a system with trusted AS (tag 1) or with no trusted AS (tag 2).

In table 3.4 the generic security functions are entered which are necessary to counteract the various threats. As can be seen, the various threats require various countermeasures as provided by the GSF. But the GSF are not sufficient by themselves in all cases. To counteract the threats, supporting organizational measures are necessary as indicated by an entry abbreviated "Org".

THREAT		NECESSARY GFS
	local	in cooperation
URA1	Vⱼ,VR,MR	CS
URA2	VR,MR	CS,VI,VR,MR
RDT1	*	*
RDT2	EP	CS,Org
PMR1	EP,CS,Org	-
PMR2	EP,CS	CS,EP,Org
PUA1	VR,MR	-
PER1	EP,ER,Org	-
PER2	EP,ER	CS,Org
MRI1	*	*
MRI2	-	CS,VI,VR,EP,Org
UPR1	*	*
UPR2	-	CS,VI,VR

VI: Verification of Identity
VR: Verification of Rights
MR: Management of Rights
CS: Communication Security
EP: Evidence Provision
ER: Error Recovery
Org: Organizational Measures
*:   No Countermeasure Possible
-:   No Countermeasure Necessary
1/2: Organization With/Without Trusted AS

Table 3.4: Threats and Countermeasures with the GSF

How to interpret table 3.4 is explained with the help of an
example: the meaning of, for example, the first row is that a specific
form of the threat URA exists which is present when the distributed
system does not contain at least one trustworhty AS. To locally
compensate for this threat the VI function must be present. Globally,
communication security is necessary. The CS function assures that the
data transfer is not tampered with so that the identity of a requester
whose password is transferred can be proven beyond doubt. With the
identity known the VR function can decide if a certain right, such as
starting a specific activity, can be allowed. In this way all entries
of table 3.4 can be interpreted. The application of the scheme as a
whole is explained in the next chapter.

4. APPLICATION OF THE CLASSIFICATION SCHEME

The analysis of a distributed system leads to all information necessary
to determine the right position in the classification scheme (table
3.3) proposed in the foregoing chapter. Depending on the actual threats
and the resulting class, countermeasures can be developed and
initiated. The whole process is an iterative one with a possibly
varying number of cycles.

Step 1: Analysis of the Subsystem Structure. This step tries to
recognize all autonomous subsystems (AS) into which the distributed
system is decomposed.
Expected result: Relevant information about all AS.

Step 2: Analysis of all Possible Transfers. There is a variety of data
transfers between the AS depending on the task to be accomplished in
cooperation with the different AS involved. Table 3.1 lists all
possible kinds of transfer.
Expected result: Identification of the threat categories to be chosen
from the ones depicted in table 3.3.

Step 3: Analysis of the System Organization. In this step the system is
analysed to find out which of the criteria mentioned in chapter 3
apply. Wheras steps 1 and 2 deal with purely technical aspects, step 3
has to rely partly on assumptions. For example, it is very hard to find
evidence that uniform rules and regulations can and will be followed by
all AS. Especially difficult is the evaluation of an AS to find out
whether it is trustworthy or not. Different evaluators can easily come
to different results. It is advisable to iterate the cycle with two or
more alternatives. Thus, the consequences of the different evaluations
of the security provided by the system can clearly be seen.
Expected result: Identification of the kind of organization to be
chosen from the ones depicted in table 3.3.

Step 4: Identification of the Appropriate Threat Matrix Entries. The results of steps 2 and 3 lead by themselves to the appropriate threat matrix entries in table 3.3.
Expected result: Determination of both all relevant threats and all possible countermeasures as shown in table 3.4.

Step 5: Final Evaluation and Rating. This evaluates the effectiveness of all countermeasurs already built into the system which are supposed to defeat the individual threats.
Expected result: Enumeration of the threats which are not dealt with properly together with their possible countermeasures.

If step 5 identifies certain countermeasures that are missing or have to be improved the evaluation cycle can be performed again after incorporation of all these changes into the system. An overview of the classification method is depicted in figure 4.1. The boxes "---" stand for steps, "***" for results of steps, and "..." for classification dimensions.

The whole process comes to an end either if there are no threats remaining or as soon as a decision is made that the remaining threats are of such a nature that the value of the information to be protected does not justify any further countermeasures.

5. DISCUSSION OF THE GENERIC SECURITY FUNCTIONS

The presence of the generic security functions (GSF) in a distributed system is not a remedy to all possible threats and problem areas. First of all, it has to be admitted that there does not exist a mathematical proof that the GSF as deduced earlier are sufficient and necessary. The same is true concerning their completeness or implementation independence. It is only the way these functions have been developed that common sense rather than pure formal reasoning tells us that the attributes mentioned above hold good. Only the notions of right and of exercise of rights have been used.

Even if the GSF are judged to be sufficient it has to be admitted that they already may have inherited potential deficiences from the security policy. Furthermore, it has to be admitted that modeling a security policy on a computer leads to threats which are not necessarily obvious, or to threats which could not be exploited in manual systems within a reasonable time span. In addition, there is the possibility of design and implementation errors in the software development process of the GSF. Since this is basically a software engineering problem, it will not be delt with further in this context.

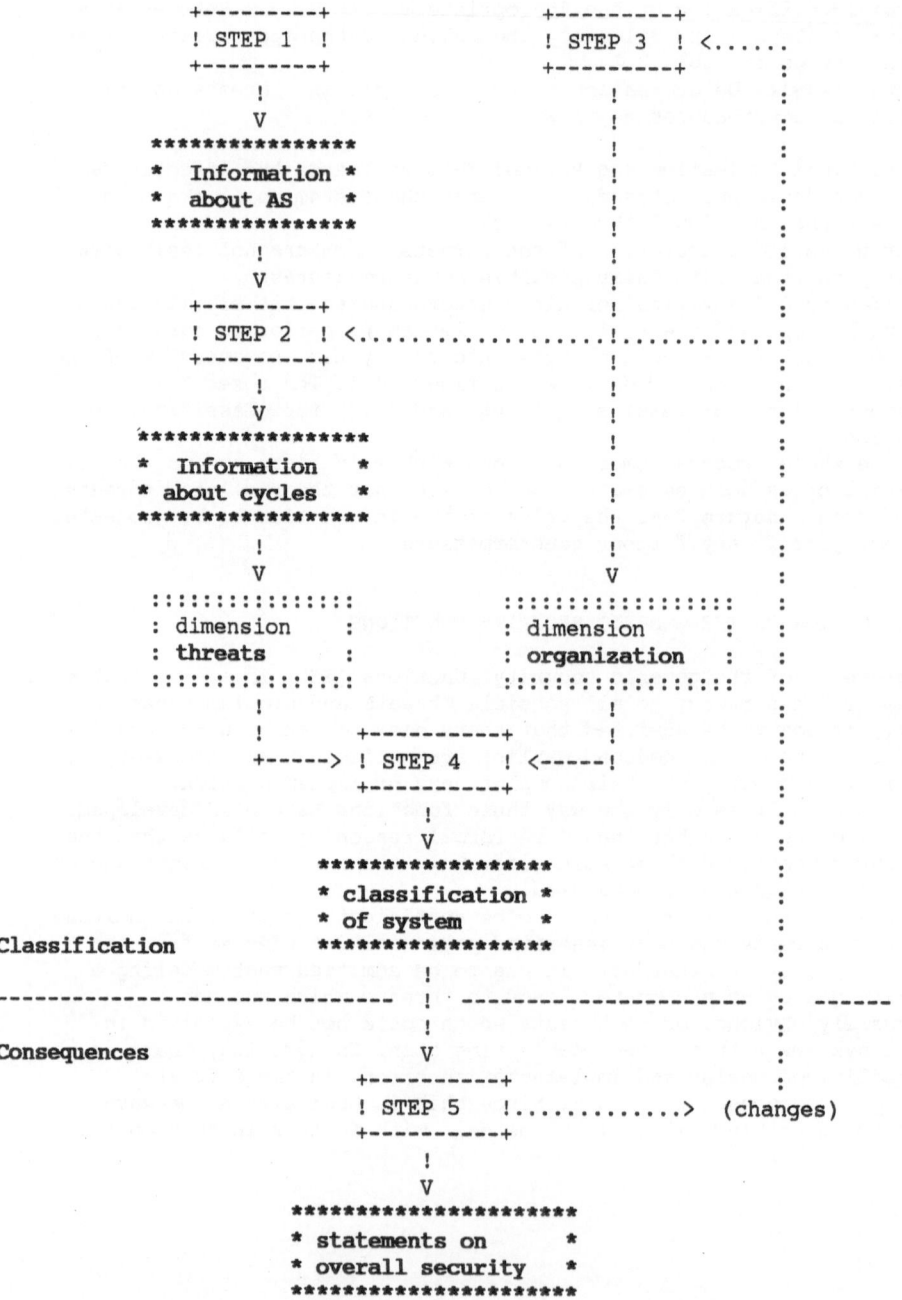

Figure 4.1: Classification Method.

The limitations of the GSF are reached in the areas:

        (1) security policy,
        (2) covered channels,
        (3) denial of service,
        (4) aggregation and inference of information.

These problem areas are now discussed to a certain extent.

(1) Security Policy

In a distributed system various security policies might be implemented
in the autonomous subsystems (AS). If these policies are not a subset
of a general system wide policy, clearly the effects of the GSF can be
hampered, especially in those cases where cooperation of the security
functions must take place to counteract a threat. Another problem
occurs when a security policy has the property that rights owned by a
subject can arbitrarily be passed on to other subjects. Then it cannot
be decided whether the system is in a secure state at a given point in
time. Thereby, "secure state" has the meaning that an access to data in
accordance with a right passed on is not possible against the will of
the owner of this data.

(2) Covered Channels

A covered channel is an unintended means of communication. By making
use of it, subjects can communicate in a way that does not conform with
the security policy. Covered channels can either be storage channels or
timing channels. A storage channel exists if two subjects have access
to the same store. A timing channel exists if one subject can modulate
a resource in such a way that time delays can be observed by a second
subject. The bandwidth of these channels can vary between 1 bit/s to
many kbit/s. Open problems with covered channels are:

- Not all covered channels can be detected. This is especially true
  for timing channels.
- There is a gradual transition from correctly using a right to
  misusing it.
- The coding of the information transmitted via the channel is
  unknown.

(3) Denial of Service

A service should be completed in a time span which looks reasonable to
an authorized requestor. Looking at the definition of a distributed
system in this paper it is obvious that denial of service is a real
problem. Considering the communication between two AS as a specific
service, the question arises when does denial of service take place and
when is it just the variable time delay imposed upon the communication
that hampers the completion of the system behavior. A solution to this

problem is only possible by means outside the system like contracts which specify average service times. The EP function can only counteract this threat in a limited way.

(4) Aggregation and Inference of Information

From the many problems that exist those of statistical databases are understood to a certain degree for a central system. A system is said to be secure if it is only possible to get statistical data but no original data. Disclosure of original data and especially of personal data of a statistical database is facilitated if advantage can be taken from additional knowledge which may be obtained from secondary data. If those secondary data reside in the same AS there is a chance that accesses to the database can be controlled in such a way that inference of information can be avoided or, at least, recognized afterwards. But what happens in an open environment? In general, the existence of data in the other system which can serve as secondary data is unknown to the local GSF. Thus, the GSF cannot decide to deny accesses to them. Also, global logging by an EP function is of no great help since the accesses can happen at different points in time and the recognition of two specific accesses which makes it possible to interfere information very difficult. Thus, controlling the posssibilities for obtaining and manipulating information becomes a tremendous problem since in the not too distant future the majority of systems is expected to be both distributed and open.

6. SUMMARY AND CONCLUSIONS

A scheme has been developed which makes it possible to evaluate distributed systems with repect to security aspects. The scheme combines the notions of organization, security threats, and generic security functions. From the determination of both the overall organization in which a given system is embedded and the threats which are a consequence of the tasks performed by the system, the generic security functions can be determinded which are necessary to guarantee security. An evaluation of the implementation of these functions results in a judgement of the security achieved. Up to now, the scheme has successfully been applied to a large distributed system, namely the socalled Btx-system (Bildschirmtext-System) of the German postal service. Many problem areas could be identified which are worth investigating in the future.

The implementation of the generic security functions has to combine organizational and technical measures properly. The more technical measures and mechanisms are made use of the fewer organizational measures are necessary. The advantage of technical measures is that they are deterministic, their disadvantage that they, if they are very sophisticated, can cause serious inefficiences in data processing. The disadvantage of organizational measures is that human beings are involved whose behaviour cannot be predicted with certainty. Especially, if a system is distributed the kind of overall organization is of tremendous relevance. Without a common and effective authority it cannot be guaranteed that the security policies of the autonomous subsystem are not in conflict and that they are followed obediently. A common authority is, however, possible only in a closed system.

The general construction process shows that the generic security functions have to be present at all system levels (With an increasing proportion of technical measures at the lower levels). This makes clear why security cannot be expected to be successfully achieved by adding security mechanisms to a system afterwards.This is particularly true for unstructured systems. A well-structured design is an absolute prerequisite for gaining trust by verification. Even, then, verification is still an extraordinarily complex task. It is one of the main goals of the construction process that the system is structured in a sound way. Quality assurance has to take care that the implementation of a system is carried out in the way prescribed by the construction process. The better a system is structured the more effective are the generic security functions and the fewer the possibilities of misuse.

Most of the considerations above apply to both centralized and distributed systems. For achieving security in a distributed system it is necessary to make a distributed system look like a centralized one. Therefore, a distributed system must be governed by a common authority of an overall organization - as is a centralized system - and must be of closed type - as, again, is a centralized system. In making it closed a reliable communication security function is inevitable.

There will be more and more distributed systems in the near futrure. Consequently, many new security challenges are emerging. Thus, there is an urgent need for a thorough understanding of security problems.

APPENDIX

The appendix lists some articles or books in chronological order which, without being explicitly referenced, influenced this paper.

1. Graham, G.S., P.J. Denning: Protection - Principles and Practice. Proc.Spring Joint Computer Conference (72).

2. England, D.M.: Capability Concept Mechanisms and Structure in System 250. Proc. Int. Workshop on Protection in Operating Systems, IRIA (74).

3. Linden, T.A.: Operating System Structures to Support Security and Reliable Software. Computing Surveys, v8n4 (76).

4. Popek, G.J.: Issues in Kernel Design. Advanced Course on Operating Systems, Technical University Munich (77).

5. Bell, D.E., L.J. LaPadula: Secure Computer Systems - Unified Exposition and Multics Interpretation. ESD-TR-75-306 (79).

6. Chamberlin, D.D., J.N. Gray, J.L. Traiger: Views, Authorization, and Locking in a Relational Data Base System. Proc. of the National Computer Conference (78).

7. Denning, D.E., P.J. Denning, M.D. Schwartz: The Tracker: A Threat to Statistical Database Security. (79).

8. Hesse, W. Das Projektmodell - Eine Grundlage für die ingenieurmässige Software-Entwicklung. Tagungsband GI-Jahrestagung (80).

9. Fernandez, E.B., R.C. Summers. C. Wood: Database Security and Integrity. The Systems Programming Series, Addison Wesley (81).

10. Liskov, B.: Report on the Workshop on Fundamental Issues in Distributed Computing. ACM OSR v15n3, (81).

11. Dittrich, K., K. Hug, P. Kammerer, D. Lienert, H. Mau, K. Wachsmuth: Protection in the OSKAR Operating System. Goals, Concepts, Consequences. Proc. IEEE Symposium on Security and Privacy, Oakland (82).

12. Schlörer, J.: Outputkontrollen zur Sicherung statistischer Datenbanken - Ein Überblick. Informatik Spektrum, Bd. 5, H. 4 (82).

13. Brück, H. vor der, C. Jahl, C. Köhler, N. Ramsperger: Untersuchung der EDV-technischen Datenschutz- und Datensicherungsprobleme in verteilten DV-Systemen. IABG Report B-SZ 1321/01 (83) - Supported by the German Ministry of Research and Technology.

Along the same lines, the IP allows a security option to be placed in the IP header. The security option can contain information regarding the classification level, the compartment, and the handling restrictions on the data contained in the packet. Included as part of the security option is the transmission control code which provides a way to separate traffic and define communities of interest among network users. (8) There is a problem, however, when classified data is labeled as such while traversing an unclassified (or lower classification) network since the packet is thus flagrantly tagged as one that is interesting and worth attacking.

The DoD will try to solve the packet labeling problem by incorporating security layers into its proposed protocol reference model. The security principles incorporated are those providing a hierarchical layering for end-to-end security which does not preclude the use of encryption techniques. An illustration of the DoD reference model with added layers for security is shown in Figure 5.

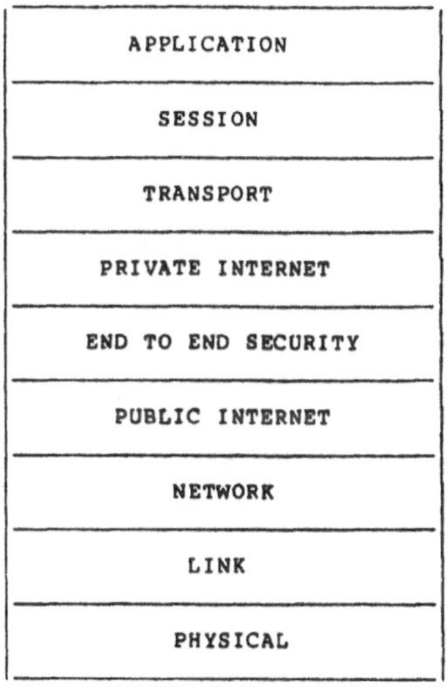

```
+-------------------------------+
|          APPLICATION          |
+-------------------------------+
|            SESSION            |
+-------------------------------+
|           TRANSPORT           |
+-------------------------------+
|       PRIVATE INTERNET        |
+-------------------------------+
|      END TO END SECURITY      |
+-------------------------------+
|        PUBLIC INTERNET        |
+-------------------------------+
|            NETWORK            |
+-------------------------------+
|             LINK              |
+-------------------------------+
|           PHYSICAL            |
+-------------------------------+
```

Figure 5:
The proposed DoD protocol reference model with security layers.

The public and private internet layers shown are incorporated in the model to allow for the hiding of classified data. The public internet header would contain nothing of interest, security wise, and would not look different whether the underlying data was classified or not. The private internet header would contain the actual security level of the data. All the data contained in the protocol levels above the end-to-end security layer might also be encrypted.

REFERENCES

1.   D.H. Barnes, "The Provision of End to End Security for User Data
      on an Experimental Packet Switched Network", Proc. 4th Internat.
      Conference on Software Engineering for Telecommunications
      Switching Systems, Warwick, England, pp 144-148, IEE (July 1981).

2.   E.J. McCauley and P.J. Drongowski, "KSOS - The Design of a Secure
      Operating System", AFIPS Conference Proc. Vol. 48, pp 345-353
      (1979).

3,   J.M. Rushby, "The Design and Verification of Secure Systems",
      Proc. 8th ACM Symposium on Operating System Principles, Asilomar,
      Ca., pp 12-21 (December 1981). (ACM Operating Systems Review,
      Vol. 15 No. 5).

4.   J.M. Rushby and B. Randell, "A Distributed Secure System", IEEE
      Computer Vol. 16 No. 7, pp 55-67 (July 1983).

SECURE COMMUNICATIONS PROCESSOR RESEARCH

Dr. Derek Barnes
Royal Signals and Radar Establishment
St. Andrews Road
Malvern, Worcestershire
United Kingdom

ABSTRACT

For several years, the Royal Signals and Radar Establishment has been
carrying out a research programme in the area of Secure Com-munications
Processors (SCPs). This work aims to realise a range of practical
Trusted Computing Bases (TCB) for a wide variety of network security
apllications. The Secure Communications Processors have been designed
to be simple , secure and efficient, whilst the underlying TCBs are
intended to be application independent. Thus, the cost of developing a
new secure component of a distributed system is minimised.
     At present, three different Secure Communications Processors have
been produced, or are being researched. These are SCP1, a limited
functionality TCB for dedicated applications, SCP2, a mid-range TCB
for a wide range of network security applications, and SCP3, a high
functionality, new architecture, multi-processor system.
     In this paper the three current Secure Communications Processors
are functionally described, together with the types of application
which they are intended to host. As an example, the roles of SCP1 and
SCP2 in the practical realisation of a Distributed Secure System are
outlined.

1. INTRODUCTION

Communications networks and distributed systems exist to provide their
authorised users with access to information, and to provide facilites
to manipulate that information. The information entrusted to such a
system must be valid and reliable, so in many environments it must be
protected from unauthorised access and alteration, or at the very least
any changes, deliberate or accidental, should be detected. Users should
not be able to make use of resources to which they are not entitled;
for example, not everyone should be able to make use of system management facilites. Equally important, though perhaps the most difficult to
achieve, is to stop accidental or deliberate attempts to prevent users

R. W. G. Herbers (ed), The Upper Layers of Open Systems Interconnection, 195–200.

from using services to which they are entitled. System security is
therefore concerned with both accidental and deliberate attacks on the
integrity of the system and the information which it contains.

Common-user distributed systems are currently very much in favour
for their ability to provide survivable, integrated communications and
computing facilites at an economical cost to individual groups of
users. However, these groups of users often wish to operate within
separate compartments, for example closed user groups, while still
communicating via the same common-user system.

It is therefore becoming increasingly important to be able to provide multi-level secure data networks and distributed systems for. a
wide range of defence and civilian applications.

The Royal Signals and Radar Establishment, part of the United
Kingdom Ministry of Defence, has for several years been carrying out a
very active research programme in this area. One outcome of this work
has been the realisation of a range of Secure Communications Processors
(SCPs) to form the basis of various network and distributred system
security schemes. Essentially, each SCP represents a real-time Trusted
Computing Base, specifically orientated towards network security
requirements.

2. TRUSTED COMPUTING BASES

A Trusted Computing Base (TCB) is defined to be the totality of the
foundation software and hardware necessary to securely enforce a
security policy upon all operations of a computer system.

At its simplest, a TCB consists of a simple Separation (1),
running on comparatively unsophisticated hardware, e.g. a computer with
a simple memory management unit. However, a TCB can also be a large
Security Kernel, together with all its related non-kernel trusted
processes, running on a larger machine and providing general purpose
computing facilities (2).

In order to discuss TCBs in more detail, it is convenient to
partition the possible range of different types of TCB into three
classes. They are:

The Dedicated TCB

This is the simplest form of TCB. It is one which is basically
dedicatated towards performing a single, very simple, static form of
security application. A dedicated TCB is usually found to be an
embedded part of a system component, e.g. providing the foundation for
a guard or one-way filter. This type of TCB is preconfigured when the
system is built, and contains no dynamic process creation facilities.
The simple separation kernel (3) represents a typical dedicated TCB.

The Mid-Range TCB

The mid-range TCB provides a common TCB for a related range of
applications. For example, a communications orientated mid-range TCB

could form the foundation for a range of network security devices. This type of TCB provides facilities for creating and deleting processes dynamically, but does not allow general online user programming. It is therefore particularly appropriate for running fixed applications, which are more sophisticated than those which can be supported by a dedicated TCB.

The General Purpose TCB

The general purpose TCB provides the basis for multi-level secure, general purpose, multi-user computer systems. Typically it allows its users to perform the general on-line computing functions offered by a large mainframe. KSOS (2) is an example of a system incorporating a general purpose TCB. This type of TCB represents the ultimate in generality for multi-level secure systems.

3. SECURE COMMUNICATIONS PROCESSORS

In 1981, RSRE launched its 'Multi-Level Secure Communication Networks Initiative', which is intended to realise a range of three principal Secure Communications Processors. The rationale behind this approach was that of concentrating the available resources on a limited number of widely applicable TCBs, rather than trying to develop a potentially large number of different secure systems from scratch. Without this approach, every new security relevant network component would need to be designed and implemented afresh upon appropiate hardware, if available. Thus, with this initiative, RSRE are pursuing the approach which provides the best long term cost benefit.

The essential properties of the three SCPs, which have been or are being produced by RSRE, are as follows.

SCP1

SCP1 is a dedicated TCB for simple, static security applications. The SCP1 work is based upon a generalisation of the SUE Security Kernel work (1) on PDP11/34s carried out at RSRE. However, it is our intention to realise the SCP1 Separation Kernel concept upon other machines as necessary.

The principle of the SCP1 kernel is to segment a computer into a preconfigured number of static isolated regimes, or virtual machines. Each regime contains either all trusted or all untrusted functions. The only way in which the regimes can communicate is via preconfigured message passing routes through the trusted SCP1 kernel. The kernel provides scheduling, timing, control and error handling functions, but all input/output operations are handled directly by the appropriate regimes themselves.

SCP2

SCP2 is a mid-range TCB for network orientated security applications
which require dynamic features, but which are removed from the com-
plexities of online user programming. The principal aim of the SCP2
project has been to produce a system with an intrinsically simple
design structure. The practical realisation of this structure will
result in a secure system, which is efficient enough to handle
demanding real-time applications.

The philosphy'behind SCP2 has been to select very carefully from
commercially available computer hardware that which best provides the
features determined to be desirable for this type of secure application, while making absolutely sure that it contains no undesirable
features. It should be noted that determining the absence of undesirable features represents an onerous task! The SCP2 work has therefore
concentrated upon the design and implementation of the software for a
network orientated mid-range TCB, given certain hardware characteristics.

SCP2 provides facilities for the dynamic creation and deletion of
protected (isolated) processes within security environments, and provides facilities for controlled message passing between processes. A
prototype SCP2 has been designed and built by TSL Communications. The
full SCP2 implementation is under way, and is expected to be completed
during 1986. A part of this implementation will result in a demonstration application. Known as the T-Host, this application will provide a simple, multi-level secure electronic mail facility over one or
more insecure networks.

SCP3

SCP3 is a mid-range TCB, similar to SCP2, but offers improved security,
integrity and denial of service properties. It is also capable of
supporting a greater range of applications (including some online user
programming).

SCP3 developed from the philosophy that all currently available
commercial hardware provide at best, something of a compromise in terms
of their features from a security point of view. Thus the SCP3 project
started with no preconceived hardware constraints. Instead, a secure
system (hardware, firmware and software) is being designed and implemented to provide a very secure real-time mid-range TCB for a wide
range of network security applications.

When complete, SCP3 will be a modular, secure, multiprocessor
system, with excellent internal integrity and denial of service
protection properties.

It is not expected that the SCP3 work will provide a usable
secure system for many years. It represents part of our long term
research into the next generation of secure systems.

4. SCP NETWORK SECURITY APPLICATIONS

Having identified the generic TCB types, and looked at the facilities offered by the RSRE range of SCPs, consider the type of network security applications for which they can be used.

SCP1 is ideally suited to the provision of simple end-to-end encryption facilities. (1). However, it can be used for a number of guard and filter applications. An example of its use for performing a number for these features is to be found in the Distributed Secure System Project mentioned below.

SCP2 will be able to support a range of applications in a secure, simple and efficient manner for a complete range of security critical components for wide area and local area networks and distributed systems. Applications therefore include the following:

    a. **Simple Hosts,** which provide predetermined, limited functionality computer systems accessed by local or remote users.
    b. **Network Front Ends,** which act as security managers between large host computer systems and various networks.
    c. **Switches.** SCP2 can provide the trusted, secure basis of packet switches, message switches, and similar devices, being specifically designed to be efficient enough to handle such demanding real-time applications.
    d. **Geteways** between two or more networks which have different security constraints and require some trusted mediator of the information flowing between them.
    e. **Network Access Control Centres,** which are required in most locally and widely distributed secure systems, providing security management functions.
    f. **Packet Assemblers/Disassemblers,** which are becoming increasingly security relevant, enabling users to dynamically gain access to multi-level secure facilities and information.
    g. **General Servers** on both local and wide area networks, which are increasingly being seen as security relevant, e.g. filing systems and electronic mail machines.

SCP3 will be able to support all of those applications outlined for SCP2, as well as more complex ones, including those which require a level of user programming.

    The SCP2 implementation will be tested in a demonstration application, known as the T-HOST. This has been very carefully chosen, so that it can form the basis for further research, demonstrates a useful application, and represents a sensible complexity of application for implementation. The T-HOST is a simple electronic mail host which can be demonstrated stand-alone, or in conjunction with other T-HOSTs attached to an inter-network. Each T-HOST requires one link to an insecure X25 network. All inter T-HOST communications are encrypted at

the transport service layer. The T-HOST provides only a simple multi-
level secure electronic mail application to users on the same, or other
T-HOSTS. Users can 'login' locally at different security compartments,
and once satisfactorily authenticated can use the mail facilites
locally or remotely on another T-HOST. A multi-compartment disc backing
store is provided on each T-HOST to support the mail application.

5. THE DISTRIBUTED SECURE SYSTEM PROJECT

It is one thing to produce building blocks for multi-level secure systems, and quite another to produce actual working systems. The Distributed Secure System project aims to provide a working demonstration of
a real multi-level secure, general purpose distributed system. Rushby
(4) has described the basic concepts of the DSS design. A working non-
secure emulation of the DSS design has recently been produced for RSRE
by Systems Designers Limited running on a number of DEC PC350 Personal
Computers interconnected by a Local Area Network. This emulation has
proved the practical feasibility of the basic DSS design.
      In the near future, the real DSS implementation work will begin.
For this Motorola 68010s will be used for the essential Trustworthy
Network Interface Units (TNIU) which enforce the security separation
between the system components. An SCP1 type of separation kernel will
provide the dedicated TCB functions required within each TNIU. Initial
multi-level secure components such as the Multi-Level Secure Filing
System will be very heavily based upon the SCP2 mid-range TCB.

6. CONCLUSIONS

The range of Secure Communications Processors currently being pursued
by RSRE represents an essential commitment to the basic building blocks
for secure computer networks and secure distributed systems. The
alternative of starting from scratch with a bare machine for each of
the many security relevant applications envisaged has been avoided.
This should mean that new, network orientated security applications can
be mounted quickly and at minimum incremental cost in the near future.

TESTING NATO NETWORK AND TRANSPORT PROTOCOLS

J.L. Robinson
Directorate of Military Communications
Communications Research Center
Ottawa, Ontario
Canada

1. INTRODUCTION

The objective of reliable, interoperable communications will not be met unless the protocols operating in the communication systems work properly. To ensure this, the protocol design must be tested for logical correctness and proper performance and protocol implementations must be tested for conformance to the standards. Progress has been made recently with the development of NATO standards for communications protocols. However very little consideration has been given to testing the protocols that are candidates for these standards. This paper reviews that subject with some special attention to the NATO Network and Transport Layer Protocols.

The paper begins with a report on the status of NATO Network and Transport Protocols and an introduction to the subject of protocol testing. Next, some background about Formal Description Techniques is given and recent Formal Descriptions of the ISO Network and Transport Layer are introduced. Finally, conformance testing is reviewed and possible NATO requirements are considered.

2. NATO NETWORK AND TRANSPORT PROTOCOLS

The development of Transport and Network Layer standards for NATO has progressed since 1981 through the work of Sub group 9 (SG/9) of the Tri Service Group on Communications and Electronic Equipment (TSGCEE-AC/302) and SG/9's working group (WG1). Following the decision by NATO to adopt the International Standards Organization (ISO) layered architecture model (1) SG/9 and WG1 have concentrated on drafting the protocol and service Standardization Agreements (STANAGs) for this architecture and on the extensions and enhancements to the civilian standards that are required to meet the military needs (2).

The protocols at the Network Layer are still under study in ISO. Two ongoing ISO activities that are important for the NATO Network Layer are the development of a connectionless internet protocol (3) and the work on X.25 at the network level (4). The development of NATO

R. W. G. Herbers (ed), The Upper Layers of Open Systems Interconnection, 201–207.
© *1987 by D. Reidel Publishing Company.*

Network Protocols cannot progress faster than the ISO work on these
standards. The inclusion of satellite and radio networks receives
little attention in ISO but is important for NATO. Appropriate Network
Layer protocols are needed. It is hoped that the draft STANAG 4263, the
Network Protocol Specification (5) will serve to organize these
developments and expedite decisions on NATO Network Protocols during
the next few years.

The definition of the service features at the Network-Transport
layer interface is given in draft STANAG 4253, Network Service Definition (6). This document states that the NATO network service is as
defined in the corresponding ISO document (7) and the addendum for
connectionless services (8). When this ISO document achieves international standard status it should be possible to finalize STANAG 4253,
provided that the provision of military features has been completed by
NATO in the interim.

The ISO transport protocol standard (9) is quite mature and hence
the NATO Transport Protocol Specification, STANAG 4264 (10) may be the
first STANAG to contain a ratified protocol. However, before the NATQ
STANAG is complete the connectionless addendum (11) must be included.
In addition, the incorporation of military features and special-case
transport protocols must be understood. Mechanisms for the interoperation of the US DoD Transmission Control Protocol (TCP) with the
ISO (Class 4) transport protocol have been described recently (12, 13)
and hence the possible coexistence of alternative Transport Layer
protocols must be studied.

3. PROTOCOL TESTING

The NATO decision to adopt the ISO model has led to rapid progress in
the development of draft STANAGS for the Network and Transport Layers.
The incorporation of military features seems likely to require differences from the ISO standards. Any unique protocol that results must be
tested for correctness and conformance. The appropriate tools should be
under development in parallel with the definition and specification
activity.

The expression "protocol testing" is used here as a general term
to include the vast array of procedures and techniques that are available or are under study to aid in the design of errorfree protocols and
in the evaluation of implementations for conformance with the specifications. Several excellent reviews are available (14, 15) and international symposiums are held annually (16).

The characteristics to be tested in a protocol design include
behaviour and performance. Here behaviour concerns the functional and
logical structure of the protocol and design errors must be avoided
otherwise unexpected and incorrect behaviour will occur. Performance
concerns those issues associated with efficiency measures, typically
throughput, delay and recovery times.

There are many approaches to testing protocols. It seems useful to
separate these into two categories: those used in designing and
specifiying protocols and those used to evaluate an implementation for
conformance to the standard specification.

The procedures and techniques that are available for the first
category include analytical modelling, simulation studies and formal
techniques (17). Analytical models and simulations have been useful to
study link layer communication protocols such as multiple access (18)
and error control procedures (19). Protocols at the middle and upper
layers of the reference model seem, however, to be too complex for
simple approaches and the research has been increasingly focussed on
formal procedures. A variety of computational models and their
accompanying analysis methods have been applied to protocols (14, 20).
In addition a sophisticated simulation system suitable for the
Transport Layer is under development (21).

In addition to concerns about the design and specification of
correct protocols, procedures are needed to test protocol
implementation for conformance to the reference specification. In the
first packet switching networks, for example ARPANET, the correctness
of implementations was tested on-the-air using iterative debugging.
However, with the growth of international standards and the proli-
feration of communication nets accessible to independent implementors,
the need for a more formal conformance testing arrangement has arisen.
Conformance testing is the subject of later section of this paper.

4. FORMAL DESCRIPTION TECHNIQUES

Protocols should be specified clearly and unambiguously so that
implementors can develop correct and compatible implementations. Within
ISO, Formal Description Techniques (FDTs) are being developed for this
purpose. In 1980 ISO/TC/97/SC16/WG1 created an ad hoc group on FDT (22)
which subsequently formed three subgroups. Subgroup A considers
architectural concepts and how these support the work of subgroups B
and C. Subgroup B is developing description techniques based on
extended finite state machines, Pascal and a state transition model
(Estelle) (23). Subgroup C is developing description techniques based
on temporal ordering of interaction primitives (Lotus) (24). The FDT
group presently spends most of its effort in the development of (trial)
formal specificaions for the existing ISO protocols.

The formal protocol and service specifications have been developed
for the Network and Transport layers using Estelle as the basis for a
performance study of alternative transport protocols in different
system architectures (25). To lay the foundation for detailed study of
performance issues a notation for performance specifications has been
developed which allows the addition of performance statements in the
formal specification of the communication protocol or service.

It is important that protocols under development in NATO have the
clarity and non-ambiguity offered by FDTs. While it is reasonable to
expect that the ISO work on FDT will be useful to the NATO protocol
designers an expertise in FDT description should be available for those
protocols which deviate signficantly from the civilian standards.

5. CONFORMANCE TESTING

If a protocol implementation is to work with other implementations then
its behaviour should be tested for adherence to the protocol standard
specification. In addition, an implementation must meet user requirements with regard to characteristics such as the range of options supported (functional range), the performance (throughput and response
time) and the robustness (degree to which an implementation is able to
recover from error situations). Conformance procedures are under development in ISO to test protocol implementations for this purpose.

The question of conformance was raised as an official question
within ISO TC97/SG16/WG 1 in 1982. The question was elaborated at such
a rate that by 1984 a checklist for protocol designers was available
and a multi-part formulation of the question was begun, starting with
the meaning of conformance and ending with questions of whether testing
methodology and test specifications need to be standardized. A rapport-
eurs group was set up to work on the technical subjects of testing
methodology and test suite specification. An excellent report on this
topic is available (26). The next few paragraphs give a brief review of
that report.

The intention of the checklist is to help protocol designers
produce standards which avoid ambiguous or untestable conformance
requirements. As yet too few protocol definers are taking notice of the
advice available in the checklist. In particular, the requirements on
the capabilities of an implementation tend to be only partially defined. Test definers will inevitably discover latent conformance problems in their standards and will have to seek their correction. In
light of this, those bodies defining protocols for NATO should become
familiar with and work to this checklist.

The rapporteur's group has agreed to concern itself initially with
abstract testing methods which are applicable to OSI connection-
oriented protocols in the Transport, Session and Presentation Layers.
These abstract testing methods are described in terms of what outputs
from the OSI protocol entity under test are observed and what inputs to
it can be controlled. More specifically, the behaviour of an (N)-entity
is defined in terms of (N) - Abstract Service Primitives (ASPs) and (N-
1) ASPs. Each of these two sets of interactions can be observed and
controlled from several different points, directly or remotely and this
has led to the definition of a suite of conformance tests for each of
three abstract testing methods. Testers are expected to select the most
appropriate suite for the implementation under test. Details are given
in (26).

The extent of the apllicability of these abstract testing methods to other layers is worth consideration. Since the application and physical layers both have a service boundary that extends out of the seven layer model, it is recognized that these methods are not easily applicable at these layers. To make them applicable to the Link and Network layers some of these methods may need adapting because the (N-1)-Service is not then end-to-end. Some further development may also be needed for connectionless protocols and services. Further study on all these issues is recommended in (22).

The level of international participation in this ISO activity is such that rapid progress can be expected at least on the technical issues. Nevertheless, with so many OSI protocols this work will take a long time to complete. The major benefit, however, of agreed conformance test suites should be much better conformance of complementations to OSI standards and thereby more reliable intercommuncication which is, of course the goal of the NATO standards activity.

The following general observations are made with regard to NATO requirements. The conformance testing capabilities developed by civilian agencies may not be suitable for NATO standards for both technical and political reasons. NATO is developing standards in close parallel to the ISO and hence should be able to take full advantage of the ISO work. However, to the exent that deviations and enhancements must be introduced to meet military needs, NATO will have unique standards with the possibility of peculiar testing requirements. The civilian facilities may not be capable of handling these tests. Also, for reasons of autonomy and security, it might be necessary that NATO have its own capability rather than have to use civilian testing facilities located in particular nations. This discussion argues for the necessity of a conformance testing capability in NATO that should be developed in parallel with the protocol standards work.

6. CONCLUSION

Rapid progress has been made in the development of NATO standards for data communications in the last few years. Parallel work must be supported to ensure that the necessary tools and techniques are available to test the protocols if the objective of reliable technical interoperability is to be achieved.

This paper has been largely a review of the subject of protocol testing with reference to the relevance for NATO standards development especially at the Network and Transport Layers. A recent Formal Description of the ISO network and transport layer has been introduced. FDTs should be considered for NATO standards because they provide clear and unambiguous specifications.

A recurring theme in this paper concerns the need for testing tools available to the NATO protocol designers. Before systems can be built and deployed the conformance fo the implementations to the standard specification must be demonstrated. Much work remains to be done.

ACKNOWLEDGEMENTS

The FDTs described in this paper have been developed by DR. G.V.
Bochmann of Cerbo Informatique Inc., Montreal. Dr. O Monkewich of the
Canadian Department of Communications is contributing to the ISO work
on conformance testing. His assistance to the author's understanding of
the issues is acknowledged.

REFERENCES

1.   Open Systems Interconnection - Basic Reference Model. ISO 7498.

2.   Approach to ISO. Enclosure 3 to DS/C/EL(82) 369, 1982.

3.   Protocol for Providing the Connectionless-Mode Network Service.
     ISO/DIS8473, July 1984.

4.   Use of X.25 to Provide the OSI Connection-Oriented Network
     Service. ISO TC97/SC6 N3148, June 1984.

5.   Network Protocol Specifications. Draft NATO STANAG 4263, TSGCEE
     SG/9 WG1, Oct. 1984.

6.   Network Service Definition. Draft NATO STANAG 4253, TSGCEE SG/9
     WG1, Oct. 1984.

7.   Data Communications- Network Service Definition. ISO/DIS-8348,
     April 1984.

8.   Addendum to the Network Service Definition Covering
     Connectionless-Mode Transmission. ISO/DP8348/DAD1, Aug. 1983.

9.   Open Systems Interconnection - Transport Protocol Specification.
     ISO/DIS 8073.

10. Transport Protocol Specification. Draft NATO STANAG 4264, TSGCEE
     SG/9 WG1, Oct. 1984.

11. Connectionless Transport Protocol Addendum. ISO TC 97/SC16
     N 1705, Oct. 1983.

12. The TCP and ISO Transport Service - A Brief Description and
     Comparison, I. Groenbeck. Shape Technical Centre TM726, Sept.
     1983.

13. Comparison of DoD (US) and ISO/CCITT Transport Layers. Cerbo
     Informatique Inc., Final Report Part II for DOC Research Contract
     OST83-00082, December 1984 (to be released).

14. Special Section on Protocol Specification, Testing and
    Verification. C.A. Sunshine (ed.), IEEE Trans.Comm., Dec. 1982.

15. Special Issue on Protocol Specification, Testing and
    Verification. C.A. Sunshine (ed.) Comp. Networks 6, Dec. 1982.

16. Protocol Specification, Testing, and Verification, III.
    Proceedings IFIP WG 6.1, Third International Workshop, M. Rudin
    and C. West (ed.), May 1983.

17. Testing and Conformance of ISO Protocols. AC/302 (SG/9) WP ....
    (draft) December 1984.

18. Multi access Protocols in Packet Communications Systems. F.A.
    Tobagi, IEEE Trans. Comm. 28, April 1980.

19. Modelling and Measurement Techniques in Packet Communications
    Networks. F.A. Tobagi et.al., Proc. IEEE 66, Nov. 1978.

20. Formal Methods in Communication Protocol Design. G.V. Bochmann
    and C.A. Sunshine, IEEE Trans. Comm., April 1980.

21. A Simulation Tool for Formal Specifications. Cerbo Informatique
    Inc., Interim Report 3, DOC Research Contract OST83-00082, Dec.
    1984 (to be released).

22. Formal Description Techniques for OSI: an Example. G.V. Bochmann,
    Proc. IEEE INFOCOM '84, April 1984.

23. A FDT Based on Extended State Transition model. ISO TC97/SC16
    N13T7 revised July 1983.

24. Draft Tutorial Document on Temporal Ordering Specification
    Language. ISO TC97/SC16N..., Aug. 1983.

25. Example of a Network Service Specification. Interim Report 1;
    Example of a Transport Protocol Specification. Annex to Part 1,
    Final Report for DOC Research Contract OST83-00082, Dec. 1984
    (to be released).

26. Conformance Testing within ISO. D. Rayner, Pg. 43, Second
    International Conference on Introduction of Open Systems
    Interconnection Standards, Ottawa, Canada, May 1984.

Session 7

Applications of OSI and Proprietary Systems

Session Chairman: Walter H.P. Schmidt

THE TELETEX SERVICE
DEVELOPMENT IN THE FEDERAL REPUBLIC OF GERMANY AND IN THE
INTERNATIONAL ARENA

Rolf Rueggeberg
Deutsche Bundespost
Fernmeldetechnisches Zentralamt (FTZ)
Am Kavalleriesand 3
D-6100 Darmstadt 3
West-Germany

CONTENTS

1. TELETEX DEVELOPMENT FROM 1976 UNTIL TO-DAY

1976 In March the "Commission for the Development of the Technical
     Communication System (KtK) recommended the introduction of the
     new text communication service "Teletex". This recommendation
     was contained in the category "New Telecommunication Services in
     existing Networks" of the Telecommunication Report which the KtK
     presented to the Federal Government.
         In the same year the German Federal Post presented a new
     study question to the CCITT, the body for International
     standardisation by Telecommunications Administrations in Geneva.
     The General Assembly accepted the new study question and thus
     created the basis for international standardisation of the
     teletex service in the study period 1977-1980.

R. W. G. Herbers (ed), The Upper Layers of Open Systems Interconnection, 211–231.
© *1987 by D. Reidel Publishing Company.*

In the same Year the German Federal Post, through the
Federal Minister Ehmke, set up the working group "Text" in which
manufacturers and user organisations together with experts from
the German Federal Post defined the conditions and
characteristics of the new service Teletex.

1979 The CCITT organised in Geneva the "First CCITT Symposium on New
Tele-communication Services" from 14-16 May. This was the first
time that the new Telematic Services such as Telefax, Videotex
and Teletex were presented to an international audience.

1980 For the first time the characteristics of the Teletex Service
were presented at the Hanover Fair. Five compatible terminals
(Olympia, Philips, SEL, Siemens and Triumph-Adler with 2 types)
were presented.

In June the terminals of about 700 subscribers were
converted to CCITT-technique.

International service with Austria was inaugurated.

1983 February: opening of Teletex Service with Canada
     September: opening of Teletex Service with USA
     October: opening of Teletex Service with Sweden
     December: opening of Teletex Service with Finland.

2.THE TELETEX SERVICE

2.1 WHAT IS TELETEX?

2.1.1. Difference compared with Telex

The Teletex Service can, simplified, be characterised by the following
statements:

The office typewriter with its full character set should be provided with communication capability. The same machine which is used for
the preparation of texts (Office correspondence) should also be capable
of transmitting and receiving text so that a part of the correspondence
which is at present still transported physically can be conveyed considerably faster and more economically using telecommunication techniques.

Here the differences to the telex service are already indicated:

1.   The Teletex terminal equipment is located at the typist's
     position and is used for preparation of texts using all the
     possibilities of a memory typewriter.

     Texts when completely prepared are stored and are
     transmitted directly from this store via the telecommunications
     network to the recipient.

     Telex terminal machines are in most cases located in an
     organisational unit. A text to be transmitted is previously
     prepared and before transmission must be again typed out.

2.   The teletex terminal is based on the functions of an office
     typewriter with its full character set.

In the telex service International Alphabet No. 2 is used. As compared with the character set of a typewriter it is limited: It uses only figures 0 to 9, only lower case (or upper case), no umlauts, no special characters and no accents.

3. The teletex terminal transmits the messages at a speed of 2400 bits/second, i.e. a DIN-A4 page with normal printing is transmitted in about 10 secs.

In the telex service which has already been in existence for 50 years (!), the transmission speed has been standardised at 50 bauds (= 6 2/3 characters/sec) so that the same message requiring a transmission time of 10 sec. in the teletex service would require a transmission time of 3 minutes in the telex service. As compared with the telex service, the teletex service offers not only improved characteristics (full character set of the office typewriter, higher transmission speed). The essential difference lies in the fact that the teletex terminal is used in the typist's position for the generation of texts. Teletex is not "improved telex" but rather extends from the "typewriter with communication facility" to "text processing equipment with communication capability".

2.2. THE TELETEX SERVICE IS A SUBSCRIBER SERVICE

In comparison with those services which are available to anyone as required, e.g. mail and parcel service of the postal authorities or the telegram service of the telecommunication authorities, the utilisation of a subscriber service is essentially limited to the group of the so-called subscribers. Due to the establishment of public telephones and public telex facilities these services are, for the origination of traffic, available to everyone, however the transmission of a message relative to the traffic destination is only possible to subscribers to the service.

The essential characteristics of a subscriber service contain the following four points:

1. Compatibility between terminals.
2. Guaranteed service quality.
3. Subscriber directory.
4. Reasonable charges.

In the first case compatibility between terminals makes it possible for traffic "anyone to anyone", which is handled according to a defined quality of service guaranteed by the administration. The subscriber directory contains the necessary information as to those taking part in the service and how they can be reached. Finally the charges which the subscriber must pay for this service must bear a reasonable relation to the service performance.

     While the compatibility between terminals can be defined on an
international basis and thus belongs to the area of responsibility of
the international body, the other three characteristics lie completely
within the area of responsibility of the national administrations and
operating companies.

2.3. ESTABLISHING PERFORMANCE CHARACTERISTICS

Here under a number of characteristics are enumerated, which have been
established for the international teletex service and outline the efficiency of the teletex service.

a) The transmission speed is 2,400 bits/sec., i.e. a normally printed
DIN-A 4 page is transmitted in about 10 seconds!

b) The format of a teletex page - the printable area of a page - has
been established in such a way that both the North American format and
the DIN-A 4 page can be used both in vertical and horizontal format.
The printable area is defined by the maximum number of lines (56 high,
40 horizontal) and the maximum number of characters per line (77 high,
92 horizontal) with a character spacing of 2,54 mm.

c) Provision of a receive store in the teletex terminal is obligatory.
To determine the size of receive memory required in individual cases,
service quality criteria are laid down by means of which the minimum
size of the receive store can be established. Thus the size of the
receive store can vary between 12k (low volume of incoming traffic) and
74k (large incoming traffic volume), assuming undisturbed local
operation for one hour.

d) To ensure international compatibility in the transmission of texts a
basic character set was defined comprising the total of all latin
characters appearing on the keyboards of typewriters in countries with
latin characters. This totalled 308 characters. Naturally the teletex
terminal generates only those characters which can be generated by the
keyboard as fitted (= minimum set of the international basic character
set). On the other hand the complete character set must be received and
printed out.

e) For unequivocal identification of a teletex terminal and to ensure
the automatic verification of the subscriber which has been reached by
the calling terminal a teletex terminal identification was established,
consisting of:

    - country identification number
    - the national subscriber number and
    - a letter group.

The data which characterises a connection is termed the communcation
data and is combined in the so-called communication data line.

On every page the first printable line is reserved for printout of the communication data line. This line consists of:

- the identification of the calling subscriber
- the identification of the called subscriber
- time and date
- reference information for document and page

with a length totalling 72 characters.

f) For interworking with telex a converter unit in the network for speed conversion (from 2400 bits/sec to 50 bits/sec), for code conversion (8 bit into 5 bit) and procedure conversion (Teletex procedure into telex procedure) must be defined. The teletex terminal operates in the so-called "telex-mode", whereby:
- only characters in the telex alphabet may be used and
- line length is limited to 69 characters (telex format).

g) For processing of teletex traffic a procedure has been defined which takes into account that

- in different countries the teletex service will be provided in different networks (circuit switched or packet switched data networks, telephone networks)
- in addition to the basic characteristics, so-called "options"

  can be used (options are characteristics which do not belong to

  the basic service but can be standardised for world-wide use e.g. national or user-oriented character sets, mixed operation with character-coded and facsimile-coded messages, other formats etc.).
- the subscriber can also use non standard functions (so-called "private non-functions") such as e.g. ciphering, industry-oriented text processing.

3. TELETEX SERVICE IN THE GERMAN FEDERAL REPBLIC

3.1 DEVELOPMENT OF TELETEX CONNECTIONS

The first forecast in 1979 of the development of the teletex service predicted that, following the introduction of the service in 1981 the number of teletex terminals would reach about 40,000 during 1985 and by 1990 would be about 120,000.

Because the introduction of Teletex was delayed the growth was somewhat slower, and the forecast was changed to the following values:

end 1983:   4,000
1985:   18,000
1990:   90,000

Table 1 and Figure 1 show the actual growth of connections:

```
--------------------------------------------------
Month                   Ttx                  Growth
                        Connections          %
--------------------------------------------------
01.06.81                150
01.08.81                230                  53
11.10.81                340                  48
01.12.81                460                  35
01.02.82                570                  24
01.04.82                640                  12
01.06.82                780                  22
01.08.82                980                  26
01.10.82                1.230                26
01.12.82                1.520                24
01.02.83                1.854                22
01.04.83                2.227                20
01.06.83                2.575                16
01.08.83                2.977                16
01.10.83                3.402                14
01.01.84                4.325                27
01.03.84                5.050                17
01.05.84                5.784                15
01.07.84                6.320                 9
01.09.84                7.070                12
01.11.84                7.806                10
--------------------------------------------------
```

Table 1: Development of Teletex Subscribers.

Given the stated conditions it is to be expected that in accordance with the forecast, by the end of 1984 - 8,000 and end 1985 - 18,000 teletex subscribers will be connected.

3.2. AUTHORISED TERMINALS

The terminal equipment market in the area of the German Federal Post is liberal, every domestic and foreign manufacturer of teletex terminals may offer, in so far as the technical specifications of the authorisation requirements are fulfilled. These authorisation requirements were compiled in collaboration with the equipment supplier industry in the "Text Working Party".

The presently valid list of authorised teletex terminal systems comprises, as at 6 January 1984, 42 Terminals and systems as set out in the following Table 2.

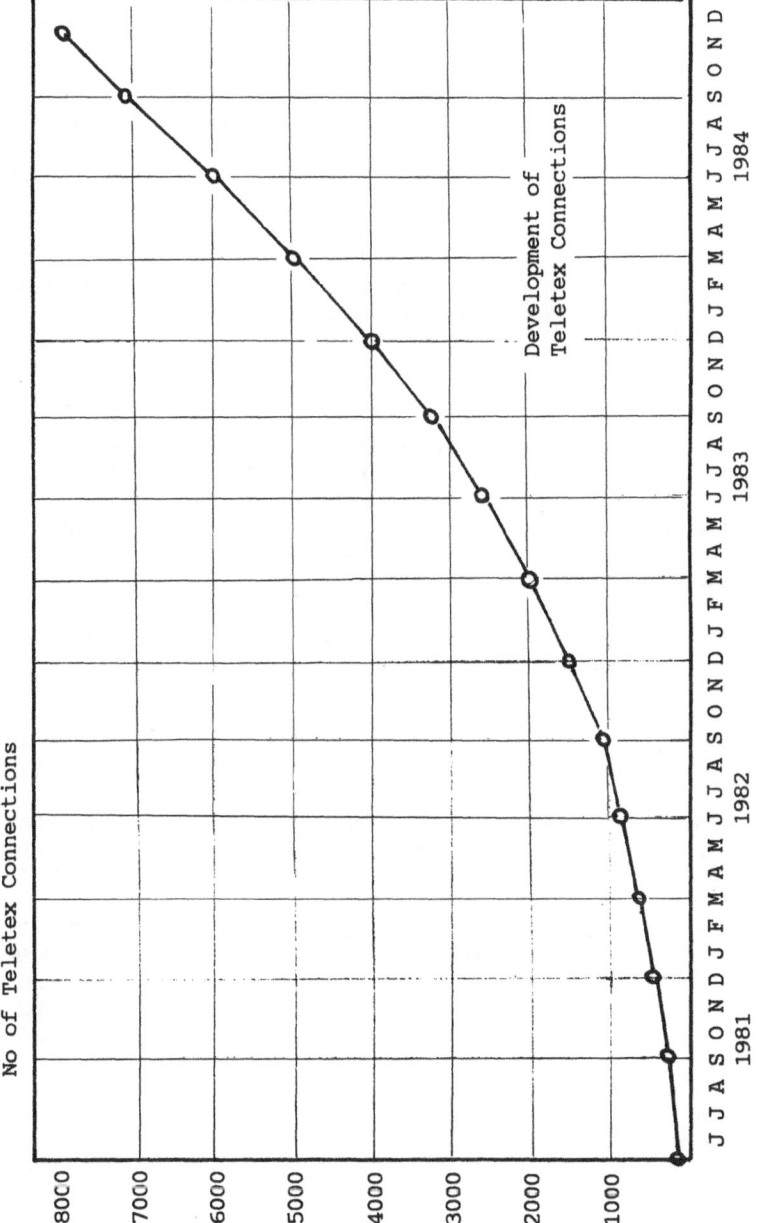

Figure 1

Firm	Type	Permit No.
Beaugrand Datentechnik GmbH	Textverarb-Systeme Alphatext	FTZ03075D
ctM Konstanz	Textsyxtem CTM TS 100, TS200, SBS	FTZ02970D
DE TE WE Berlin	cobos 10 ttx	FTZ02786D
DE TE WE Berlin	cobos 100 ttx	FTZ02982D
Deutsche Olivetti, Ffm	ET 351 Ttx	FTZ02779D
Digital Equipment GmbH	System Rainbow 100	FTZ03100D
egs mbH, Erkrath	MINI, MINITRITEX, QUINTEX, egs 45	FTZ03120D
Ericsson Duesseldorf	Eritex 10	FTZ03000D
Exxon Hamburg	Textsystem Exxon 500	FTZ02934D
Hasler GmbH, Olching	Hasler Silk 500	FTZ03071D
Hasler Precisa Eschborn	Hermes top-tronic/Teletex	FTZ02797D
IBM Stuttgart	Schreibsystem ibM 6580	FTZ0271500D
IBM Stuttgart	Electron.Kugelkopfsp.- Schrbm. IBM 85	FTZ02878D
Kienzle Apparate GmbH	Datenverarb.Anlage Modellreihe 9000	FTZ02857D
Kneisler electronik Brschwg	TurboTTX	FTZ03023D
Kneisler electronik Brschwg	TurboTTX-N	FTZ03025D
Nixdorf Paderborn	Datenverarb.Anlage System 886X	FTZ02858D
Olympia Wilhelmshaven	Disque mit IKBS	FTZ02911D
Olympia Wilhelmshaven	ES 340 mit IKBS	FTZ02912D
Olympia Wilhelmshaven	FP 40 mit IKBS	FTZ02913D
Olympia Wilhelmshaven	Textautom. ES 110,150, 180,340, FP 40	FTZ02707D
Olympia Wilhelmshaven	wie oben, mit KBS 203	FTZ02708D
Philips Data Systems	Textsystem P5002/P5003	FTZ02946D
Philips Data Systems	Text-Datenverarb. Serie P 3000/4000	FTZ02946D
Philips Data Systems	Textstation P5020	FTZ02947D
Ricoh Deutschland	Teletex-Terminal EX 5120	FTZ02919D
SEL Pforzheim	SEL Textsystem 3150	FTZ02590D
Siemens AG	Siemens 5505 ttx	FTZ02803D
Siemens AG	Textstation T 4200 Modell 40	FTZ02817D
TEKADE Nürnberg	P 5700	FTZ02818D
TEKADE Nürnberg	TEKATEXT 40	FTZ02078D
Telefonbau & Normalzeit	TENOTEX 10, 15 u. 20	FTZ02928D
Telefonbau & Normalzeit	TENOTEX 15 mit IKBS	FTZ03020D
Telefonbau & Normalzeit	ttx-Ergänzungsbaugruppe TEB	FTZ03082D
Telefonbau & Normalzeit	Konzentrierende Ein- richtung KET	FTZ03083D

Triumph Adler AG	SE 1042 mit EDK 201	FTZ02789D
Triumph Adler AG	SE 1042 mit EDK 202	FTZ02808D
Triumph Adler AG	Bitsy 1, Bitsy 10	FTZ02828D
Triumph Adler AG	Alphatronic	FTZ03126D
Wang Deutschland GmbH	WANG PROFESSIONAL COMPUTER	FTZ03126D
Wang Deutschland GmbH	Büroinformationssystem WANG OIS	FTZ03128D

Table 2: List of Permitted Terminals (Status 6.1.84)

3.3. TELETEX FIELD TRIALS

3.3.1. General

Between 1979 - 1981 several extensive field trials were carried out by
the industry, and supported by the German Ministry for Research and
Technology. These included the following projects under the overall
designation "Research Project Office Communication":

1. ALLIANZ
   User: Allianz Insurance Company
   Manufacturer: AEG/Telefunken, T&N, Olympia

2. TEKOM
   User: Siemens AG
   Manufacturer: Siemens AG

The accompanying scientific research was in the hands of:

    Professor Picot (University of Hannover)
    Professor Reichwald (Military Academy, Munich)

In addition to the testing of terminals under normal operating
conditions, the aims of the field trials included the following:

-   acceptance of the new service
-   economic viability in consideration of qualitative and

    structural aspects
-   influence on office organisation
-   influence on personnel

The field trials were carried out in the following three phases:

Phase I: Investigation of existing organisation and
            structure/quality of text traffic (before introduction of
            the new technique)
Phase II: Testing of local functions by operators
Phase III: Testing of communication functions, influence on office
            organisation.

3.3.2. Extent of Field Trials

Teletex terminals were installed in the offices of the named nation-
wide organisations. In all these were:

        635 Users (Departements)
        142 Typists
         77 Terminals.

Figure 2 provides a survey of the communication network which was used
in the teletex field trial:

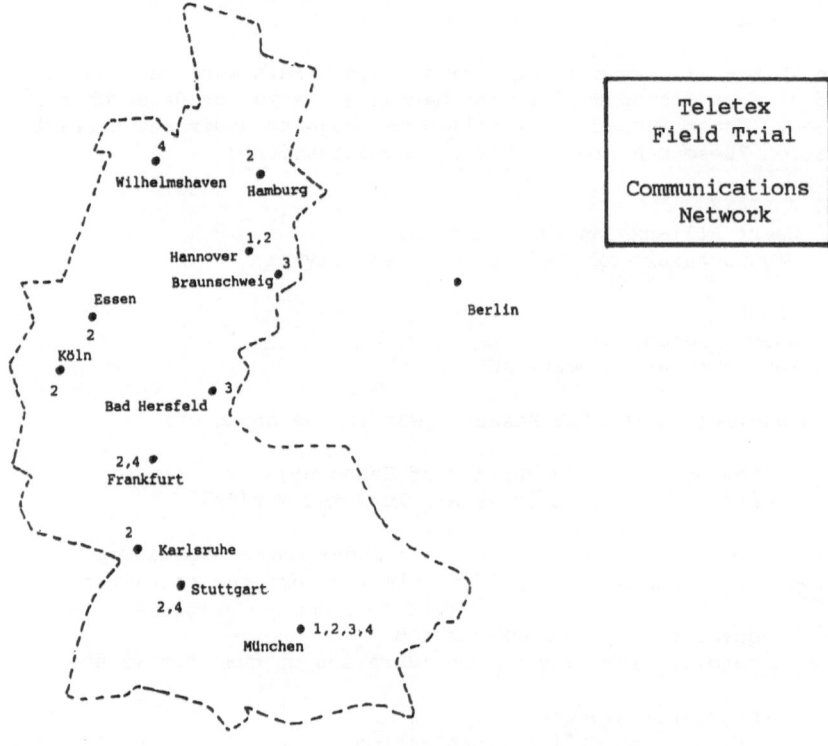

Fig. 2

(1) Universities
(2) Offices of Allianz Versicherungsgesellschaft
(3) Offices of Siemens Organisation
(4) Location of Manufacturers: Wilhelmshaven: Olympia
                               Frankfurt: T&N
                               Stuttgart: AEG/Telefunken
                               München: Siemens AG
                               Berlin: all

3.3.3. Some Results

Figure 3 shows one result from Phase I.
    In large organisations only 10-20% of the total correspondence is
external communication. The balace is subdivided 50% each traffic
within the Department and within the organisation.
    Consequently large organisations will use teletex primarily for
the handling of internal traffic.

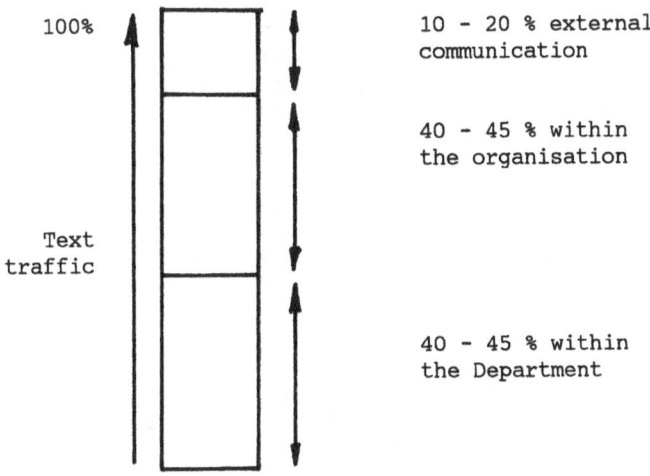

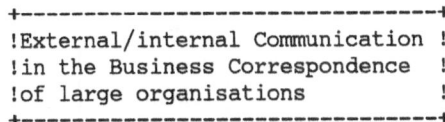

Fig. 3

The users were asked how they assess the usefulness of the teletex
service in their organisation in respect of the following criteria:

- time-saving
- necessary
- useful
- practical
- helpful

The answers were very positive (no negative or neutral answers). The result acknowledged already in an early phase that teletex was accepted by the users:

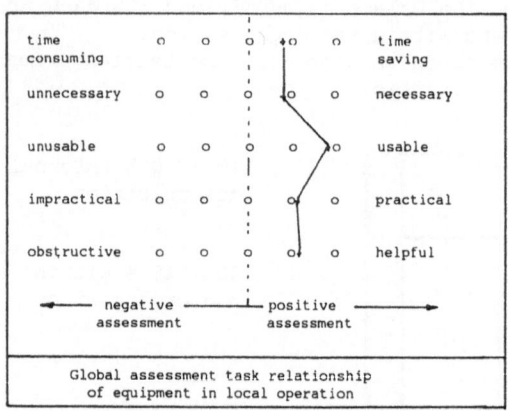

Fig. 4

The typists were questioned about the operation and service of the teletex terminals. The answers (Fig. 5) were likewise very positive with one exception: the printing was too loud.

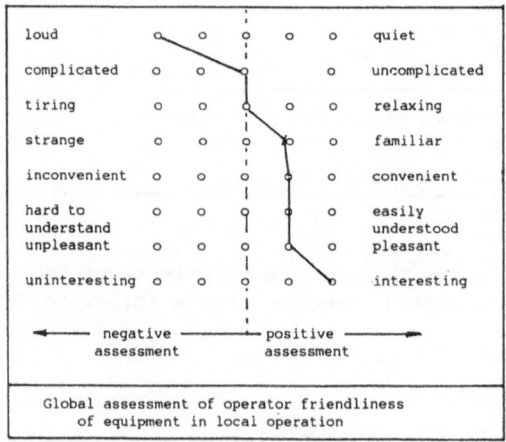

Fig. 5

To be fair: These terminals were prototypes from the year 1975. Present
day terminals are quieter. However, it appears to one typist that the
automatic printing at a speed which is faster than the typing speed, is
always more irritating than "normal" operation with manual input.

The secretarial positions were equipped with Telex, Telefax and
Teletex terminals. Furthermore telephone and internal post were also
available. The decision was left to the secretary as to which
communication channel she would employ for each required communication.
Figure 6 shows how these channels for internal and external
communications were used.

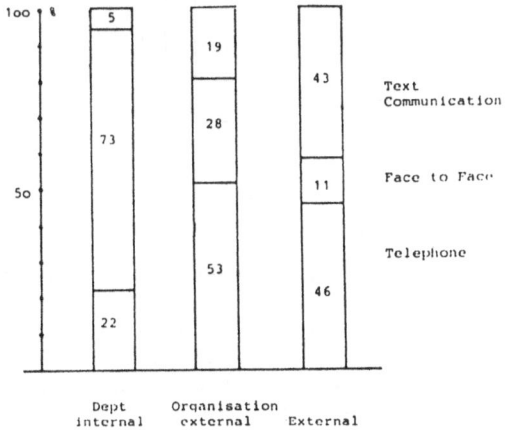

Usage of communication channels
between Internal/External
Communication partners
(Industry Management)

Fig. 6

Within the Department 73% of communications were made by personal
contact, only 22% by telephone and 5% in writing.

Within the Organisation telephone communication was used or more
than 50%, however only 28% by personal contact and 19% by written
communication. In external communication 11% took place by personal
contact, 64% by telephone and 43% written.

The participants were asked how teletex would possibly influence
the use of communication channels and substitute for it.

The answers are set out in Fig. 7.

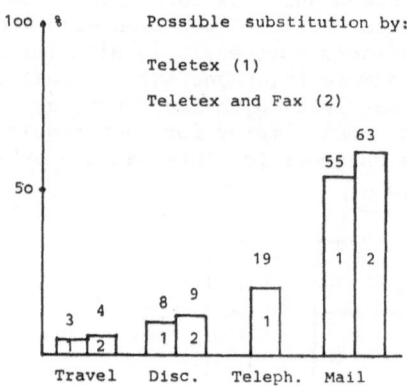

Fig. 7

The possible substitution of teletex for travel is neglectable, the possible influence on personal discussion is similarly relatively slight. The large traffic proportion lies with letter post. Within the business area more than 10 million letters are sent daily. If 63% of these could be replaced by teletex, this corresponds to a traffic share of 6.3 million teletex transmissions per day. Assuming each terminal on average 5-10 letters per day (certainly too high) the potential market for teletex terminals is 0.6 - 1.2 millian installations!

4. THE INTERNATIONAL TELEX SERVICE

At the end of last year from the CCITT in Geneva, a "Circular Letter" with a list of questions covering the plans for the introduction of teletex service in the various countries was sent to all telecommunications administrations world wide. It included the following questions:

  1. In which network is Teletex being introduced?
  2. Which procedure is used for interworking Telex/Teletex?
  3. When will national service be opened?
  4. When will international service be introduced?
  5. By whom are terminals supplied?
  6. By whom are terminals maintained?
  7. Are terminals authorised? If yes, by whom?
  8. How many terminals are expected to be connected by 1983, 1985, 1990?

The answers to this - in all 31 - are set out in Table 3.

Comments:

To 1: According to CCITT Recommendations the Administrations are free
to chose which network is to be used for the teletex service.
Undoubtedly the Datex-L Network is the most suitable network. All
countries which have such a network available use it also for Teletex.
Overall the following subdivision results:

1. Datex-L* Network	13 countries	41,9%
2. Datex-P* Network	7 countries	22,6%
3. Switched Telephone Network (PSTN)	1 country	3,2%
4. Datex-L + PSTN	2 countries	6,5%
5. Datex-P + PSTN	4 countries	12,9%
6. Datex-L + Datex-P	3 countries	9,7%
7. Datex-L + Datex-P + PSTN	1 country	3,2%
Datex-L oriented (1 + 4 +6 + 7)	19 countries	61,3%
Datex-P orientated	15 countries	48,4%

* Datex-L generally means "Circuit Switched Data Network"
* Datex-P means "Packet Switched Data Network"

To 2: The CCITT accepted standard for interworking from Telex to
Teletex is the so-called "1-stage selection procedure".
       An essential criterion for this procedure is that the calling
telex subscriber receives in the beginning the answer back of the
teletex subscriber and remains connected to the Teletex-Telex
conversion facility until completion of transmission.
       A pre-condition for the use fo this method is that the call number
of the teletex subscriber including the telex country code and the
access code is not longer than 12 digits.
       In all countries which use the Datex-P network and for access also
the PSTN, this condition is not fulfilled. For this case a new method,
the so-called "2-stage selection procedure" has been developed.
       With the "Real-Time Method" the teletex terminal is connected via
two logical channels. The calling telex subscriber has via one channel
direct access to the teletex subscriber.

To 3 and 4: In contrast to the Federal German Republic many countries
commenced intensive work on the teletex service only in 1980. The
introduction of the teletex service has resulted correspondingly late
in these countries.
       At the end of 1984 the teletex service in Europe will be available
on a wide basis. In all these are eleven countries, 1985 seventeen,
1986 nineteen and 1987 twenty countries.

To 5 and 6: In six countries teletex terminals will be offered also by
the administration. This question was not discussed in the other
countries.

To 7: In almost all countries the terminals will be authorised by the administration. In England there is a separate authorising authority which is responsible to the Goverment (not British Telecom): (BTAB = British Telecom Approval Board).

To 8: Only in a few countries are there forecasts as to the future number of teletex terminals. In Europe the most optimistic forecast is that of the Norwegians when one considers it in relation to population. Of all the forecasts that from Telecom Canada (here unfortunately without an answer) is the most extreme.

In total 150,000 teletex terminals are expected, whereby every office work place which is equipped with a typewriter is seen as a potential work place for a teletex terminal.
Following the questionnaire the following total result:

1984	19,180
1987	134,430
1990	345,840

Nine countries provided no information.

5. DEVELOPMENT OF INTERNATIONAL STANDARDISATION

The recommendations for the Telex service compiled during the Study
Period 1977 - 1980 have been consolidated during the current Study
Period (1981 - 1984). The established principles for the basic Teletex
Service remain unaltered and have proved to be good. The following
supplements have been studied and to some extent already decided upon:

1. Two-stage dialling procedure for interworking from Teletex to
   teletex (see Part 4, Point2):
2. Procedure for dialoge-operation.
3. Procedure for "mixed-mode" operation.

Dialoge method of operation has been requested by some users e.g. for
access to Data Bank systems.

   In "mixed-mode" operation the possibility exists to transmit both
character-coded text transfer (=Teletex) and facsimile coded
information.

   For this application many Teletex subscribers indicate a large
requirement. In this application it does not concern only the
transmission of drawings or diagrams in addition to text, but above all
already prepared texts, which are not in memory, to be sent as
attachments.

   In addition by means of "mixed-mode" operation individual
letterheads may be created.

   At the moment it is not yet certain whether it will be possible to
finalise the standardisation work within this study period. Only after
completion of the standardisation work will the manufacturing industry
be able to implement the first terminal devices. At the earliest it can
be reckoned that "mixed-mode" equipment will come on the market by the
end of the 1980's.

6. OUTLOOK

In looking towards the future the question should also be answered as
to whether the expectations have been fulfilled. Multiple answers to
this question are necessary:

1. The characteristics for the Teletex service as defined by CCITT have
been justified. In its basic features Teletex has been fully accepted
by the users.

2. The standardised procedure for communication has likewise proved
correct. It can already be seen that this procedure finds wide
application beyond Teletex (see FAZ, Glimpse into Business dated19. 1.
1984 "Teletex becomes a most important standard", growing market, mixed
transmission of Text, Data and Pictures.

3. The fact that already following finalisation of the international
standards in 1980, three years later at the "Telecom 83" inGeneva, the
Teletex service is considered by all participating companies and
administrations (world-wide) as being taken for granted, is undoubtedly
a positive development.

4. Assuming the statements of overseas administrations prove to be
true, by the end of 1984 Teletex will be widely available throughout
Europe, and in overseas areas about one or two years later. That is
indeed a very rapid development, which however as viewed by the first
subscribers in the German Federal Republic is not happening quickly
enough.

5. A high percentage of possible users still delays their use of the
Teletex service because the number of subcribers is still relatively
small and the so-called "critical size" has not yet been reached. In
this respect the manufacturing industry and also the customer advisory
service of the German Federal Post should be intensified further and in
particular information should be made available concerning usage, concepts for small- and medium-size businesses.

6. The number of permitted terminals at more than 40 is unexpectedly
high and is constantly being added to. This development is unprece-
dented in the world.

7. Concerning the future development two statements should be
considered in parallel:

> The prognosis of the German Federal Post is
> considered by other European Administrations to
> be too optimistic, while industry indicates them
> as too pessimistic.

When one considers the results of the Teletex Field Trial (Referpara
3.3), the potential market for Teletex terminals is seen as an increase
above the forecast value of the German Federal Post by more than 0.6-
1.0 Million terminals (!)
    This is also supported by the Canadian forecast,with aprognosis of
150.000 Teletex terminals by 1990. Every work place which is equipped
with a typewriter is considered a potential site for a teletex
terminal.
    Canada has about 20 million inhabitants, about one third of the
German Federal Republic. When this forecast is transferred to the
German ratio, the forecast by the German Federal Post must lie at
3450.000 Teletex terminals (!). In comparing the telex development of
the two countries, it corresponds to this ratio:
> about 50,000 Telex subscribers in Canada/
> are to be compared with about/
> 150,000 Telex subscribers in the German
> Federal Republic.

In the light of these perspectives undoubtedly we are only at the beginning. Much work in customer advisory and information is necessary until the usage of the Teletex service in the offices of businesses in industry and administration becomes a matter of course.

Annex

Responses to the Teletex Questionnaire (December 1984)

Administration/ RPOA	Network (1)	Interworking Telex/Teletex (2)	national service (3)	Internat. service (4)	Provision of termin. (5)	Maintenance of terminals (6)	Approval (7)	1984 (8.1)	1987 (8.2)	1990 (8.3)	Comments made by the Administrations/RPOAs concerned (9)
AUSTRIA	CSDN	one stage	1983	1983	private	private	PTT	600	2000	4000	
BELGIUM	PSTN	real time	1984	1984/85	priv./PTT	priv./PTT	PTT	50	1500	4500	
DENMARK	CSDN	one stage	1984	1984	priv./PTT	priv./PTT	PTT	350	3000	7200	All terminals are connected via an Administration provided DCE, that protects the network. Therefore type approval will only be a protocol testing.
FINLAND (PTT)	CSDN	one stage	1984	1984	priv./PTT	priv./PTT	PTT	800	3300	n.a.	A CSDN test traffic started 1983, domestic in may. International in Nov. The full service started in June 1984. CSDN/PSTN national interworking is u.s. The provision of PSTN terminals by PTT is u.s.
FINLAND (TEL.CO.)	PSTN	u.s.	1984	u.s.	priv./ Tel.co.	priv./ Tel.co.	Tel.co.	n.a.	n.a.	n.a.	Tel.co. = private telephone companies in Finland
FRANCE	PSTN/ PSDN	two stage	1984	1985	private	private	PTT	3000	30000	100000	The French Administration is implementing a specific equipment called CEGT (Centre d'exploitation et gestion teletex) which will provide functions such as remote loading of the Teletex identifier, updating of the Teletex directory and assistance to the fix-user.
GERMANY, F. R. of	CSDN	one stage	1981	1982	private	private	PTT	7000	40000	90000	
GREECE	n.a.	n.a.	n.a.	n.a.		n.a.	n.a.	n.a.	n.a.	n.a.	1) The Teletex service is not available in our country at this moment. 2) At present we are in the initial phase of configuring the greec national data network, most probably packet switched, which is not expected to be operational before 1987. 3) As we are planning to incorporate facilities for a teletex service in our national data network, this service does not seem to be introduced in our country before the above date.
HUNGARY	CSDN	n.a.	n.a.	n.a.	private	n.a.	PTT	n.a.	n.a.	n.a.	We consider the possibility of the introduction of the teletex service, but it is not yet elaborated and so our answers are incomplete and our present expectations may change as well. We have a teletex pilot service on the circuit switched data network in service from 1981 on the character transmission rate of 2400 bit/s of which intend to start the Teletex service.
ITALY	CSDN	one stage	1984	1984	private	private	PTT	730	10000	30000	
LUXEMBOURG	PSDN/ CSDN	one stage	1985	1985	private	private	PTT	-	n.a.	n.a.	
NETHERLANDS	PSDN	two stage	1984	1984	priv./PTT	priv./PTT	PTT	500	4000	10000	1) For the Teletex service subscribers will be taken into a database control facility instead of a closed user group. 2) Electronic directory and on-line information services are being planned for.
NORWAY	CSDN	one stage	1984	1984	priv./PTT	priv./PTT	PTT	550	2600	5900	
PORTUGAL	PSDN	two stage	1986	u.s.	u.s.	u.s.	u.s.	-	100	1300	
SPAIN	PSDN	two stage	1984	1984	private	private	CTNE	1050	5750	12000	CTNE = Compania Telefonica Nacional de Espana
SWEDEN	CSDN	one stage	1983	1984	priv./PTT	priv./PTT	no	2500	10000	20000	
SWITZERLAND	PSTN	one stage	1985	1985	private	private	PTT	-	3500	7700	
TURKEY	CSDN	one stage	1985	1985	PTT	PTT	PTT	800 (1985)	2000	4000	
UNITED KINGDOM	PSTN/ PSDN	two stage	1984	1984	priv./BT	priv./BT	BABT	n.a.	n.a.	n.a.	BT = British Telecom, BABT = British Approval Board for Telecommunications

Administration/ RPOA	Network (1)	Interworking Telex/Teletex (2)	national service (3)	Internat. service (4)	Provision of termin. (5)	Maintenance of terminals (6)	Approval (7)	Terminal forecast 1984 (8.1)	1987 (8.2)	1990 (8.3)	Comments made by the Administrations/RPOAs concerned (9)
USA (ITT)	PSTN/ CSDN	one stage	1984	1984	private	private	no	n.e.	n.e.	n.e.	
USA (WUTCO)	CSDN PSDN	one stage n.a.	1983 1985	1983 1985	private private	private private	WUTCO WUTCO	n.a. n.a.	n.a. n.a.	n.a. n.a.	WUTCO = Western Union Telegraph Company
CANADA (CNCP)	CSDN	two stage	1983	1983	priv./u.s.	priv./u.s.	CNCP	n.a.	n.a.	n.a.	CNCP = Canadian National Canadian Pacific
CANADA (TC)	PSTN	two stage	1984	1984	private	priv./PTT	TC	n.a.	n.a.	n.a.	TC = Telecom Canada
ARGENTINA	PSDN	one stage	n.a.	n.a.	private	private	ENTEL	n.a.	n.a.	n.a.	ENTEL = Empresa nacional de telecomunicaciones
SURINAME	PSTN/ CSDN	one stage	1984	1985	PTT	PTT	PTT	50	1000	2500	
MOROCCO	CSDN	u.s.	1985	1986	private	private	PTT	n.a.	800	n.a.	PTC = Post & Telecommunication Corporation. Connection from Telex network to PSDN will be possible. Teletex is only scheduled for possible introduction in 1986. No detailed planning or market surveys have been carried out. So all figures are only assessments. The introduction of Teletex is dependent on funds being made available.
ZIMBABWE	CSDN (Telex)	one stage	1986	u.s.	PTC	PTC	PTC	n.a.	100	300	
IRAN	CSDN	one stage	u.s.	u.s.	priv./ICI	priv./ICI	ICI	n.e.	n.a.	n.a.	ICI = Telecommunication Company of Iran Establishment of Teletex service in Iran is under further study
AUSTRALIA	PSTN/ PSDN	two stage	1985	1986	priv./TA	priv./TA	n.a.	-	5000	35000	TA = Telecom Australia The Teletex service will be part of a total text services strategy which will also include a computer based message service (mailbox) and enhanced telex facilities.
NEW ZEALAND	PSTN/ PSDN	n.a	n.a.	n.e.	priv./NZPO	priv./NZPO	NZPO	n.a.	n.a.	n.a.	NZPO = New Zealand Post Office. This information is tentative only. No decision has yet been made to offer Teletex service in New Zealand.
INDIA	CSDN/ PSDN	one stage	n.a.	n.e.	private	private	PTT	n.e.	n.a.	n.a.	Teletex service is proposed to be tried out as a pilot project both with CSDN and PSDN being planned for installation in the next 2 or 3 years. Commercial service and terminal requirements will be firmed up only on completion of these pilot projects.
JAPAN (KDD)	CSDN/ PSDN	one stage	-	1985/86	private	private	KDD	-	70-80	190/200	KDD = Kokusai Denshin Denwa Co. Ltd. For the time being, KDD will not regard international teletex as an independent service but will admit the subscribers of Venus-P (PSDN) or Venus-C (CSDN) to connect their Teletex terminals to these networks. Whether KDD will open an independent international Teletex service or not depends on customers' requirements in the future.
JAPAN (NTT)	PSTN/ CSDN/ PSDN	u.s.	1984	n.a.	priv./NTT	priv./NTT	NTT	u.s.	u.s.	u.s.	NTT = Nippon Telegraph & Telephone
THAILAND	CSDN	one stage	1987	1987	PTD	PTD	no	-	10-20	50-100	PTD = Post and Telegraph Department. Administration will provide terminals. No type approval is necessary.
HONGKONG	PSDN	one stage	1984	1984	private	private	yes	100	3000	9000	Approval jointly provided by national and international Teletex service providers
SINGAPORE	CSDN/ PSDN	two stage	1985	1985	priv./TS	priv./TS	TS	-	800	1500	TS = Telecom Singapore PSDN by 1985, PSDN and CSDN by 1986

Abbreviations:
PSTN — Public Switched Telephone Network
PSDN — Packet Switched Data Network
CSDN — Circuit Switched Data Network

PTT — generally used for Telecommunication Administration
n.a. — no answer
u.s. — under study

OPEN SYSTEMS INTERCONNECTIONS WITH BULL
(STRATEGY AND PRODUCTS)

Guenter Boehmer
Honeywell Bull AG
Theodor-Heuss-Str. 60-66
D-5000 Koeln 90
FRG

After the declaration of the 12 Europeans on the adoption of international communication standards, BULL announces the availability of
ISO/DSA specifications enabling inter-operation of its equipment with
those of other manufacturers.

The full set of DSA connection specifications called S.I.D. (ISO/DSA
specifications) will enable our customers to build DSA networks open to
other suppliers.

R. W. G. Herbers (ed), The Upper Layers of Open Systems Interconnection, 233–240.
© 1987 by D. Reidel Publishing Company.

Beyond the European agreement on the implementation of standards in the products offered, BULL shows its will to pursue the effort for standardisation in the field of distributed applications.

1. REMARK

The choice made by the 12 European industrialist to follow international standards is justified by the fact that it is necessary in order
to enable the market to develop through the existence of standards:

- Recognised by all,
- Under control of independent organisations
- Stable, that is which do not evolve to the will of a single supplier
- Which can be defined in advance with respect to product in order to favorise innovation.

All these conditions are effectively fulfilled as long as there is the engagement on the part of a large amount of industrialists who support them.

This engagement will effectively provide an industrial validity to the standards when products begin to appear.

2. HISTORY

1976 Start of DSA definition activities
1977 Launching of the "OPEN SYSTEM" activity at ISO.
     Active participation of CII HONEYWELL BULL and HIS.
1978 ISO agreement on the "OSI" model with seven layers identical to
     the model used for DSA.
1979 First worldwide announcement for DSA and first delivery of
     DN 7100
     "CONFORMITY TO STANDARDS" message.
1980 Start of the opening of the X25 and X21 public networks.
1981 Progressively, the "OPENING BY CONFORMITY TO STANDARDS" message
     becomes a key-message.
1982 Second worldwide DSA announcement - message: implementation of
     exchanged media without jeopardising applications.
1983 Approval of "5 out of 7" layers at ISO
     European actions around the inter-operation between the products
     of the main European manufacturers.
     Delivery of 1000th BULL Datanet.
1984 - March
     Declaration of 12 European manufacturers on the adoption of
     communication standards - Selection of OSI standards,
     implementation in products.

STATE OF STANDARDISATION OF
INTERCONNECTION OF OPEN SYSTEMS

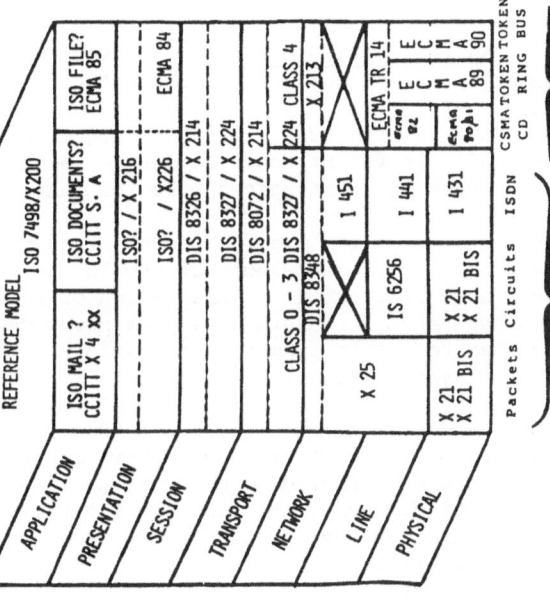

BREAKDOWN OF COMMUNICATION FUNCTIONS
SIMILAR TO TELEPHONE

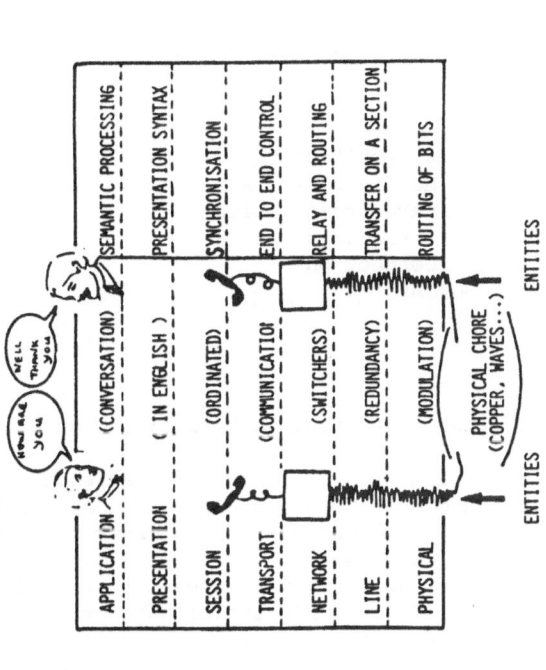

REFERENCE MODEL
ASSIGNS A SPECIFIC FUNCTION TO
EACH LAYER

3. THE EVENT

Standardisation : DSA and ISO : 5 out of 7. 5 layers out of 7 which an
ISO reference model in the network architecture field includes, have
been standardized.
        This result, to which the BULL group has largely participated
through an active and perseverent contribution for numerous years,
validates and reinforces the strategic choice for DSA in all hardware
and software products.
        To have participated in the elaboration of standards is for the
BULL group to have an intimate knowledge of the ISO reference model,
therefore the assurance of correct implementation of this model in DSA.
And it is also an assurance for users of a continuous development,
thereby enabling them to profit from the telematic services offered
from the distributed system market.
        These standards benefit from the supports of the set of competent
and recognised standardisation organisations (AFNOR, ECMA, CCITTT) in
which representatives of the BULL group have participated actively.
        Also, the presence of worldwide user organisations (banks,
airlines) to this meeting, marked the epso facto officialisation of the
impact of these standards on the distributed systems market.
        For the BULL group it is a success and the concretion of a policy
and the role it has decided to play concerning a global offer based on
a catalogue of DSA products.

Legends:

AFNOR: Association Française de Normalisation
CCITT: Comité Consultatif International pour le Télégraphe et le
         Téléphone
DIN: Deutsche Industrie Normen
DSA: Distributed Systems Architecture
ECMA: European Computer Manufacturer Association
ISO: International Standard Organisation
NBS: National Bureau of Standards
OSI: Open Systems Interconnection
SID: Specification ISO/DSA

4. STRATEGY

As early as 1979 the group's strategy in this field was always very
clear
                -    integration of international standards as soon as approval.
                ··   implementation of BULL protocols as close as possible to
                     current international definitions in order to offer complete
                     solutions to our customers.
In October 1983, this strategy was intensified with the adoption of the
newly approved Transport and Session Protocol international standard
which constitutes the proof that this strategy was founded on a solid
base.

Also, the evolution of worldwide telecommunications as well as the requirements of interoperation between products caused the European reaction at the level of the manufacture of data processing and tele-communications equipment as well as the national PTTs, the single alternative: the adoption of common standards based on the international standards.

Hence, the group strategy, which in the beginning was oriented towards our users, now takes an international dimension within the framework of the cooperation agreements between European industrial companies.

5. OFFER DESCRIPTION

The product concerned by this announcement is a set of documents, variable in number, enabling implementation on a foreign device (mini-computer, micro-computer, office automation station, work station) of a set of software used to connect this device to BULL systems.
The connection is applied at two levels:
- communication level
- application level

The communication level is based on ISO protocoles (levels 1 to 5) and because of this fact, is completely aligned on international standar-disation and does not depend on a specific manufacturer's architecture.

On the other hand, the application level is entirely dependent upon the application accessed in BULL systems and consequently depends entirely on the architecture and implementation of the manufacturer.

Because of its independence with respect to manufacturer, the communication level can be used for an interconnection between two foreign devices with the specific application level.

The connection is made through a specific entry point called "ISO/DSA Plug" available on a DN 7100 communication processor.

This proposal is a guaranty for those acquiring these specifi-cations to have interconnection means.
- perfectly in conformity to standards for the communication part
- offering a communication interface stable with respect to time (independent of Manufacturers' architecture and protocoles), with high performance since it integrates all of the most modern means for connecting to networks (x25, x21, local network, ...).

6. FUNCTIONAL DESCRIPTION

6.1. GENERAL

This chapter is devoted to the functional description of the various
tools enabling the connection of an ISA/DSA work station to a DN 7100:
-      on the same station (ISO/DSA specifications)
-      on the DN 7100 (ISO/DSA plug),
-      on the central systems (specific applications).

6.2. CONNECTION SPECIFICATIONS

The protocols and function which must be implemented in an ISO/DSA
station are described in the set of documents composed of three main
parts.

1. A basic part corresponding to the first five layers of the OSI model
(including the overall communications management and the session), in
conformity to international standards.
       The implementation of its contents supplies the necessary services
for establishing and using a session between a work station and any DSA
system.
       This documentation will reference international standards used and
will indicate the options chosen amongst these standards. The delivery
of this document will not require the signature of a confidentiality
contract since the information contained therein are public.

2. A description of the rules of usage of the services for the ISO
session in order to reach DSA applications for an ISO/DSA work station.
This document will require the signing of a confidentiality contract in
order to qcquire it and the signing of a secrecy agreement letter if
the implementation is made by a third party.

3. The set of documents corresponding to the various applications
accessible on BULL data processing systems and a specific document
describing the test functions will be developed on an ISO/DSA work
station.
       Each document will also be covered by a confidentiality contract
and if required a secrecy agreement letter.

6.3. ISO/DSA ENTRY POINT ON DN 7100

The next version of the DNS software (DNS C) will contain modules
necessary to support the ISO/DSA plug enabling the connection of
ISO/DSA work station.

7. DESCRIPTION OF PRODUCTS

General Description

In conformity to the functional description, a complete set of specifications is broken down into three sub-assemblies where each sub-assembly covers a precise functional area and, depending on its contents, justifies a commercialisation mode a s well as a given price.

Sub-assembly No. 1
SID 1.00 ISO specification (levels 1 to 5) for connection.

Sub-assembly No. 2
SID 2.00 General and common rules for the use of an ISO session by DSA applications.

Sub-assembly No. 3
SID 3.XX Descriptions of protocols required for access to DSA applications (a document per accessed application).
The documents composed in sub-assembly No. 3 available now are:
    SID 3.00 Tests
    SID 3.40 UFT.

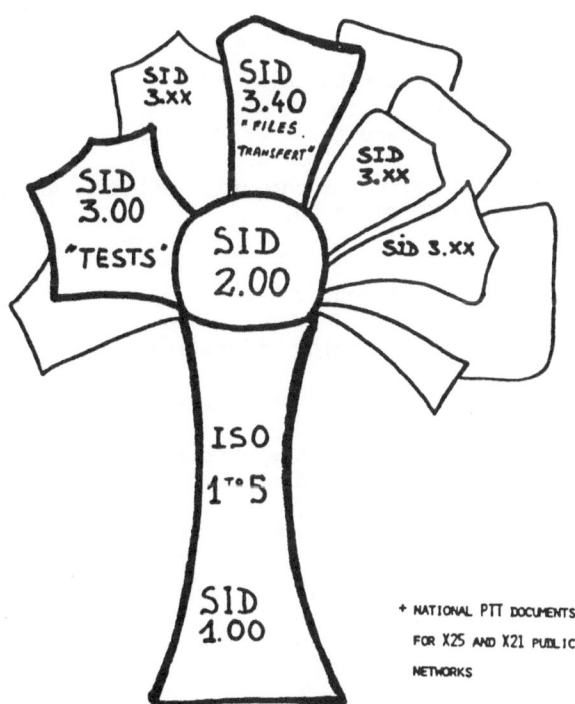

ISO/DSA SPECIFICATIONS

8. CONTENTS OF ANNOUNCED DOCUMENTS

SID.1.00   Communications management: description of the four ISO
             levels for the following communications means:

             - HDLC private line
             - X25 access (public network included)
             - X21 access (public network included).

             Message management: ISO session's description.

             The access to the X25 and X21 public networks are indicated
             in the document in the form of reference to utilisation
             specification

SID 2.00   ISO session access method.

             Presentation rules.

             Rules common to applications.

SID 3.00   Rules for the utilisation of test and debugging tools
             present in the DN 7100.

             Interpretation of test results.

             Description of test results.

             Implementation of rules for the utilisation of an ISO
             session described in SID 2.00.

SID 3.40   Description of UFT dialogue rules.

             Format of commands and coding of utilised fields.

             Format of exchanged data.

             Implementation of rules for the utilisation fo the ISO
             session described in SID 2.00.

NETWORKING STANDARDS
AT DIGITAL

Peter Gulick
DIGITAL Equipment Corporation
12, Av. des Morgins
CH-1213 Petit Lancy
Switzerland

1. INTRODUCTION

This talk will examine DIGITAL's products, plans, and positions regarding computer networking standards. Of particular importance is the work currently under way in ISO (and elsewhere) on Open Systems Interconnection, although there are other standards developments which must be taken into account.

2. DECNET - A LITTLE BACKGROUND

It is impossible to discuss networking at DIGITAL without involving DNA and DECNET. DECNET is the name given to a family of products, running on virtually all DIGITAL computers and operating systems which allows these systems to communicate with each other very easily. The DECNET products are built in accordance with the DIGITAL Network Architecture (DNA).

The first DECNET products where announced in 1974, for what were then the major DEC operating systems. All of the protocols used were designed specifically for DECNET, since at that time there were absolutely no suitable standards available. DECNET has since then been very substantially enhanced, to add many new networking functions, to support new interconnection technologies, and to improve performance. A major emphasis for DECNET has been to simplify the user's problem in managing a large network. This has resulted in a comprehensive management architecture which allows remote management, event notification and control.

DNA/DECNET development has proceeded in phases, each phase corresponding to a significant enhancement to the architecture. The most recent phase is "Phase IV", which includes support for Local Area Networks (The ETHERNET) and for large networks. Support for packet-switching networks using X.25 has been included for some time.

R. W. G. Herbers (ed), The Upper Layers of Open Systems Interconnection, 241–245.
© *1987 by D. Reidel Publishing Company.*

We know that it is not feasible to update all of the systems in a network at the same time. Because of this, it is a feature of DECNET that each new phase will interwork successfully with all implementations of the previous phase. This gives DECNET users a period of, generally, several years to complete the migration to a new phase. Intermediate versions of the products, between phases, must work with both the current phase and the previous phase, regardless of how many intermediate versions there may be.

It is worth mentioning that DECNET is used for DIGITAL's internal network of several thousand computer systems spread across the entire world. This massive network, one of the largest computer networks in the world, is an essential tool for our company and is in constant use for all aspects of our business.

3. THE EMERGING OSI STANDARDS

The OSI Architecture, the Seven-Layer Reference Model, is well-known. When the OSI model is compared with the model used in the DIGITAL Network Architecture, it will be seen that the two models are identical up to the transport layer (Layer 4). Above this the differences are fundamentally descriptive rather that substantive. The similarity between the two architectures means that it is, in principle, a straightforward matter to perform piecemeal migration of DECNET towards OSI. For example, it would be possible to replace the present proprietary transport protocol in DECNET (NSP), with its OSI equivalent. This would not affect any of the other layers of DECNET.

DIGITAL is participating heavily in the definition of OSI standards. The principal international forum for standardization is the international organization for standardization (ISO), which takes its input from national and industry bodies. DIGITAL has representatives on these bodies for all of the OSI layers. We are very pleased as a company to be able to apply the experience we have gained in ten years of DECNET, to such an important topic as an Open Multi-Vendor Networking Architecture. We are also pleased to find that, in general, this experience is welcomed.

We are certainly very well aware of the desire, by computer users, for Multi-Vendor Networks, in particular because of the procurement freedom which such networks appear to be able to offer. At the same time, we are also conscious of the need that users have for reliability, performance and a high level of integration of networking with other system functions. Many DECNET users are already taking advantage of these features of DECNET. It would not be fair to them to sacrifice these features simply in the name of conformance to standards. In other words, incorporation of OSI standards into DECNET must not compromise the usefulness of the products which the company currently has.

This means that the introduction of OSI standards into DECNET will be undertaken very carefully. If there is a clear requirement for some particular OSI standard (which will generally arise once it has been approved in the standards process, together with any necessary supporting standards), then, if it is not possible to use it without compromising the features already available through the use of a proprietary protocol, DECNET will have to support both protocols. This has already happened, for example, with X.25. X.25 does not offer the flexibility and management advantages of the DECNET Routing Layer, and therefore operates as an alternative at this layer where Open Multi-Vendor communication is required (It is also integrated for use between DIGITAL systems).

4. IMPLICATIONS OF THE STANDARDIZATION PROCESS

There are some aspects of the standardization process which create difficulties for a computer manufacturer when looking at OSI.

One of these is the very slow process of development and approval for international standards. This is inevitable, given the need to obtain consensus among many different organizations and nations, each with their own background and requirements. Nevertheless, it does mean that standards are very slow to evolve and adapt to, for example, possibilties introduced by new technologies or user requirements. It typically takes around five years from when technical work starts on standardization in a particular area, to the approval of an international standard. In many cases, this will be too long for computer users to wait for access to the required function. Therefore, proprietary or ad-hoc solutions may need to be applied to satisfy users in the meantime.

Another problem is created by the later stages of the approval cycle for ISO. It is natural that as soon as there appears to be a technically stable proposal for a standard, users want to see it implemented. This follows from the very natural desire to have open networks. However, there is a long gap between the production of a so-called "Draft Proposal" and an approved standard, generally about two years. During this time, the proposed standard may change, possibly quite drastically. There is no requirement for these changes to be made in a way which would allow intercommunication between implementations designed before and after the change. This is not just a theoretical possibilty. Exactly such a change was made, for example, at the very last stage in the approval of the ISO transport protocol. Therefore, there is a serious risk in making implementations of proposed standards available before final approval. This can lead to conflict between the objectives of satisfying user desires, and of building stable procucts which can work successfully with both previous and future versions.

In DIGITAL, we are very excited by the prospect of Multi-Vendor Networking. This is a new opportunity for all of us involved in information technology, and we are looking forward to the future provision of open networks having comparable size and function to today's proprietary networks. We know that the DIGITAL Network Architecture and the DECNET product family are an excellent basis from which to proceed with OSI.

Nevertheless, moving forward towards OSI will not be without its problems. It would not be fair to DIGITAL's customers to pretend that moving from today's closed environment to an open environment can be done as quickly as they may like.

It is our objective in DIGITAL to move towards open, Mulit-Vendor Networking, but to do this in a way which does not compromise the quality of networking which we are able to offer today.

5. OSI/DNA COMPARISON

Now let us look at each layer regarding the capabilities offered

1. PHYSICAL
2. DATA LINK
3. NETWORK
4. TRANSPORT
5. SESSION
6. PRESENTATION
7. APPLICATION

6. DIGITAL'S COMMITMENT IN REAL TERMS

DIGITAL has spent considerable energy helping to develop these standards. We believe in logical, helpful standards that are easily implemented and universal. We have also worked to incorporate these standards in our own DIGITAL Networking Architecture (DNA), and DECNET.

DIGITAL will modify its leading network products, DNA and DECNET, to fully support standard protocols wherever possible. In some cases, this will mean that existing proprietary protocols used in DECNET will be replaced by standard protocols which accomplish the same objective. In other cases, DIGITAL will support both a standard protocol and a proprietary protocol. This will ensure that our customers will continue to enjoy the functions and performance they have come to expect from DIGITAL networks.

DIGITAL Leadership: A standard in itself.

DIGITAL is today the leading open system vendor, and takes the following steps to ensure the future of our leadership in open, Multiple-Vendor Computer Networking.

o We will continue to support standard protocols as they become technically stable and sound.

o We will replace existing and future proprietary protocols with standard protocols, as long as they offer comparable or better functionality or performance.

o   We will migrate to standard protocols while ensuring that ex-
    isting networks are disturbed as little as possible, and that
    existing software can work correctly with new software.

o   We will participate in the ongoing activity to establish con-
    formance, testing standards to ensure that implementations of
    these standards supplied by different vendors will work to-
    gether.

INDEX

STANDARDS
(Status as of 1985)

1. CCITT-Standards

X.2, 40
X.21, 35
X.25, 23, 31, 131, 243
X.32, 40
X.75, 40
X.213, 39
X.215, 138
X.225, 138
X.400, 34, 107-108, 125-151
X.409, 140
X.410, 129
X.411, 129, 142
X.420, 128
X.430, 143
P1, 137
P2, 136
P3, 137, 142
P5, 143

2. ISO-Standards

7498 (IS), 17
8072 (DIS), 60
8073 (DIS), 60
8208 (DIS), 29, 40
8325 (IS), 34
8326 (IS), 34
8348 (DIS), 24, 34, 47
8473 (DIS), 28
8802 (DIS), 34

3. Other Standards

IEEE 802.3, 60
NATO ACP127, 125, 131, 138